PELICAN BOOKS

THE PELICAN HISTORY OF MUSIC

VOLUME THREE

D1551002

*The Pelican
History of Music*

3
CLASSICAL AND
ROMANTIC

＊

EDITED BY ALEC ROBERTSON AND
DENIS STEVENS

PENGUIN BOOKS

Penguin Books Ltd, Harmondsworth, Middlesex, England
Penguin Books Inc., 7110 Ambassador Road, Baltimore, Maryland 21207, U.S.A.
Penguin Books Australia Ltd, Ringwood, Victoria, Australia

—

First published 1968
Reprinted 1969, 1971, 1973

—

Copyright © Penguin Books, 1968

—

Made and printed in Great Britain by
Cox & Wyman Ltd, London, Reading and Fakenham
Set in Monotype Imprint

Contents

CONTENTS

CONTENTS

Preface to Volume Three

THE third and final volume of this *History of Music* is mainly concerned with the eighteenth and nineteenth centuries but, as arbitrary divisions cannot be drawn, it takes into account approximately the first two decades of the twentieth century. Professor Arthur Hutchings ends his contribution on the nineteenth century with a coda which he calls 'The Indian Summer of Romanticism' and in which he asks whether music is not essentially a romantic art. 'Can no musician,' he concludes, 'claim greatness until he shares the appeal to our common humanity notably achieved by the great romantics?'

If, as the editors believe, the answer to that question is in the affirmative it follows that what is called romanticism can be found, for example, in plainsong and Palestrina, Bach and Beethoven, Haydn and Henze. We have nevertheless given the title of *Classical and Romantic* to this volume, using these terms in their generally accepted, though indeterminate, sense.

The volume, like its two predecessors, has been designed to satisfy the needs of intelligent and open-minded readers who know something about the history of art and literature yet lack the opportunity to link their knowledge with the more detailed aspects of musical art-forms. It cannot be, and is not intended to be, a comprehensive account of composers and their works, but rather an account of music seen against its various backgrounds – social, aesthetic, religious and historical. The brief bibliographies are offered as a guide to further reading rather than an indication of works consulted in the compilation of individual chapters.

The original intention of the Editors was to conclude the *Pelican History of Music* at the end of the first half of the present century, but it became plain that so much material could not be encompassed in one volume. Professor Hutchings has therefore added to his section the coda mentioned above. This enables him to take account, in some detail, of twentieth-century works by Strauss, Mahler, Rachmaninov, Bloch, Sibelius, Elgar, Delius, Bax and Charles Ives, and to make useful comment in passing on a number of other composers. Further historical developments may be studied in the Pelican volume edited by Howard Hartog, *European Music in the Twentieth Century*.

1967   ALEC ROBERTSON
                                                     DENIS STEVENS

I · THE ENLIGHTENMENT AND THE REVOLUTION

Hugh Ottaway

1. Music and Society in the Age of Enlightenment

> Mozart is a child of the *Encyclopédie*, Beethoven of the Revolution; their very greatness lay in the fact that they expressed the humanity of their own time, not the sentimental hankering after the emotions of the past.
>
> EDWARD J. DENT

BY 1750 the baroque state had passed its zenith. Absolute monarchy and feudal landlordism were to remain the dominant features of European society for many years to come, but the forces of change – bourgeois, rational, contemptuous of dogma – were already building up their pressure. This had much to do with the expansion of trade and the development of science. The scientific achievements of the seventeenth and early eighteenth centuries, culminating in the work of Newton, had given men renewed confidence in the power of independent thought. If human reason could 'reconstruct' the universe, then equally it could remake society. While pleasure-loving aristocrats, the arbiters of taste and fashion, were delighting in the rococo, a new technique of criticism was being sharpened under their noses. One thinks first of Voltaire and the French *philosophes*: men like Montesquieu, imbued with the liberalism of Locke; Diderot and the Encyclopedists; Jean-Jacques Rousseau. . . . There are many differences here, but a desire for freedom and toleration, an awareness of human potentiality, and, with the striking exception of Rousseau, a passionate belief in reason as the key to enlightenment and progress – these were the all-pervading influences. In asserting the supremacy of 'feeling' and of 'nature', Rousseau released tremendous hidden energies; both the Revolution and romanticism were profoundly indebted to him.

Whatever its contradictions and cross-currents – Voltaire *v.* Rousseau; reason *v.* feeling – the Enlightenment was a movement of immense optimism and promise. Significantly, its centre was France, the country in which autocracy had been most crushingly imposed and had conspicuously failed to justify its God-like pretensions. But the ideas of the Enlightenment were not the possession of any one country; nor did they express themselves exclusively in literature. In one form or another, they coloured every aspect of eighteenth-century culture, not least the world of music.

Quite apart from their wider importance, Rousseau and Diderot, like d'Alembert and Grimm, have an immediate bearing on the history of music. When the Neapolitan *opera buffa* 'hit' Paris in 1752, they were among its most polemical champions. They were quick to recognize that the *buffo* style, however slight, was human and alive and therefore capable of growth, whereas the French heroic opera (*tragédie lyrique*), even in the hands of so great a master as Rameau, represented a dying tradition, tied irrevocably to the forms and myths of autocracy. And so they acclaimed the 'new music' based on naturalness, simplicity and reason – ideals to be reiterated again and again in the years ahead. Rousseau attacked Rameau in his *Lettre sur la musique française* (1753) – also in the *Encyclopédie* (1751–72), to which he was the principal contributor on music – and himself became an influential amateur composer. Grimm declared that one aria by Hasse or Buranello was more valuable than all Rameau's operas put together! It is easy to smile and say how wrong he was. At the time, he was right. The *Guerre des Bouffons* was a battle for the future, based on principle, and was not at all concerned with the niceties of historical judgement.

However clear-headed its protagonists, history is always richer and more original in its creations than anyone can foresee. Even the Encyclopedists had a limited appreciation of the way in which the Enlightenment would reveal itself musically. In particular, their theories effectively concealed from them the importance of instrumental and orchestral music. Grétry, who realized their ideals more persuasively than anyone – except the creator of *Le Nozze di Figaro*! – was first and last an operatic composer; he thought the new instrumental forms inadequate, even inept, *as means of communication* and believed that Haydn, too, would have written operas rather than symphonies if only he had met Diderot!* Small wonder, then, that France, so

* Grétry would have known little or nothing of the operas Haydn

fertile in ideas, contributed little to the rise of the sonata outlook. Compared with Mozart and Haydn, Grétry and Gossec
are minor figures indeed. The sonata style was largely the creation of Austrian, Czech and German musicians, and it developed in a milieu hitherto dominated by the highly artificial
Italian opera of the courts. Just as we look to Paris for the main-
stream of enlightened thought, so we turn to Mannheim and
other German cities, and most of all Vienna, for a comparable
ferment in the world of music.

STYLE GALANT

Wherever artists challenged the baroque tradition, they
stressed the importance of communication and simplicity. One
thinks of Telemann advising his students to keep away from
'the old fellows who believe in counterpoint rather than
imagination'. 'Music', he argued, 'ought not to be an effort, an
occult science, a sort of black magic. . . . He who writes for the
many does better work than he who writes for the few'. Such
views imply the existence of a new, middle-class public not
content to participate vicariously in the culture of the courts.
Meanwhile, aristocratic art was itself changing. The salon and
the boudoir supplanted the opera-house, the painter the archi-
tect, as the essential expression of the late baroque. A private
sensibility emerged from beneath the public grandeur, and
strength of line became dissolved into rococo elegance. The old
world had entered its autumnal phase: as Max Graf has splendidly put it, 'the giant of the Baroque style had been transformed into an effeminate worldling with refined tastes and
impotent longings'.

Frequently, a single term is made to cover both these trends.
The *style galant*, we are told, is characterized by melodic and
formal elegance and a light, homophonic texture (melody and
accompaniment) with a slow rate of chord change. Good
enough. And then we find the term applied to music as diverse

---

did write. These were for his own productions at Esterház and did not
travel like the symphonies, quartets, etc. Only very recently has a
revival of interest in them taken place.

as Telemann's *Musique de Table*, a coloratura aria by Hasse or Graun, the opening movement of a Stamitz symphony, the lean, two-part texture of a sonata by C. P. E. Bach, an *affettuoso* movement from a Quantz trio sonata – and so on. If we compare the two extremes here, Hasse and Stamitz, we experience quite different worlds of feeling. With its elegant ornamentation and embellishment, Hasse's coloratura is pure rococo. This is indeed *galant* ('courtly'). In Stamitz, however, the 'effeminate world-ling' displays an unwonted masculinity: the homophonic texture is part of his music's assertiveness; it is a forceful, anti-baroque gesture, matched by dynamic contrasts and instrumental fire.* Exceptionally, the term *style bourgeois* is used to mark this distinction, which is historically an important one. For although the *galant* and the *bourgeois* are aspects of the same cultural situation and share the same basically homophonic technique, their content is different; on the one hand a dissolution of the old 'heroic' ideals, on the other a burgeoning of the new tonal drama of conflict and development. True, this distinction is immediately blurred in the pleasantries of polite social music, which doubtless explains why '*galant*' is so freely used. The vast quantity of social chatter which glutted the expanding music market of the 1760s and 1770s aimed at pleasing both the old and the new consumer. That this established a new 'norm of expression' is shown again and again in contemporary musical journalism. One critic, writing in 1787, complained that Mozart's string quartets (the six dedicated to Haydn) did not 'unanimously please', whereas the music of Kozeluch was 'welcomed everywhere'. Kozeluch, a prominent market name, is now 'unanimously' forgotten (see also p. 67).

It is to the *style bourgeois* that the great classical works of the last two decades of the century are indebted for their dramatic boldness. Classicism marks the climax of the anti-baroque movement.

* For illustration, listen to the first movement from the Symphony in E flat (*La melodia Germanica*, No. 3) recorded on HLP 18 (see also p. 54). The second movement, too, is revealing; its sentiment is 'domestic' rather than 'courtly'.

'GOOD TASTE': A POPULAR FALLACY

The new universal language of the so-called *style galant* forms the background to the achievement of C. P. E. Bach, Gluck, Haydn, Mozart and many lesser men.

From time to time one still meets with the assumption that, however great their individuality, the composers of the pre-revolutionary era, even Haydn and Mozart, worked within the well-defined limits of 'good taste'. The remedy for this is to read what their contemporaries had to say. 'Good taste' is frequently the invention of the next generation. When Frederick the Great of Prussia resisted the music of the pre-classical symphonists, he did so precisely in the name of good taste, by which he meant the style of Hasse, Graun and Quantz. What he thought of Haydn and Mozart – if, indeed, he ever allowed their music to sully his ears – remains obscure. However, the views of others are well known.

At least from the time of *Figaro* (1786), Mozart was generally regarded as an over-rich, extravagant composer, of 'more genius than taste'; his music was 'too strongly spiced' and 'overloaded with instruments'. *Don Giovanni* was denounced for its 'exaggerated, debauching contrasts'. *Die Zauberflöte* was said 'to make war on good taste and sane reason in a spectacle that dishonours the poetry of our age'. These were the judgements of contemporary critics, the guardians of 'taste'. It was only when belaboured by the revolutionary Beethoven that they began to use Mozart as a model of propriety, and for this they 're-created' him in their own chosen image. Even that was not the end. 'After he was dead people began to make him into a romantic. *The Marriage of Figaro* was almost a revolutionary manifesto; later generations, especially where the opera was patronized by a court and aristocracy, interpreted it as a piece of Dresden china prettiness'.*

On the whole, Haydn got away with it far more lightly. There were many warmly appreciative notices. But one cannot escape the conclusion that he was also considered more lightly: 'the

* Edward J. Dent, *Opera* (Penguin Books, 1945).

most original humour and the most vivacious and most pleasant wit' – this is the aspect of his work most frequently commented on, both ways. Some were agreeably amused, for Haydn was 'naturally playful and alluring'; others dismissed him as altogether frivolous. His apparent whimsicality, not good taste, is the predominant impression. (It must be stressed that these were the reactions of critics, not of the new musical public.)

Haydn was the great creative innovator of the second half of the century – 'one of the great men against their time', Einstein calls him – and in a curious, negative way this seems to have told to his advantage. From the critics' point of view, he was always something of an outsider; his music was *expected* to behave unconventionally, unpredictably. But Mozart was an insider, aristocratically trained, a brilliant exponent of the courtly graces who had unaccountably 'gone wrong'. His later music was fraught with a strange, enigmatic passion, subversive of good order; and as everybody knew, it was the music of a man who had rebelled against his patron. At least to the composer Naumann, Mozart was 'a musical *sans-culotte*'.

CLASSICISM

Perhaps this blanket term, as difficult to define as its supposed opposite, Romanticism, is largely responsible for the fallacy of 'good taste'. For it does imply a certain composure, control and restraint. 'Passions,' wrote Mozart, 'whether violent or not, should never be expressed when they reach an unpleasant stage; and music, even in the most terrible situations, should never offend the ear, but should charm it and always remain music'. This is one aspect of eighteenth-century classicism, and it explains how lesser artists could hope to mask their mediocrity with a show of good manners. Hence the hollow conventionality of the minor music of this period.

We must distinguish between form and formality, the truly classical and the merely 'classicist'. Only in this way can we hope to see classicism as a positive and not a negative. When Tovey remarks on 'all that variety of colour and rhythm and continual increase of breadth which is one of the most unapproachable powers of the true classics', he is directing us to a vital creative process, full of energy and life: the process creates the form, not vice versa.* It is a pity we have to generalize about classical 'forms', as if they were moulds for casting or plans to be fulfilled; for as soon as they become such, formality has taken over, and this is as true for us as listeners as it is for a composer. Ideally, we should concern ourselves only with the form each movement reveals – the particular way in which themes, rhythms, keys, etc. interact and are held in equilibrium. In the classical style this sense of equilibrium is repeatedly threatened and disrupted, however subtly, but always renewed, re-established. This is Tovey's 'continual increase of breadth', and in Chapters 4–6 the nature of it will occupy us a good deal.

Another necessary distinction is that between the classical outlook of the 1780s and 1790s, of which the German scholar Winckelmann was the foremost prophet, and the heavier, more doctrinaire classicism of the beginning of the century. Winckelmann's 'noble simplicity and tranquil greatness' was liberal in intention, largely Hellenic in inspiration, and consciously opposed to the rococo and baroque. Humane and enlightened, this Hellenic revival had as its aim, not art for art's sake, but rather the triumph of art over the sorrows and imperfections of life. In music, probably the clearest and most helpful illustration is Mozart's G minor Symphony (K.550): Schumann was right in hearing this as 'Grecian lightness and grace', though he seems to have missed the suffering which Mozart's imagination had encompassed and subdued.

Finally, a further point of historical perspective. It is often assumed that, if the Enlightenment was predominantly classical, the Revolution must have been romantic. It ought to be clear from Beethoven that this won't do at all; but Beethoven invariably has the force of a special case, and so conclusions go undrawn. The root of the trouble lies in a fondness for categories considered more or less in isolation: not surprisingly, the categories lose their meaning and become mere labels.

* Tovey is still unsurpassed for his insight into 'the true classics': see his well-known *Essays in Musical Analysis*, and his little-known *Beethoven* (O.U.P., 1944).

When Beethoven revolutionized eighteenth-century music, he vastly expanded the classical forms and gave them a content that was highly charged with the romantic virtue of enthusiasm; like most major artists of the Revolution, he remained fundamentally classical in outlook, though his music repeatedly modifies our conception of the term. The Revolution certainly cleared the way for romanticism but practised it only marginally.*

COMPOSER AND PATRON

In the Age of Enlightenment the forward-looking composer had greater problems than the writer. The writer had only to outwit the censorship: despite a struggle with church and state, the *Encyclopédie* appeared in print; by substituting *Freude* ('joy') for *Freiheit* ('freedom'), Schiller could publish his celebrated *Ode* (1785) and nobody was long deceived.† Music, however, is not fully realized until it is performed. And while the means of music-making were largely controlled by the courts and the aristocracy, aristocratic patronage was virtually indispensable. Only gradually, with the growing importance of the middle classes, did public concerts become a prominent feature of musical life. In this and in the publishing of music, London and Paris led the way. Beethoven made a living of sorts, in Vienna, by selling and performing his own music. Mozart conspicuously failed to do so. Haydn served a princely family until he was nearly sixty and then, free at last, took the plunge into a completely different world, that of Salomon's London concerts.‡

* For a wider discussion of this situation, see Arnold Hauser, *The Social History of Art*, Vol. 3 (Routledge Paperbacks, 1962), especially Chapter 5, 'Revolution and Art'.

† On the other hand, a composer of instrumental music, however revolutionary, could hardly be sentenced to ten years' imprisonment for 'criminal outspokenness', as the poet Schubart was, in Württemberg.

‡ Eighteenth-century London was the first great music market, which makes the feebleness of English-born composers all the more remarkable. Apart from Thomas Augustine Arne (1710–78), a *galant* composer of talent, and the younger Thomas Linley (1756–78), hardly one is worth mentioning.

Times were changing, yet the terms of patronage remained much the same. To their patrons many musicians were liveried servants, superior artisans, in standing comparable with cooks and valets. Mozart, we know, found his status quite intolerable. Haydn was a great deal better placed, and more equable in temperament, but shortly before his unexpected release he described himself as 'a slave', 'a poor wretch', 'constantly harassed with much work and all too little leisure'. With the decline of the aristocracy, the role of such an artist became increasingly equivocal. He had still to meet his patron's demands, and this could mean a more personal control than that imposed by any censorship; at the same time, he was an innovator, developing in music an outlook that was fundamentally liberal and middle-class.

This does not mean that the great composers of the Enlightenment – Beethoven's predecessors – were revolutionaries anxious to proclaim the Year One. They were not. To some extent the courtly milieu could represent for them the continuity of civilization, within which the forces of reason and enlightenment would prevail. Haydn's Austrian Hymn was both a patriotic gesture and an expression of esteem for the Habsburg monarchy. Nevertheless, as Wilfrid Mellers has remarked, it is at least symbolical that three of the most noted composers of *opera buffa* – Piccinni, Paisiello and Cimarosa – spent part of their lives in prison for political reasons. *Opera buffa* was 'comic' entertainment, and because it was comic the tensions in society could be given expression; there was a good deal of veiled satire – and, with the aid of 'ad-libbing', not so veiled. It is very significant that virtually all the greatest operas from the end of the period – *Le Nozze di Figaro, Don Giovanni, Die Zauberflöte*, even *Fidelio* – are in the so-called comic or popular tradition. *Fidelio* is in the form of a *Singspiel*, the German popular opera, but the form is revolutionized by the subject and its treatment: we can actually point to the moment when it ceases to be a *Singspiel* in any recognizable sense – Leonore's great recitative and aria '*Abscheulicher! wo eilst du hin!*'. In this moment heroic opera is reborn. Far from belonging to a mythological Golden Age, like the heroines of *opera*

THE ENLIGHTENMENT AND THE REVOLUTION

seria, Leonore is Beethoven's own ideal of womanhood, precisely in the year 1805. And Beethoven, we remember, treated his patrons as equals, or, if they let him down, as scoundrels. These two facts are intimately related, and each should be interpreted in the light of Beethoven's belief that music is 'a higher revelation than the whole of wisdom and the whole of philosophy'.

A NEW AESTHETIC PRINCIPLE

We have seen something of the impact made by *opera buffa* on minds seeking a new, liberal culture. The early symphony stands in much the same relation to *opera buffa* as does the baroque *concerto grosso* to *opera seria*; it is a projection, in terms of instruments alone, of cultural values established in the theatre. What has come to be thought of as the language of 'pure' music was hammered out as a means of expression in which the absence of words and action gave an opportunity, not to be 'abstract' in the modern sense, avoiding human content, but to embody new forms of content in music possessing its own inner drama. The sonata style represents a change in aesthetic principle among the most far-reaching in musical history; for it introduces a dynamic view of musical structure, and in particular a dynamic approach to tonality.

The long-term effects of key-change are so important in the music of this period that their technical basis is well worth understanding. The task implied is less formidable than is sometimes supposed, though it is, in the main, beyond the scope of the present survey.*

A brief backward glance at harmonic development may be useful. What the textbooks call the 'harmonic revolution' of *c.* 1600, associated with Monteverdi and the rise of opera, was a late achievement of Renaissance humanism. This revolution had much to do with the realization of personal emotion by a

---

* For a thorough treatment of this and related matters the reader should turn to *Harmony for the Listener*, by Robert L. Jacobs (O.U.P., 1958), an excellent book which shirks nothing yet assumes only the merest rudiments.

solo singer in a grand, heroic context; the changing harmonies added depth to the expressive qualities of the vocal line. This does not mean, however, that composers suddenly ceased to think polyphonically. Neither does it mean that harmony, as such, was a new resource. The so-called revolution was three parts evolution, the remaining one part being the attitude to harmony rather than harmony itself. By 1600, however, the exuberance of the humanist movement was being disciplined and controlled by the Counter-Reformation and the rise of the great autocracies. In music this was to lead to a reaffirmation of linear thinking, but within the unequivocal framework of the major–minor key-system. The great 'monolithic' forms, the fugue and the passacaglia, are its most highly organized expressions – and its sternest disciplines. Discipline, as understood according to the 'doctrine of temperaments and affections', was the foundation of baroque expression, and it lay in the close adherence to a single mood or emotion throughout the length of a musical movement. There was scope for all manner of invention and embellishment, but ideally nothing was permitted to disturb, and therefore weaken, the 'affection'. This is the root of the intensity and concentration of the great baroque structures. But the 'affective' concept was fundamentally non-dramatic, statuesque, a fact which is immediately evident in the formal and expressive character of the *da capo* aria. Hence the long-term use of key-change was limited and of a purely spatial (architectural) significance; it did not involve tonal conflict. Hence, too, the impersonal, monolithic character of baroque music and of baroque art in general, itself a reflection of autocracy.

When, after the religious and dynastic struggles of the seventeenth century, the courts of Europe staged a revival of Renaissance splendour in the manner of Versailles, a new humanism was already waiting in the wings. The sonata, with techniques of conflict and development among its conscious resources, was the characteristic new creation, the form in which a hopeful, expanding view of the world opposed itself to the feudal and clerical dogmas of the old order. It was historically inevitable that the music of the Enlightenment, however else it might develop, would break away from the unitary, 'affective' principle, replacing it with thematic contrasts and tonal drama. Something of the way in which this happened – the tentative, unconscious groping, as well as the moments of acute self-awareness – will be considered in the following chapters.

2. Dynastic Opera

OPERA SERIA

AT the centre of baroque culture stood the opera-house. There, in music, architecture, painting and drama, the rulers of Europe proclaimed their 'awful majesty' and vied with one another in the pursuit of noble splendour. Performances of heroic opera were more than entertainment; they were a part of the court ceremonial, even a ritual, in which the arts were brought together to glorify a dynasty and to 'act out' the values which were supposedly the basis of aristocratic society.

By 1750 almost every court in Europe that could afford it had established its own Italian opera. From London to St Petersburg, Italian or Italian-trained musicians held the centre of the stage. Only in France was an independent tradition maintained.

The rigid conventions of Italian *opera seria* have been described in Volume 2 (pp. 259–63). Perfected by the Imperial Court Poet and 'arch-librettist' Metastasio, the form was inherently undramatic and statuesque. Metastasio was a master of language, a fastidious craftsman whose libretti were set again and again by innumerable composers. What he achieved was the maximum provision for the singer's art, especially that of the revered *castrati*, within an orderly and dignified framework related to the principles of the French classical drama. It was the perfection of a method, and the method was unyielding. Thus the typical Metastasian opera was in three acts, with six principal characters, each of whom was given the 'correct' number of arias. No two arias of the same type could follow one another; nor could two successive arias be given to the same character. There was usually a duet for the principal pair of lovers, but in general dialogue was limited to the recitatives, which alone advanced the action. Any larger ensemble was virtually unknown, except in the short finale, where all the principals took part. Choruses, too, were generally excluded. One or two of Handel's operas are exceptional in introducing substantial choruses and even ballets, but these features derive from the French tradition (Lully–Rameau), not the Italian. Any notion of musical characterization was subservient to the 'doctrine of temperaments and affections', which restricted each aria to a single mood. Indeed, the principal 'characters' were not really characters at all but embodiments of qualities or emotions, literally mouth-pieces in an idealization of the 'heroic way of life'. The plot, though invariably based on classical mythology or Roman history, had nothing to do with the real world of antiquity. The hero and heroine were endowed with an inflated chivalry and set in a timeless, dream-like world that never was. Which is another way of saying that Metastasio's reforms, unlike Calzabigi's and Gluck's (see p. 35), were untouched by the spirit of the Enlightenment.

In the 1750s the most notable exponents of the purely Metastasian *opera seria* were Johann Adolph Hasse (1699–1783) and Carl Heinrich Graun (1704–59), both Italian-trained Germans. Hasse was *Kapellmeister* to Frederick Augustus II of Saxony, and in his time the court at Dresden was musically the most brilliant in Europe. The true equivalent of Metastasio's libretti, Hasse's music was in a flawlessly polished *galant* style which gave the singers every opportunity and represented the furthest point in the trend towards a non-dramatic, concert-like performance (see Volume 2, pp. 272–3). Graun, a lesser talent, slightly heavy where Hasse was effortless, pursued the same objectives at the Prussian court of Frederick the Great. Some of his operas were composed to libretti which the King himself had written. One of these, *Montezuma* (1755), is of interest for several reasons: the subject is 'modern' – the Spanish conquest of Mexico – and its treatment reminds us that Frederick, as Crown Prince at least, was the hope and joy of the *philosophes*; secondly, it reduces the *secco* recitative to a minimum, favours the cavatina in place of the *da capo* aria and achieves some genuinely dramatic situations; finally, the music is reputed to be Graun at his best. Though it was not repeated, this partial break with convention was a sign of the times. Probably it was inspired by Algarotti, whose *Saggio sopra l'opera in musica* was published in the same year.

Algarotti was one of a number of writers who, in step with the Encyclopedists, pressed the claims of naturalness, simplicity and reason.* This movement for operatic reform could only grow. Even in the citadel of *opera seria*, Naples itself, the Metastasian conventions were being undermined; the aria was becoming more flexible, both in structure and in function, and *recitativo accompagnato* was tending to displace the usual *secco* form. Something of this is revealed in the operas of Niccolò Jomelli (1714–74), a Neapolitan composer who worked at Stuttgart in the wildly spendthrift days of the Duke Carl Eugen (of Württemberg). The Duke demanded a lavish spectacle, and Jomelli sought to match it in musical intensity.† He adapted Metastasio's libretti, gave importance to the chorus and elaborated both recitative and aria by means of orchestral expression. But he did not attack the *da capo* aria: his *Didone abbandonata*, *Demofoonte*, *Vologeso* and *Fetonte*, all composed in the 1760s, represent the utmost expansion of the old *opera seria* rather than a new conception.

If Jomelli owed something to the French heroic style, still more so did Tommaso Traetta (1727–79), another Neapolitan composer who modified the conventions. By the time he composed *Sofonisba* (Mannheim, 1762), Traetta had absorbed much from Rameau, and for his *Ifigenia in Tauride* (Vienna, 1763) he had the stimulus of a libretto by Coltellini, another of the advocates of operatic reform. After this, however, only *Antigona* (St Petersburg, 1772) – libretto again by Coltellini – reached the same imaginative level: Traetta remained, at bottom, the suave Neapolitan, and his true successor was not his rival, Gluck, but

* cf. *Candide* (1758): 'If a man can experience transports of pleasure on seeing a eunuch warbling the part of Caesar or Cato and strutting awkwardly across the stage, then let him enjoy it by all means. But for my part, I have long ceased to attend such wretched entertainment, though it is the glory of modern Italy and the expensive plaything of kings.' (Trans. John Butt, Penguin Classics, 1947.)

† 'In the winter, when the theatre [at Stuttgart] was heated only by 3,000 candles, a full house was assured by forcing the burghers and the soldiers of the guard to fill the empty seats.' For some interesting background to dynastic opera, especially at Stuttgart, see A. Fauchier-Magnan, *The Small German Courts in the Eighteenth Century* (Methuen, 1958).

Antonio Sacchini (1730–86), who was later influenced by Gluck.

The apparent ambiguity of Jomelli and Traetta has a certain fascination for us. There are moments when they seem to reach out towards a new scale of dramatic values; more often, though, they merely rationalize and refurbish the old dynastic opera, much as the 'enlightened despots' whom they served sought to rationalize autocracy.

If the revival of *opera seria*, other than as a curiosity, is quite impossible today, this is not only because the basic structure of recitative and aria seems fundamentally undramatic but because the values represented are so utterly remote and unreal. This unreality was felt increasingly by the eighteenth-century aristocrats themselves. They tended to turn more and more to *opera buffa*, except on the great ceremonial occasions – coronations, weddings, name-days. Indeed, performances of *opera seria* came to assume the sort of significance that religious ceremonies have for the English upper classes on the 'great' occasions today; they represented a social myth in which few continued to believe but which was felt to be an indispensable pillar of civilization.

Dynastic wars and financial stringency also contributed to the decline. In her struggle for survival, the Empress Maria Theresa reduced the musical establishment of the Austrian court from something like 130 to about twenty.* Among the criminal stupidities of the Seven Years War (1756–63) was the destruction of the Dresden opera-house, and with it most of Hasse's manuscripts, by Prussian artillery. In its turn, Berlin was occupied by Russian armies, and when the Royal Opera was later re-established, it was little more than a relic from the past; the operas of Graun were still the staple fare. Frederick's last *Kapellmeister*, Johann Friedrich Reichardt (1752–1814), found relief in the musical life of the city, where *Singspiel* and the *Lied* were both thriving (see p. 33). A similar decline set in at Stuttgart, where at long last the tax-oppressed citizens brought the Duke to heel; drastic economies were introduced,

* See Adam Carse, *The Orchestra in the Eighteenth Century* (Heffer, 1940), p. 64.

the public played an increasing part, and *opera buffa*, *Singspiel* and *opéra comique* largely took control.

By the end of the century *opera seria* was virtually extinct. When, in 1791, Mozart received an imperial commission to set Metastasio's *La Clemenza di Tito* – already set many times, by Caldara, Leo, Hasse, Gluck, Jomelli, etc. – the text was substantially revised: the three acts were reduced to two; the number of arias was drastically cut, and duets, trios and choral finales were added. Such was the ground gained by Gluck's reforms and by the techniques of *opera buffa*. But *opera seria* could not be saved by compromise or even by using a Mozart's gifts. Significantly, it is *Die Zauberflöte*, composed for the Freihaus Theatre on the outskirts of Vienna and interrupted by the imperial commission, that is universally remembered.

TRAGÉDIE LYRIQUE

The French heroic opera had more variety than the Italian. With its ballets and choruses, *tragédie lyrique* was more spectacular, more episodic, and gave less attention to vocal gymnastics; but it was dominated by the same underlying values and could in fact be still more pompous.

The last great composer in this tradition, Rameau, has been discussed in Volume 2, where he properly belongs. Some of his later work, however, has a unique relationship with the new age. Like Handel, he was forward-looking. Unlike Handel, he did not react positively to the spirit of the Enlightenment. At bottom he was an elegiac composer, for while he could mock the heroic values of the civilization which he served, the only alternative 'belief' he had to offer was a scientific comprehension of his craft. In this respect, the *opéra bouffon*, *Platée* (1745), is a very revealing work. Rousseau considered it 'Rameau's masterpiece'. *Platée* satirizes 'civilization', not from the standpoint of the Enlightenment, but from that of a mythological Golden Age. The dream-world of the pastoral episodes alone escapes parody. Only this, he seems to say, is real; and if the nobles of Versailles had been able to overlook the other reality so pointed in the parody, they would certainly have agreed. Instead, *Platée* was condemned for its 'bad taste'.

No wonder Rameau infuriated the Encyclopedists! He could see yet would not see. And no wonder his lively mind returned at last to an early passion, musical theory. After the triumph in Paris of *opera buffa*, Rameau became little more than a court composer: the subsequent history of French opera is that of *opéra comique* and of Gluck's triumph in the 1770s. Yet there is much in Rameau's music, especially his later music, that shows him thinking in terms of the Parisian musical public rather than the charmed circle of Versailles. The orchestral writing in his operas reveals a wide range of descriptive and dramatic effects which anticipate not only Gluck but the Mannheim symphonists (see p. 51). It is not too much to say that, as the last great composer of baroque opera, Rameau embraces everything from the austere grandeur of Lully to the *galant* manner of early Mozart. But the forward-looking elements in his work emerged almost in spite of himself; they arose from his insatiable inquiry into every aspect of his materials. It is Handel, the Handel of the dramatic oratorios, whose technique was less 'advanced' than Rameau's, who strikes us as the truly progressive artist. To musicians of succeeding generations, Rameau's theoretical work seemed his most valuable contribution, and this, in all essentials, was the achievement of his earlier years: the epoch-making *Traité de l'harmonie* appeared as early as 1722. His scientific rationalism had more in common with Descartes than with Diderot: for Rameau 'Nature' was scientific and acoustic rather than 'the natural in expression'.

With his great gifts, and greater intellect, Rameau is a fascinating yet frustrating figure at the parting of the ways. Voltaire was his friend, the Encyclopedists his enemies. He is a figure of peculiar significance for us today – the cultivated intellectual who holds aloof from a changing world.

3. New Operatic Forms

OPERA BUFFA

THERE is musical justice in the way that the comic element, having been expelled from 'serious' opera, developed a vigorous life of its own and played a vital part in the formulation of new cultural values. The Neapolitan 'comedians' debunked the heroic and sublime, and although they used the traditional figures of the *commedia dell'arte*, by then wearing thin, their performances sparkled with natural dialogue, often in dialect, musical freshness and a spontaneous invention that sprang directly from the life of the streets and inns. As Paul Henry Lang has written, 'the *opera buffa* . . . was indeed the opposition of the healthy theatrical and musical instinct of the people to the pompous and garbled concert opera; and the first comic operas were, as later in France, virtual caricatures of the *opera seria*, until Vinci and Pergolesi elevated them from slight comedy to a true portrayal of life and characters'.*

Uninhibited by the rules of 'good taste', *opera buffa* was notably flexible in its resources. The *secco* recitatives became more natural and speech-like, the arias blossomed freely into duets and larger ensembles, and from Galuppi onwards the concerted finale opened out into a form of major proportions, culminating in the *buffo* works of Mozart. Perhaps the most important innovations were the 'ensemble of perplexity', an opening ensemble and the *canzonetta*. This last is a popular song, usually in 6/8 and sung by one of the humblest characters: Susanna's *'Deh vieni, non tardar'* (*Le Nozze di Figaro*) shows how firmly the *canzonetta* established itself, claiming a place in the richest and most highly developed works. The influence of popular music was, indeed, pervasive, bringing naturalness to the word-setting, revitalizing the accepted dance metres and strongly colouring the crisp orchestral style which formed the basis of many an early symphony. From the symphonic point

* Paul Henry Lang, *Music in Western Civilization* (Dent, 1942).

of view, the vogue enjoyed by *opera buffa* in Vienna came to be of great historical importance.

After 1750 *opera buffa* travelled as extensively as *opera seria*, and an ability to handle it became essential to every Italian or Italian-trained musician. It was now a fully-fledged, three-act form; musically, it became both more sophisticated and more mannered, and the plots tended to a certain sameness, yet the *buffo* stage remained in touch with its popular roots. A vast number of empty, shoddy works appeared, of course, and not only by third-rate composers, for the demand was insatiable; only too often the stock situation inspired the music it deserved. As always, much depended on the librettist. A good librettist – Goldoni, for instance – could give a composer immense opportunities for characterization and the achievement of psychological truth; the 'comic' could embrace the tragic, or at least the pathetic, in a human counterpoint of laughter and tears – literally counterpoint in the great ensembles which more than anything mark the maturity of the form.

In the best works of Niccolò Piccinni (1728–1800) and Giovanni Paisiello (1740–1816) this breadth of sympathy is clearly evident. Piccinni's *La Buona Figliuola* (1767), based on Richardson's novel *Pamela*, began a period in which middle-class sentiment increasingly replaced popular realism: the *buffo* label became inadequate, some such term as *dramma giocoso* or *opera semi-seria* being a fitter description of the more ambitious works. With Paisiello's masterpiece, *Il Barbiere di Siviglia* (1782), we enter a world that is close to Mozart's. Until supplanted by Rossini's *Barbiere* (1816), this was perhaps the most successful of all comic operas, its characterization, robust humour and sheer fertility of musical invention winning acclaim all over Europe. From the end of the century only Paisiello and Domenico Cimarosa (1749–1801) can stand the comparison with Mozart which modern revivals inevitably entail; and of the two, Cimarosa has the advantage, for while he lacks the Mozartian depth of feeling he achieves a briskness and an ebullience that point towards Rossini. Thus the comparison is survived because it is only partially valid. The Cimarosa of *Il Matrimonio segreto* (1792) belongs to the central *buffo* tradition – comic entertainment barbed with social satire – and is wholly contained by it; the Mozart of *Figaro* (1786) and *Don Giovanni* (1787) reaches out to a penetration of human behaviour that is many-sided and without precedent on the lyric stage (see 'Mozart and the Opera', p. 78).

OPÉRA COMIQUE

The impact of *opera buffa* on mid-century Paris has been touched on in the first chapter. The *Guerre des Bouffons* opened up a new creative front in the battle against the baroque. Brandishing a pamphlet and a musical play, Rousseau did much to lay the basis of the *opéra comique* which came to maturity in the work of François Philidor (1726–95), Pierre Monsigny (1729–1817) and, above all, André Grétry (1742–1813). But as so often in French operatic history, it was an Italian, Egidio Duni (1709–75), who provided the crucial stimulus: Duni was the true father of the *opéra comique*, as Rousseau was indisputably its 'father-figure'.

Rousseau's little comedy, *Le Devin du village* (1752), served as a model for many composers, including Mozart (*Bastien et Bastienne*), and by the time it finally left the stage, around 1830, the four-hundredth performance had been reached.* As an adaptation of the *buffo* style, it is hardly more than competent, though it has an undeniable charm. Rousseau was an amateur musician; but he was also the apostle of a new sensibility, a world of feeling destined to transform the arts out of all recognition, and this is where his influence lay. *Le Devin du village* established an attitude; it became the prototype of the 'village opera', the musical expression of a new democracy conceived in the spirit of 'back to nature'. Of course, the 'nature' portrayed is a sentimentalized rusticity, at the opposite pole from the Arcadian myth of Versailles but likewise an idealization.

For all its indebtedness to the Neapolitans, *opéra comique* did

* Berlioz, in his *Memoirs*, refers to the night when a huge powdered periwig was thrown at the heroine's feet – and *Le Devin* was heard no more! 'Wretched little drivel', he calls it.

not acquire the vigorous realism fundamental to the true *buffo* spirit; it became 'romantic' where *opera buffa* remained urbane. Quite apart from Rousseau's influence, the difference in background shows us why. *Opera buffa* came from within the court tradition, was strongly rooted in the *commedia dell'arte* and established its values, at least in part, by means of a parody of the heroic. Thus the relationship between *opera seria* and *opera buffa* resembles that of the master and servant in many a *buffo* plot, the master grandly ridiculous, the 'humble' servant worldly wise. There is no such relationship between *tragédie lyrique* and *opéra comique*, though the latter, like the English ballad opera, often ridicules serious opera.* Accordingly, *opéra comique* started out from 'low life' and proceeded to idealize it. The tradition on to which Rousseau and others grafted the *buffo* style was that of the French popular theatre, the *théâtre de la foire*, which had already evolved the *comédie avec ariettes*: the satirist Favart, who translated Pergolesi's *La Serva padrona*, is the key figure here.

Unlike their Italian, Czech and Austrian contemporaries, the French composers of this period have attracted little attention from modern historians. Some of them seem overdue for reconsideration, and none more so than Philidor, whose *Tom Jones* (1765) is one of the masterpieces of French comic opera. Philidor was a highly gifted musician and in his best work strikingly foreshadowed some of his younger contemporaries, notably Mozart. But he is remembered now, if at all, less for his music than for his brilliance as a chess player.

The eighteenth-century *opéra comique* reached its climax in the work of Grétry, who has been described as 'the Molière of music' and, more justifiably, 'the French Pergolesi'. It is generally held today that Grétry's creative powers did not match his lively intelligence. Even so, his melodic gift, theatrical sense and masterly lucidity make him a striking and sympathetic figure. That he was a force in his own day is undoubted, and in one respect – thematic association – he foreshadowed the

---

* The history of ballad opera is disappointing: apart from Arne's *Love in a Village* (1764) and the best of Charles Dibdin (1745–1814), interest is limited to the period of *The Beggar's Opera* (1728).

dramatic technique of Weber and even that of Wagner. His
most ambitious work, *Richard Cœur-de-Lion* (1784), brings out
the romantic tendency inherent in *opéra comique*: emphasis is
given to the Blondel legend, so that the minstrel, who has his
own 'reminiscence theme' (cf. the Wagnerian leitmotive), is as
much the hero as is Richard himself. Here we have a heroic subject treated in terms of middle-class sensibility, an early
example of the 'rescue opera' which was popular during the
Revolution and remained in vogue for some years (cf. Cherubini's *Les Deux Journées* and, at a deeper level, Beethoven's
Fidelio). Even here, though, an early mastery of the *buffo* style
– his training was Italian, his idol Pergolesi – remains the basis
of Grétry's music, a basis that has been transformed by the
influence of the *chanson* and by a keen response to the inflexions
of the French language.

<h2 style="text-align:center">SINGSPIEL</h2>

Like the English ballad opera and the French *opéra comique*, the
German *Singspiel* is a musical play with spoken dialogue.
Sentimental rather than comic, this popular *Volksoper* became
established in the larger northern cities, especially Leipzig and
Berlin, where it expressed the feelings of the lower middle
classes. Many of the early *Singspiele* were adaptations of ballad
operas or *opéras comiques*, the two earliest dating from the 1740s.
Coffey's *The Devil to Pay* was reworked at least three times, and
the final version, of 1766, with music by Hiller, marks the
beginning of the *Singspiel* in its 'classic' form.

Johann Adam Hiller (1728–1804) had a rare gift for simple,
popular melody. His collaboration with the playwright Weisse,
a disciple of Favart, produced a succession of works in which
the clear, natural feelings of ordinary folk were opposed to the
wiles of aristocratic sophistication. His sympathy with the
'humble' was as genuine as Haydn's. Unlike Haydn, however,
Hiller sentimentalized: country life became idyllic (cf. Rousseau
and the 'village opera'), tenderness child-like, and reality
almost a fairy tale. We need to be careful here, for, as Mozart
showed in *Die Zauberflöte*, the fairy tale could be a vehicle for

33

the expression of profound ideas; in general, though, it is true to say that the later *Singspiel* inclined heavily towards a world of fantasy. This provided a point of departure for German romantic opera, as in E. T. A. Hoffmann's *Undine* (1816) and Weber's *Der Freischütz* (1821). The latter is indebted to both the classic *Singspiel* and the later 'fairy opera'.

The history of the *Singspiel* is closely bound up with that of the *Lied*. This domestic song form sprang from the same desire for simple, heartfelt expression; related to folk song and to urban popular music, it represented a middle-class revolt against the stylized conventions of the Italian aria: Hiller's *Kinderlieder* make the point with a characteristic charm and effectiveness. For the most part it was the north Germans, notably Johann Schulz (1747–1800), Carl Friedrich Zelter (1758–1832) and Reichardt, who developed the *Klavierlied* and prepared the way for the Viennese tradition of Schubert and Brahms. Johann Zumsteeg (1760–1802), Schubert's early model, composed both *Lieder* and *Singspiele* of a high quality.

Of the Viennese *Singspiel* little need be said. In so Italianate a city, German opera was almost bound to be a bastard form, part home-spun, part *buffo*. The *Nationalsingspiel*, promoted by the Emperor Joseph II in 1778, was short-lived and seems to have relied heavily on adaptations from *opéra comique* and *opera buffa*. The north German *Singspiel* was generally looked down on by the more sophisticated Viennese public. Like so many of Joseph's reforms, the plan for a national opera was an idealistic conception which took little account of social pressures. A German spirit could not be conjured by imperial decree! The most successful *Singspiele* were those whose style was most Italianate: Dittersdorf's *Doktor und Apotheker*, produced in Vienna in 1786, was 'the opera of the year' – the year of Mozart's *Figaro*!*

Occasional attempts at *opera seria* in German – Holzbauer's *Günther von Schwarzburg* (1777) is the principal example – led nowhere. More interesting as an experiment is the melodrama, a form associated mainly with Georg Benda (1722–95), a

* For *Die Entführung aus dem Serail* and *Die Zauberflöte*, see 'Mozart and the Opera', p. 78.

follower of Hiller. Benda's *Medea* and *Ariadne auf Naxos* impressed Mozart, and Beethoven used the same technique – speech with instrumental accompaniment – in the gravedigging scene in *Fidelio*.

GLUCK AND THE NEW TRAGIC OPERA

Despite the growth of the popular or 'comic' forms, many composers remained attached to *opera seria*, not so much for what it was as for what it might become. Their temperament and their musical gifts demanded the treatment of 'serious' (tragic) themes, and this gave a creative impetus to the theoretical movement for operatic reform. The way in which the task was viewed is not always clear. Sometimes, it seems, the urge to reform went no deeper than a desire for more variety and flexibility; often it was concerned with reducing the tyranny of singers. These were serious intentions, so far as they went; but the Metastasian type of libretto (see p. 23) limited the effectiveness of a purely musical reform. As we have seen, Jomelli and Traetta, distinguished composers of both serious and comic works, to some extent pointed the way; but it was Gluck, a decidedly un-Neapolitan Germanized Czech, who made the crucial break with the past.

Christoph Willibald Gluck (1714–87) was a controversial figure, at least in Paris, and assessments of him have varied greatly ever since. To Berlioz he was one of the supreme artists. Romain Rolland compared him with Beethoven. Some, however, have denied him even his historical importance. According to Cecil Gray, 'the only crucial difference between, say, the *Orfeo* of Gluck, and the average Neapolitan opera consisted in the rejection of the old Metastasian formal conventions, but this innovation was not due to Gluck, but to his librettist Calzabigi, who wrote his text before the former had conceived the project of reform'.* In other words, Gluck merely trimmed his sails to a changing wind. There is something in this view, despite the fact that Gray was guilty of an almost wilful overstatement. It is true that Gluck composed conventional

* Cecil Gray, *The History of Music* (Kegan Paul, 1931).

Metastasian libretti, both before and after his 'reform' operas. It is also true that the assault on operatic conventions was led by writers rather than musicians: 'I begged him', wrote Calzabigi, 'to banish *i passagi, le cadenze, i ritornelli* and all the Gothic, barbarous and extravagant things that have been introduced into our music'. To leave the matter there, however, is to saddle Gluck with far too passive a role. He impressed his contemporaries as a man of fiery integrity who would spare no pains in the cause of 'truth to nature'. To disagree with Berlioz is one thing; to fail to credit Gluck with one of the greatest achievements in dramatic music since Monteverdi is quite another.

By the time *Orfeo* appeared, in 1762, Gluck had gained a wide experience as a composer of opera – wider, perhaps, than most of his contemporaries – and his extensive travels had given him contact with the *tragédie lyrique* of Rameau, the *opéra comique* and, in London, the dramatic oratorio of Handel. Whether or not he 'drifted' into working with Calzabigi, there can be no denying that he was well equipped for the task. Significantly, Gluck's crowning achievement was not so much the reform of *opera seria* as the re-creation of *tragédie lyrique*: the two *Iphigénie*s, written for Paris in the 1770s, were a logical step from the three reform operas already given in Vienna. The Lully–Rameau tradition, despite its pomposity and heroic unreality, was a good deal closer to genuine drama than the Italian 'concert opera'. Gluck was not alone in recognizing this; both Jomelli's *recitativo accompagnato* and Traetta's dramatic choruses were French in inspiration.

Gray's remark about *Orfeo* disregards the *musical* implications of the libretto – and, indeed, Gluck's response to them. The abandonment of the Metastasian conventions in the interest of the drama meant the breaking down of the relentless succession of recitative and aria into a far more flexible, and more continuous, musical structure governed by dramatic considerations. Once the framework had been broken, a new conception of musical unity had to be found. In place of the self-contained symmetries of *opera seria*, interspersed with *secco* recitative, Gluck created a continuous orchestral commentary which linked together the various 'numbers' within a scene. Coloratura and those conventions clearly opposed to natural expression – needless instrumental *ritornelli*, the *da capo* repetition in an aria – were discarded. This called for dramatic integrity as well as musical imagination, for unity was only to be achieved by underlining the development of character and situation and so establishing, in musical terms, the dramatic perspective latent in the libretto. Gluck's dependence on his libretti has often been remarked, not least by Gluck himself: where the text is right, the music is right.

With the possible exception of Handel in some of his oratorios, no other composer had taken music quite so deeply into the drama. The means were mainly symphonic. Gluck adapted the new techniques of orchestral expression pioneered by the Mannheim symphonists; he saw the way in which key-contrasts, as well as colour and instrumental rhetoric, had an immediate bearing on his intentions. In *Orfeo* his method is already clear, but its possibilities are more richly explored in *Alceste* (1767), the second of the reform operas. By the time he came to grips with *Iphigénie en Aulide* (1774), the first of his Paris operas, Gluck had acquired a flexibility which enabled him to blur the distinction between declamation and song. It is here, at the moment when recitative and aria flow into each other, that we glimpse the future of the music-drama. The set 'numbers' remain, of course, but the handling of them is subtler and more varied. In their resources, *Iphigénie en Aulide* and its successor, *Iphigénie en Tauride* (1779), owe much to Rameau, a composer of infinitely greater learning, but Gluck's respect for his dramatic material makes Rameau seem an opportunist by comparison. Grimm, whose polemics against the Lully–Rameau tradition have already been noted, was quick to see the uniqueness of Gluck's achievement. 'I do not know whether this is song,' he wrote, 'but perhaps it is something more than that. . . . I forget that I am in an opera-house and think I am hearing a Greek tragedy'. Grimm may have underestimated the 'song', but he paid the composer a greater tribute than he knew.

Gluck's success in Paris was accompanied by a further round in the *Guerre des Bouffons*, with Piccinni as the main weapon of

Gluck's opponents. The issues, however, were less clear-cut than in the 1750s. As Mahler once said of Strauss and himself, Gluck and Piccinni were, in a sense, tunnelling through the same mountain from opposite sides; they were both using opera as a means of human expression. Even so, the instinct of those who supported the *buffo* cause was sound enough; for that was the tradition in which eighteenth-century opera was to attain its final glory. Compared with Mozart's achievement, Gluck's is cold and scholarly, lacking in breadth of sympathy and richness of characterization. The difference is not really one of degree, of Mozart's genius compared with Gluck's talent, but a more fundamental difference of approach. In broad terms, what Gluck accomplished was the re-creation of heroic opera in the spirit of eighteenth-century Hellenism. Noble simplicity was his ideal.* His plots are based on Greek myth, but with none of the fatuous complications found in conventional *opera seria*. His characters are neither mouth-pieces for the 'affections' nor aristocrats of the *ancien régime* disguised as Greek heroes; they are human beings, often remote and statuesque, but with hearts and minds to call their own. They move us through the fitness and directness of their music. There are many points of psychological and symphonic interest – the two are closely connected – which reveal Gluck as an artist of the Enlightenment, and yet the total impression he leaves has as much to do with a harking back to the first principles of heroic opera as with the humanism of his own time. In Mozart, however, a passionate interest in the workings of the human mind, and especially in 'unheroic' people, was combined with a power of identification which Gluck could not approach. We are moved by the inwardness of the characterization, never merely by a sense of fitness. As the humanity of Mozart's operas has become increasingly recognized, so Gluck's reputation has declined, inevitably. His influence, though, is a fact of history: Cherubini

* In the preface to *Alceste*, he wrote: 'I tried to remove all the abuses against which good taste and reason have long raised their voices. I believed that I should dedicate the greatest part of my work to aspire to beautiful simplicity and to avoid boasting of artificial devices at the expense of clarity'.

and Berlioz – even Mozart himself in *Idomeneo* – were deeply indebted to him. Not until Wagner and the flood-tide of Romanticism was Gluck's conception of tragic opera finally outmoded.

4. Symphony and Sonata

THE SYMPHONY: ORIGINS AND EARLY
DEVELOPMENT

IT was in the opera-house that new orchestral techniques were first developed. To underline the dramatic action, portray events and depict the forces of nature, the weightiest composers of the late baroque, especially Rameau, contrived some very remarkable effects. At about the same time Vivaldi's concertos began to feature descriptive programmes, and in northern Germany theories about *Tonmalerei* (tone-painting) were fervently expounded. These are all significant pointers; yet it was only with the emergence of the symphony that the power of orchestral expression was consistently developed for its own sake.

The new approach should not be credited to any one composer or group of composers, and certainly not to Haydn, who used to be called 'the father of the symphony'. By 1750, when Haydn was still in his teens, the classical symphony orchestra had been pioneered at Mannheim, though its composition remained fluid. The earliest known symphony in four movements dates from 1740. This is a work by the Austrian composer Georg Matthias Monn (1717–50), one of many able musicians – Austrians, Czechs, Germans and Italians – who took an active part in establishing the form. There are symphonies in three movements, without the minuet, of a still earlier date, and from these it is only a short step to the Neapolitan overture, or *sinfonia avanti l'opera*, whose conventional three sections – fast, slow, fast – had been fixed by 1700.* This is the principal origin but not the only one. There are early symphonies in four, five

---

* The term *sinfonia* had long been used for any purely instrumental section, not necessarily the overture, in operas, oratorios and church music. In this general descriptive sense – familiar to English audiences from the 'Pastoral Symphony' in Handel's *Messiah* – it did not imply a formal principle, and certainly not symphonic form.

and six movements whose general lay-out is clearly indebted to the *concerto grosso* and the suite: see, for instance, the symphonies of William Boyce (1710–79). The minuet, with its *da capo* structure, was itself a survival from the suite.

The content of many of these symphonies points emphatically to the *opera buffa*. The short, incisive melodic figures with bustling rhythmic accompaniment; the sentimental, aria-like slow movements; the brilliantly busy finales in triple time – these are unmistakable features. It was largely the popularity of the *buffo* style which led to the performance of operatic overtures (*sinfonie*) as concert pieces and thence to the demand for independent symphonies. To name Pergolesi among the 'founding fathers' may seem a little far-fetched, and yet the music of Giovanni Battista Sammartini (1701–75), the most prolific of the early symphonists, is a continual reminder of his style. Sammartini has gone down to history as a facile, superficial composer – Haydn called him a 'scribbler' – but there is no denying that his influence was extensive. Working in northern Italy, he kept up a prodigious output and his music became well known in Vienna, Paris and many of the principal German cities. He is credited with being the first symphonist to introduce a distinctive second theme, in the dominant key, an important step in the evolution of 'first-movement form' (see 'The Sonata Principle', p. 43). Especially striking is his grasp of the kind of harmonic and rhythmic activity on which the reality of opposed key-centres, and therefore of the whole sonata principle, ultimately depends. This is where his influence was important. His style, however, is characterized by a *buffo* zest and tunefulness.

The symphony, then, was mainly Italian in origin, but the initiative in developing it quickly passed elsewhere. In Berlin, and subsequently in Hamburg, the German structural genius asserted itself in the contribution of C. P. E. Bach, a composer of high seriousness who is frequently underestimated as a mere 'forerunner' of Haydn. Simultaneously, a group at Mannheim, mainly Czechs and Austrians, created a vigorous orchestral style that was full of contrast and dramatic fire. In Vienna the trend was less radical, more Italianate, but the fusion of many influences – northern and southern German as well as Italian – characteristic of the Viennese classical school is already hinted at in the symphonies of Georg Christoph Wagenseil (1715–77), Florian Leopold Gassmann (1723–74) and others. There is still much to be learnt about the 'pre-classical' symphonists, and it is only lately that a systematic inquiry has really been begun.

The overall pattern is certainly complex, with a good deal of parallel development as well as distinctive pioneering. Furthermore, the symphony did not develop in isolation. The cultural forces it represented were also at work in shaping the solo concerto and *sinfonia concertante*, the *divertimento*, *cassation* and serenade, the string quartet and kindred forms of chamber music, and, of course, the keyboard sonata. These forms were so closely related that clear-cut distinctions are sometimes difficult to make. How, for example, shall we classify Haydn's Op. 1? Composed in the early 1750s as six *divertimenti* for strings, the same music appeared in Paris in 1764 as *Six Sinfonies ou Quatuors dialogués*. These works are published today as string quartets; but the important point, and this is confirmed by much of Haydn's early music, is that the composer himself made little or no distinction between orchestral and chamber-musical style, or between the content appropriate to a *divertimento* and a symphony. There is nothing odd about this; it is typical of the period. That *we* make such distinctions is largely due to the subsequent achievements of both Haydn and Mozart. As late as the 1780s, however, there is much to upset the tidy categories of the textbooks. The work we know as Mozart's *Haffner* Symphony (No. 35 in D) was written for use as a festive serenade, complete with a second minuet (the minuets may even have been danced to) and a processional march at the beginning. Then there is that remarkable C minor work for eight wind instruments (K. 388) which Mozart called Serenade and later presented as a quintet for strings (K. 406). All this can be very misleading, for it is apt to suggest confused intentions which in fact did not exist. It is true to say that as soon as we recognize the same underlying impulse, the same principle of construction, in each of these types of composition, the *apparent* con-

fusion disappears. Such forms as the symphony, serenade and
string quartet are all expressions of the sonata principle, the
creative force which revolutionized eighteenth-century music,
and so their histories are interwoven.

Some mention of 'sonata' has already been made (see p. 20),
but its implications are so far-reaching that a fuller account
must now be given. We shall then return to the Mannheim
symphonists and the music of C. P. E. Bach.

THE SONATA PRINCIPLE

First, the term itself. The meaning of *sonata* is literally 'a piece
sounded' – as opposed to *cantata*, 'a piece sung' – and it was
not until the eighteenth century that a more specialized meaning
attached itself: namely, a piece of chamber music, usually in
three or four movements, for one or two instruments. It is from
the style and structure of a revolutionary type of sonata, especially the opening movement, that the expression 'sonata principle' is derived; but it is used in reference to *all* compositions,
symphonic as well as chamber-musical, whose basic structure is
of the new sonata type. The fact that we say *sonata* principle, not
symphonic principle, is really a tribute to the important role of
the keyboard sonata in fashioning the new approach.

Tonal drama and thematic contrasts – these are the essence
of the sonata principle. Not only in structure but in musical
content, we are confronted here with a creative outlook quite
different from that of the previous period. The 'affective' concentration of baroque music, with its tendency to the monothematic and statuesque, is supplanted by a dynamic style in
which many contrasting shades of expression are freely,
deliberately sought. To the baroque mind this opening-out of a
movement's potential range seemed almost wilful and icono-
clastic. Here is a typical comment on the 'new symphonies'
[my italics]: '. . . it is true that one can find some well written,
beautiful and effective movements among them . . . but *the
strange mixture of the serious and the comical, the sublime and the
lowly, which is so frequently blended in the same movement*, often
creates a bad effect'. This is very revealing. True, the 'bad

effect' might in part be explained by the clumsy joins and short-windedness of many a 'pre-classical' symphony; yet it is clear that the critic's objections are not concerned with faulty or inadequate realization but with the quality of expression. From the standpoint of a mature sonata composer – Mozart, for example – the blending of 'the serious and the comical' was a key to the human heart and a means of attaining psychological truth ('truth to nature'); to the baroque musician it was simply bad taste.

This far-reaching change in outlook did not occur suddenly. Though revolutionary in significance, the sonata style was an evolutionary development to which many composers contributed. Between its first tentative stirrings and its mature expression in the later works of Haydn and Mozart nearly half a century elapsed. Moreover, certain of its features were already latent in the music of the baroque. This is not a paradox; every style contains within itself the germ of its own dissolution.

Before we attempt to trace this development, it may be useful to jump ahead and examine the sonata principle in its most highly organized impression, i.e. classical 'first-movement form'.* This will establish a point of reference. That some such generalization was consciously used by Haydn, Mozart, Beethoven and a host of lesser composers is absolutely clear; but in every work of the imagination its implications were rediscovered, re-created.

Reduced to a ground-plan, the form consists of three sections, usually known as exposition, development, and recapitulation:

Exposition. This begins with the principal theme, or group of themes, in the tonic key; 'first subject' is the usual description. After a modulatory 'bridge' passage the 'second subject' enters in a related key; the commonest key is that of the dominant, or, if the movement is in a minor key, the relative major. Having established this opposition of theme and key, the exposition ends with a 'closing section' or *codetta*, which may possess a

---

* Not a very satisfactory term, for the form it denotes is by no means peculiar to first movements. But perhaps the alternative, 'sonata form', is even more misleading; the suggestion of a whole sonata, instead of a single movement, is unavoidable.

theme of its own or simply rely on some cadence-making figure such as was used in the bridge passage. (The function of the *codetta* is to affirm a key, thereby throwing into relief the key-changes of the ensuing development.)

Development. Often described as 'a working-out of the themes from the exposition'. Good enough, so far as it goes. The crux of the 'working-out' is tonal drama, an exploration of more or less remote keys; thematically, this may depend on little more than a salient figure from *one* of the themes or a mere tag from the closing section.

Recapitulation. The tonal drama is now resolved; both subjects are restated, in the tonic key. (Ideally, the exposition is *re-created* in the light of the development; often, though, its course is followed almost exactly, except for the changes brought about by the transposition of the second subject – at the very least, a rewriting of the modulatory bridge passage.) The restoration of the tonic key is underlined in the *coda* (literally 'tail-piece'), which sometimes uses material from the first subject but is in general an enlargement of the *codetta*.

The reality of this scheme depends entirely on a new kind of rhythmic and harmonic activity. Directed to the establishing of successive key-centres, in such a way that one key is not only succeeded but *supplanted* by another, this activity is founded on the special relationship of tonic and dominant: the dominant of the new key has the power to push the old key into the background, almost as if the latter had never been established. This 'almost' is important, for the ultimate return to the main key of the movement should carry with it a true sense of homecoming, and so eliminate the claims of all possible rivals.

The classical 'equilibrium' thus achieved effectively reconciles a high degree of contrast, not only tonal and thematic but in rhythm, texture and dynamics, with an underlying unity related to the *da capo* principle. And this is where the analysts start to disagree. Is it a binary or a ternary form? Theoretically, it cannot be both, so absolute positions are at once taken up. But as usual, theory fails to take into account the changing practice of composers. The vast majority of examples from Haydn, Mozart and their contemporaries are clearly binary:

we are directed to repeat (i) the exposition, and (ii) the development-and-recapitulation *as a single unit*. As the development expanded, both in key-range and duration, so the binary conception was gradually transformed: the *da capo* aspect of the recapitulation became accentuated, inevitably, and the second 'repeat' was duly dropped. What had once been binary was now ternary. In one respect, however, the binary sense persisted, for the exposition was still repeated and thought of as balancing the other two sections.

The principal stages in the evolution of 'first-movement form' are shown diagrammatically in Ex. 1. This should not be interpreted too literally! It represents a kind of highway, though perhaps a more circuitous one than we can well imagine. There were also many sidetracks, and routes leading in from other points. For example, the first-generation symphonists who favoured minor keys for their second subjects were clearly on a road connecting with the operatic aria, a form whose middle section had lately been treated more dramatically. ('He was despised', from *Messiah*, is a familiar aria of this type.) If the *da capo* aria, refurbished, is felt to embrace a 'dual affection', the modern bisectional aria is quite overtly dualistic. This might be represented as Ex. 1(iii) (*Messiah* again provides a good example: 'But who may abide?'). Sonata dualism is also foreshadowed in the Vivaldi type of *concerto grosso*, both in matters of key and in the contrast between the opening *tutti* and the *concertino*. The forceful rhythms of the *tutti* theme are immediately recognizable in the first subject of some of the early symphonies.

Despite these roots in the late baroque, the support which the first sonata composers derived from inherited techniques must often have seemed to them slight enough, for where they were most in need of support there was simply none to be had. Baroque ideals could not teach them how to organize thematic and rhythmic contrasts into a coherent dramatic structure, or to impart thematic interest to passages of adventurous modulation. Worst of all, perhaps, the traditional method of writing for orchestra was quite at odds with the new (homophonic) conception of musical expression.

1   (i)   Simple binary form (mainstay of baroque dance forms):

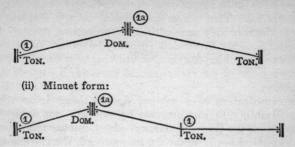

(ii)   Minuet form:

(iii) 'Semi-sonata' form (Scarlatti's 'closed' form):

(iv) Primitive 'first movement' form:

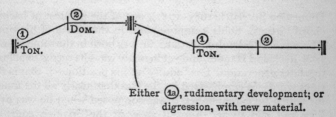

Either ①ₐ, rudimentary development; or
digression, with new material.

① and ② —first and second themes
①ₐ —first theme modified

The *galant* symphony relied heavily on melody-and-accompaniment, the more melodic, song-like sections being linked together by non-thematic material of a kind that facilitated modulation. This had two main disadvantages: the separation of thematicism and modulation, which weakened the total effect, and the limitation of most of the orchestra to an accompanimental role. That these were closely related features is shown in the way they were ultimately overcome; the one, in fact, could scarcely be tackled without the other. What was wanted was a new kind of thematic thinking which would open up the resources of the orchestra and pervade all parts of the composition.

This combination of a subtler, deeper thematicism with greater flexibility in instrumental lay-out was not achieved until the rise of the Viennese classical school, but to some extent it was pioneered in music for the harpsichord, the clavichord, and later the fortepiano, which was widely taken up in the 1760s. By the mid-eighteenth century the harpsichord almost amounted to an orchestra in itself, and its technique had an equal capacity for lines and chords. To a greater extent than the organ, it had freed itself from the 'tyranny' of polyphonic texture – due largely, no doubt, to varied work in the opera-house – and it had found a composer of extraordinary crystalline brilliance.

DOMENICO SCARLATTI

Domenico Scarlatti (1685–1757), one of the greatest of harpsichord virtuosi, holds a unique place in the music of his time. The son of Alessandro Scarlatti, he was born in the same year as J. S. Bach and Handel, and yet in many ways he seems to belong to a later generation. The 'oddity' of his position – if that is the right word – is emphasized by the fact that nearly all the music for which he is remembered was composed when he was over fifty and had tucked himself away at the Spanish court in Madrid.

In his single-movement sonatas – some 600 of them in all! – Scarlatti achieved a wonderful variety of expression, largely because his intense interest in keyboard technique was perfectly matched with his lively imagination: the many contrasts in texture, the subtle extensions of his thematic ideas, the intricate figuration – these, it seems, exactly mirror his flexibility and

48

resourcefulness as a player. He was probably the first composer to develop the use of two contrasting themes as a conscious principle of construction, and this alone would make him important in the early history of 'sonata'. Scarlatti described his pieces as *Essercizi* ('lessons' or 'exercises'), and the vast majority of them are not what we would call sonata-type movements. They are binary in form, and the thematic contrast between the two sections is sometimes very arresting; but more remarkable are those sonatas which create the illusion of 'first-movement form', or something very like it: what Ralph Kirkpatrick calls Scarlatti's 'closed' form (as distinct from the 'open' form of his simpler binary movements).* This is experienced when a marked contrast occurs within the first section, and the second section, reintroducing the opening material in a different key, sounds at first like a development. A rudimentary development or digression may in fact ensue before the secondary material returns in the tonic key, as in Ex. 1 (iii).

In some of his sonatas, Scarlatti used a language of contrasts that is terse and incisive almost to the point of truculence. Take, for instance, No. 29 in D (L. 461, Kk. 29) from the original *Essercizi* of c. 1738 (Ex. 2): (i) is followed by semiquaver figuration, and then by (ii), whose ardent homophony is immediately countered by (iii) – and so on. What sort of man wrote this music? Outwardly, he is the brilliant executant, the entertainer of the court. But behind the mask of 'impersonality' there is a passion, a savage irony, that mocks and parodies the conventions. His tone is aristocratic, in a way that Mozart would have appreciated; yet such freedom of invention was hardly known outside the framework of the *fantasia*.

Scarlatti's combination of freedom and coherence, admittedly within a small compass, makes the customary description of his style – 'half-way between the world of the old polyphony and that of the *galant* era' – seem irrelevant and meaningless. For it was not until the last quarter of the eighteenth century that these two qualities were as finely matched in the orchestral symphony. By that time another composer of keyboard music,

* Ralph Kirkpatrick, *Domenico Scarlatti* (Princeton University Press, 1953).

Scarlatti *Sonata in D (L. 461)*

C. P. E. Bach, had developed a more revolutionary type of sonata: even in his early *Prussian* and *Württemberg* sonatas, he had shown a capacity for dramatic expression that was destined to have far-reaching effects, influencing the music not only of Haydn and Mozart but of Beethoven too. However, before we consider Bach's achievement we must turn to the Mannheim composers, for it was they who dominated the 1750s and 1760s and consolidated the *galant* symphony.

THE MANNHEIM SCHOOL

From about 1740 onwards, the Electoral court at Mannheim was one of the liveliest centres of German cultural life. This was due to the enlightened patronage of the Duke Carl Theodor, Elector Palatine, whose enthusiasm for the arts and sciences came second only to his lechery. Music was a particular interest, and for many years the musical establishment flourished under the Elector's personal supervision. A wide range of talent was drawn to Mannheim, mainly from the Habsburg lands, new standards of performance were attained and creative innovation was actively encouraged. Moreover, music at Mannheim was open to the public.

Throughout Europe the Mannheim orchestra was famous for its precision and fiery brilliance. Its leading members were not only carefully chosen instrumentalists but composers too, and so there developed a distinctive style of composition. By far the most important of these musicians was the Czech violinist Johann Stamitz (1717–57), whom the Elector appointed as *Konzertmeister* (leader) in 1745. In composition as in performance, the Mannheim style was to no small extent the creation of Stamitz himself. None of the others really equalled him in boldness of invention, though Franz Xaver Richter (1709–89) and Anton Filtz (1725–60) – also Czechs – were noted composers whose music travelled widely: before he was influenced by Stamitz, Richter was an impressive exponent of baroque techniques. Two more members of the first generation, an Austrian and an Italian, deserve a mention in any account of the 'pre-classical' symphony. They are the *Kapellmeister* Ignaz Holzbauer (1711–83), who is credited with some two hundred symphonies and concertos, and Carlo Giuseppe Toeschi (1724–88). A younger generation headed by Stamitz's pupil, Christian Cannabich (1731–98), and later by Stamitz's son Carl (1746–1801), carried forward the Mannheim traditions, but when the

Elector moved his court to Munich in 1778 the great days were over.

In the music of Stamitz, and to a lesser extent in that of his colleagues, the slender language of the *style galant* found an unsuspected vehemence and masculinity. Such striking effects as the 'sky-rocket' – a soaring arpeggio played by the strings – and the Mannheim *crescendo*, built up over a repeated bass note, became proverbial; even the commonplaces of rococo sentiment – trills, sighs and the like – were transformed into dramatic gestures. Probably none of these devices was Stamitz's invention: the *crescendo* had its origin in the opera and may well have reached Mannheim through Jomelli. What was new was the context in which they appeared, and hence the total effect; for never before had a composer exploited them so deliberately, as ends in themselves. The typical Stamitz symphony, however, is more than a succession of stylish tricks and mannerisms. The urge to dynamic expression is counterbalanced by a valid sense of design; or rather, the music's dynamism, even the rolling *crescendo*, is of form-making significance and not a mere surface quality. A clear distinction of character, as well as of theme and key, is made between the first and second subjects: the first is arresting and incisive, the second mainly lyrical. Especially interesting is Stamitz's method of building up the first subject from a number of terse, pregnant motives. This not only makes for contrast *within* the subject but is also important in the struggle to wed thematicism and modulation. Ex. 1 (iv) (p. 47) represents the basic plan of many of his first movements, but various alternatives may be found. The developments lean heavily on the sequence (repetition of a phrase at a higher or lower pitch), and the recapitulations are often incomplete, as in the second part of many a sonata by Scarlatti.

The Mannheimers did much to establish the four-movement symphony, at a time when the Italians and the north Germans, and even the Viennese, still preferred the original three-movement pattern. But their greatest influence undoubtedly lay in their handling of the orchestra. Except in the slow movements, which were usually scored for strings and continuo alone, the whole apparatus of the *basso continuo* was made redundant.

True, the man at the harpsichord still directed the orchestra; not until the next century was he to disappear entirely. (When Haydn came to London in 1791 and 1794, he directed his symphonies from the piano.) For the most part, though, he was now to be seen rather than heard, and the role of the leader was becoming more important. It was no longer necessary for the harpsichord to fill out the harmonies; in a homophonic texture the 'holding' instruments, mainly oboes and horns, used in pairs, could fulfil this function more effectively. At the same time the nature of the bass part was undergoing a significant change. In baroque music the bass was a firmly drawn melodic line, fundamental to the counterpoint as well as to the harmony; like any other melodic part, it was meaningful in itself. In Ex. 3 we find a completely different conception. Here the bass is meaningless without the middle and upper parts, for the music it supports is emphatically homophonic. Turning to the horn parts, we find that the E flat of the first four bars is sustained there too; so even as a self-denying support for the harmony, the bass part is not altogether indispensable. With the increasing use of the horns as the 'holding' instruments *par excellence*, the bass was going to be free to share in the thematic work from time to time. Stamitz, however, made only tentative moves in that direction. It was not the Mannheimers but the Viennese who were eventually to bring freedom and flexibility into the new symphonic texture. Meanwhile, flutes, oboes, horns and even clarinets were breaking down the dominance of the strings, and 'colour' was becoming important in the contradistinction of thematic ideas.

The Mannheim symphony was designed to make a direct appeal to a new and wider audience: the sense of public address is in marked contrast with the chamber-musical quality of the contemporary Viennese symphony. The cultural values it represented were those of the rising middle classes, and wherever a middle-class public was a serious factor in the promotion of musical entertainment its impact was immense. In Paris especially, the confident self-assertion of Stamitz's music found an enthusiastic response: Mozart's *Paris* Symphony (K. 297), composed in 1778 for the 'Concerts Spirituels' and consciously

J. Stamitz *Symphony in E flat (La melodia Germanica, No.3)*

See *The History of Music in Sound*, Vol. VII, *The Symphonic Outlook.*

aimed at Parisian taste, gives some idea of the lasting influence which the Mannheim school established there.* So does the

* The Mozarts, father and son, were contemptuous of the Mannheim style: 'nothing but noise' was the verdict of Leopold Mozart (1719–87); 'a hodgepodge, with here and there a good idea, but introduced very awkwardly . . .' (see letter to Wolfgang, 29 June 1778). Without a doubt there were many shoddy works which fully deserved these strictures.

music of François Joseph Gossec (1734–1829), the leading symphonist of the French school. In London the symphonies and concertos of Johann Christian Bach (1735–82), though Italianate in many respects, were indebted both in orchestral method and expressive detail to the music composed at Mannheim. This can be heard in his Symphony in B flat (Op. 18 No. 2), composed in 1776 as the overture (*sinfonia*) to *Lucio Silla*.

Why is it, then, that the works of Stamitz, Richter and others are quite unrepresented in the modern concert repertoire? Briefly, because the classical symphony not only superseded but also surpassed the 'pre-classical'; it is richer, deeper and more highly organized in every way. There is one feature in particular which even the boldest of Stamitz's music seems to share with the slightest products of the period and which, in the light of Haydn's and Mozart's achievements, is bound to be felt as a weakness: the melodic interest is limited almost entirely to the top line. Thus, for all its vehemence and fire, this music seems to us to lack depth and inner power. Even so, Stamitz at his best is a distinctive and exhilarating experience; his confidence and cheek make a lasting impression.

FROM 'EMPFINDSAMKEIT' TO 'STURM UND DRANG': C. P. E. BACH

While the Mannheimers were creating their bourgeois symphonic style, Carl Philipp Emanuel Bach (1714–88) was also changing the character of *galant* music, but in a way that was subtler and less obvious. His influence, therefore, took longer to become assimilated. Many a minor composer was quick to follow Stamitz, for the outward appearance of his style could be reduced to a few simple formulas and copied effectively, if crudely, in and out of season. That is how the Mannheim *crescendo* became notorious. Bach, however, had nothing so catchy to offer; he was an artist of the 'inward' sort, to be emulated by those sufficiently gifted, but scarcely borrowed from or copied. Only a Haydn, a Mozart or a Beethoven could hope to exhaust the implications of his sonatas and fantasias. Haydn was his immediate beneficiary – 'everything that I know I have learnt from Emanuel Bach' – yet the tone and temper of Bach's music frequently reminds us more of Beethoven; it is decidedly German, not Austrian – German in its self-awareness and intense deliberation. Again, we are reminded of Beethoven in Burney's description of Bach at the clavichord: 'He played till near eleven o'clock at night. During this time he grew so animated and *possessed*, that he not only played, but looked like one inspired. His eyes were fixed, his underlip fell, and drops of effervescence distilled from his countenance'.

If that is a valid description, and there is much in the music to bear it out, then Bach's approach to his art was far more personal and subjective than that of any other composer we have discussed. Instrumental music was becoming more and more dependent upon the composer's inner resources, not only for its emotional intensity but for the *ordering* of its emotion. This trend may be said to have begun as soon as the concept of a 'basic affection' was undermined by the sighs and flourishes of rococo sentiment. Rococo art itself, however, was insubstantial and effete: the emotions embodied in the *style galant* were so artificial that the ordering of them could scarcely have presented a serious problem. As we saw in the case of Stamitz, it was those who sought to transform this shallow, courtly art into something more robust, more genuinely human, who came face to face with problems of form and content.

Now Bach's position was a peculiarly challenging one. The culture in which he developed was that of the *Empfindsamkeit* (i.e., the culture of 'sentimentality', the German equivalent of the French rococo), and he spent the larger part of his creative life at the court of Frederick the Great, where French taste was paramount. The concertos and trio sonatas of Johann Joachim Quantz (1697–1773), in the so-called 'mixed taste', are representative of Prussian court music, which changed hardly at all during more than forty years. The flute-playing King was rigidly conservative, which he himself attributed to his own discernment. As a keyboard musician, Bach was confronted with the mannered excesses of the *Empfindsamkeit* at their most extreme, for the accepted style of playing reduced melody to a flurry of ornamentation. In his important *Versuch über die wahre Art das Clavier zu spielen* (*Essay on the True Art of Playing Keyboard Instruments*, 1753), he sought to show that the expressive aims of the rococo might be better realized if the music itself were permitted to speak. He argued the need for discretion in the player's use of ornaments; at the same time he absorbed the *principle* of ornamentation into the substance of his own composition (Ex. 4). To that extent he gave his age a lesson in its own terms. But the expressive power of Bach's

C. P. E. Bach *Sonata in C minor*

music – the latent Beethovenian element – far surpasses whatever may have been possible in a reformed rococo style. Consider Ex. 5: no matter how we look at it – rhythmically, harmonically, melodically – this music points forward to the early piano sonatas of Beethoven. Particularly striking, both here and in the previous example, are the sudden dynamic contrasts and the equally expressive silences. Not for nothing has Bach been labelled 'the musical representative of the *Sturm und Drang* epoch'.*

The upsurge of individualism in German literature which

* In 1768 Bach moved to Hamburg, where he succeeded Telemann. The six collections of sonatas, rondos and fantasias 'for connoisseurs and amateurs', the symphonies and most of the choral works date from the Hamburg period.

takes its name from Klinger's play *Der Wirrwarr oder Sturm und Drang* (*Confusion or Storm and Stress*, 1776) was as sudden as it was short-lived. The impulses behind it were turbulent and undisciplined, and many of the works that it produced – Goethe's *Werther* was the most influential – were characterized by a sense of desperation and emotional excess. Outwardly, the movement was a revolt against established conventions; against formality and hypocrisy, and aristocratic complacency

masquerading as enlightenment. Inwardly, it was fraught with self-pity – self-pity disguised as sympathy for the sufferings of humanity; and it mistook its own extravagant outbursts for expressions of inspired genius. Even so, as Roy Pascal has argued, 'if we disregard the more juvenile and erratic forms that the *Sturm und Drang* longing for full development of all their faculties took, it remains an assertion of human claims on life which is a permanent inspiration – just as Goethe's *Faust* remains a supreme symbol of spiritual endeavour'.* Its limita-

* Roy Pascal, *The German Sturm und Drang* (Manchester University Press, 1953): a most stimulating and sympathetic study, invaluable for its insight into the German situation.

tions are curiously appropriate to the environment from which it sprang, and its excesses are far more meaningful than those of the *Empfindsamkeit*. This German 'pre-romanticism' had much to do with Rousseau and the primacy of feeling, but much more with the uniqueness of the German scene. Within a decade (1770–80) the storm had blown itself out: the real geniuses, Goethe and Schiller, matured and increased their stature; most of the lesser figures faded into oblivion.* What emerged in the 1780s and 1790s was a new classicism, Hellenic in inspiration; a *tempered* individualism which culminated in Part 2 of Goethe's *Faust*.

The question at once arises as to how far there was a parallel movement in music. Was C. P. E. Bach really an artist of 'Storm and Stress'? What of Haydn and Mozart, who were splendidly active in the 1770s? There was indeed a comparable ferment but modified by the nature of the medium and by various other factors. Music is resistant to untutored genius; it imposes certain technical demands, and where there is technique there is usually discipline. The composers of the period were highly trained professionals, and the courts where they worked provided an environment very different from that of the universities which cradled the writers. The division of Germany into many small states and the consequent lack of a great metropolitan centre – a London or a Paris, or even a Vienna – was one powerful obstacle to the development of a new German literature: such centres as existed were largely dominated by the courts, where French literature was venerated and German despised. Yet these were the conditions in which music tended to flourish, for every petty ruler aspired to possess his own musical establishment: German composers had both a tradition and a milieu in which to work; the new writers had neither.

So strong was the undercurrent of cultural revolt that it cut right across these important differences. Composers too sought to reveal 'the supreme value of dynamic feeling and direct experience' (Pascal): if we listen to Bach's Fantasia in C minor,

* See H. B. Garland, *Storm and Stress* (Harrap, 1952), especially Chapter 10, 'The Abortive Romantic Revolt'.

or Haydn's C minor Piano Sonata (No. 20), or one of Haydn's symphonies in a minor key – especially No. 49, *La Passione* – or Mozart's early G minor Symphony (K. 183), we find a quality of personal expression that is far removed from *galant* entertainment and different again from the classical spirit of the 1780s. If we try to describe the emotional content of these works, we tend to use such words as passionate, melancholy, pathetic, tormented; and musical equivalents for the 'interjections, half sentences, and inarticulate exclamations' which Professor Garland finds in Klinger readily suggest themselves. (Basil Lam recently described C. P. E. Bach's 'paradoxes' as 'the too-easy surprises of *a style where anything may happen*'.) Many of the more tensely emotional passages depend upon a subtle form of shock tactics: a sudden, calculated disruption of the music's equilibrium or norm of expression; a deliberate denial of the listener's expectation. This is, of course, a dramatic technique that was later used by Beethoven and by the Romantics after him. But the greater the apparent disruption, the greater the need for an underlying sense of unity and purpose. In their grasp of this necessity and their resourcefulness in meeting its demands, the composers of the *Sturm und Drang* epoch not only avoided the looseness and extravagance of the dramatists but made discoveries without which the larger classical structures would have been unimaginable. For Haydn especially the experience was crucial.

To return to C. P. E. Bach. In his finest music the overall structure is as striking as the expressive detail. Where his contemporaries thought in sections, Bach could encompass an entire movement. In some of his sonata structures the sense of fusion and follow-through is so impressive that historians used to credit him with the creation of 'first-movement form'. Particularly notable is the way in which the first and second subjects are sometimes not only contrasted but thematically related (cf. Haydn). In this and in his use of key-conflict, Bach contributed much to the development of the sonata principle. His impact on the next generation was immense: 'Bach is the father, we are the children; those of us who can do a decent thing learned how from him, and whoever will not admit it is a scoundrel'. These are the words of Mozart, who was not given to flattery.*

Not all of Bach's music was on a high and influential plane. Some of it, written to order, was more or less conventionally *galant*. Even the best has been overshadowed by the work of Haydn and Mozart, by that 'continual increase of breadth which is one of the most unapproachable powers of the true classics' (Tovey). Bach, however, is more than an 'interesting historical figure', a precursor of greater men; he deserves to be listened to in his own right. Three works, all of them available on records, are especially recommended: the Fantasia in C minor (1753), the Symphony in F (No. 3 from a set of four composed in 1776), and the Double Concerto in E flat for harpsichord, fortepiano and orchestra (1788). (See also p. 77.)

---

* Mozart, however, learned at least as much from Bach's youngest brother, Johann Christian, whose 'singing *Allegro*s' are often prophetic of his own symphonic style.

5. The Viennese Classics: Haydn and Mozart

VIENNA, the seat of the Habsburgs, was a highly cosmopolitan city, susceptible to Italian, French and German influences, and these it transformed into something unique. Long before the emergence of the classical school of composers, Vienna had a reputation for its music. Until the dynastic wars of the 1740s and 1750s, the Imperial family lavished a mighty patronage, fostering Italian opera and drawing musicians from far and wide; and the Austrian nobility was said to be the most genuinely musical in Europe. From about 1760 the middle classes became an important factor; their prosperity, however, 'even that of small tradesmen and merchants, was tied up with the expansion or retraction of court society in all its branches, and with the functioning of a vast officialdom, first of the court proper, then of the imperial administration'.* The Viennese 'pre-classical' composers – men like Wagenseil and Monn – owed something to the Mannheimers and much to the Italians, but in their absorption of these influences they made a specifically Austrian contribution. Of particular interest are their use of Austrian folk-music, their liking for major–minor contrasts, and the frequent inclusion of a minuet in their symphonies and sonatas.

It was in this atmosphere that Joseph Haydn (1732–1809) took his first steps in composition. Dismissed from St Stephen's Cathedral choir at the age of seventeen, he experienced a very different kind of music-making in the serenading street-parties which were a common feature of mid-century Vienna. This outdoor music dispensed with the harmony-filling harpsichord and was often made by a mere handful of wind or stringed

* See Ilsa Barea, *Vienna, Legend and Reality* (Secker & Warburg, 1966), Chapter 2, 'The Legacy of Baroque': a thoughtful, realistic account of Vienna in the eighteenth century, by far the best thing of its kind.

instruments. Much of Haydn's early instrumental writing, with its simple, bold textures and frequent *concertante* treatment, bears the unmistakable stamp of the street serenades. The music of his Viennese forerunners, the sonatas of C. P. E. Bach, *opera buffa* and the folk music of Austria and Croatia were the most important of his other formative influences. Unlike Mozart, Haydn was largely self-taught and slow to mature; little that he wrote before his thirtieth year shows any hint of his later stature.

It was an exponent of *galant* techniques whom Prince Paul Anton Esterhazy appointed to his household in 1761. Haydn served the Esterhazys for almost thirty years: given his equable temperament and acceptance of his status, he was well off, for if his personal freedom was limited his artistic opportunities were immense. 'My Prince was always satisfied with my works. Not only did I have the encouragement of constant approval, but as conductor of an orchestra I could make experiments, observe what produced an effect and what weakened it, and was thus in a position to improve, to alter, make additions and omissions, and be as bold as I pleased. I was cut off from the world; there was no one to confuse or torment me, and I was forced to become original.' It is odd to think of Nicholas the Magnificent – successor to Paul Anton – giving his 'constant approval' to Haydn's innovations. Perhaps he never doubted that the work of his liveried servant was a projection of his own majestic being, like the Versailles-inspired castle of Esterház which he conjured from the marshes of the Neusiedler See. The point is worth remarking, for a less conventional, sycophantic art than that of the mature Haydn is difficult to imagine. An unequivocal love of life, expressed with energy, tenderness and humour; a sense of the open air that is part of his peasant birthright; a 'truth to nature' surpassing anything in the instrumental music of his predecessors: these are Haydn's essential qualities, together with a strength of purpose clearly lost to those who persist in misapplying the epithet 'papa' – 'Papa Haydn'. There could hardly be a sillier nickname for the man who carried the music of the Enlightenment to so high a pitch of symphonic cohesion and expressiveness. When used by the court musicians, in whose

T – C

interest Haydn often interceded with his patron – see, for instance, the story of the *Farewell* Symphony (No. 45) – it was simply a term of endearment unconnected with his qualities as a composer.

That Haydn was 'cut off from the world' is doubtless true in the physical sense, especially after the opening of Esterház, but he did not develop in isolation from other men's music. The secret of many of his innovations lay precisely in his responsiveness to the right influences, most of all the keyboard sonatas of C. P. E. Bach. In striking out on his own Haydn synthesized and carried forward all that was most progressive in the work of an older generation – 'progressive' because it contained the germ of a richer, more highly organized expression. At a later date he was equally responsive to the genius of Mozart. To attempt to trace his symphonic development from the pleasantries of *Le Matin*, *Le Midi* and *Le Soir* – Nos. 6–8, composed in the first year of his appointment – through the *Sturm und Drang* and Paris symphonies to his crowning achievement in London – Nos. 93–104 – would far exceed the scope of this chapter. A note on the classical symphony, more or less as Haydn left it, must serve to bridge the gap. (See also 'The String Quartet', p. 68.)

HAYDN AND THE CLASSICAL SYMPHONY

The 'pre-classical' symphony had two main weaknesses: a chronic short-windedness, due to excessive cadencing and a failure to connect the 'sentences' thematically; and a dull homophonic texture which restricted most of the orchestra to an accompanimental role. Haydn overcame the first by building up his motives – the short, pregnant ideas essential to symphonic development – into melodious themes. The principal theme from the opening movement of Symphony No. 104 in D will show this clearly (Ex. 6): the crucial motive (a) is embedded in a spacious, singing melody, whose every phrase has motivic possibilities. The second weakness (texture) was overcome by the reintroduction of counterpoint. For the most part it is a terse, motivic counterpoint, very different from the sustained flow of baroque polyphony: see, for instance, the amazing finale of Symphony No. 103. This is especially striking in passages of thematic development, where the exploration of successive keys is often associated with a motivic-contrapuntal type of propulsion. Interacting, these two advances did much to enrich the content of the symphony and to strengthen its organization. They were the means of achieving both greater flexibility and greater cohesion, of connecting sentences into paragraphs, and of giving the cadence a truly form-defining function. Thus the total expression became not only broader and deeper, but clearer too.

Haydn's use of the sonata principle was infinitely varied, resourceful and free. One has only to compare the first movements of the London symphonies to see that this is so. By increasing the substance of both the development and the recapitulation, Haydn consolidated the ternary scheme which is known to us as 'first-movement form' (see p. 44); but the only 'rules' he followed were those dictated by expression, and by his accumulated experience in building up a large-scale dynamic structure. His structural sense is strongly felt in the interrelation of his first and second themes and in the derivation of much connecting tissue from facets of the themes. In the first and last movements of Symphony No. 104, as indeed in many earlier movements, the two 'subjects' embrace the same theme and a thematic contrast is introduced in the closing section. As early as the 1760s Haydn was already moving in this direction; his first step was to abandon the multiple second subject established by his predecessors. These structural innovations are brilliantly matched by his original use of instrumental colour, which in itself makes a fascinating study.

In eight of the twelve London symphonies – see especially Nos. 95, 100 and 101 – the finale is a 'sonata rondo', a form that was largely Haydn's own creation. This may be represented as follows, though here again we are dealing with a principle of construction, not a rigid framework ('A' is the first subject, or rondo theme, in the tonic key; 'B' is the second subject, or episode):

$$A — B — A : \text{development of } A : A — B — A$$
$$\text{(dom.)} \qquad \text{(modulating)} \qquad \text{(ton.)}$$

By fusing the principles of rondo and sonata, Haydn gave the finale a wider range of expression, and in particular a dramatic quality, while preserving much of its *buffo* gaiety. He opened up the slow movement by means of variation form, including variations on two alternating themes (No. 103), and in the minuet (especially No. 94) his liking for the *Ländler*, or country dance, gave rise to a manner far removed from the ballrooms of the mighty.

The popular note is not confined to the minuets, for Haydn's melody is steeped in the music of the Austrian and Croatian peasantry. Indeed, so strong is the popular in Haydn that there were many, especially in Vienna and Berlin, who thought it an affront to cultivated taste. One contemporary account mentions that as early as about 1760, when the first quartets became known, some 'laughed and were amused' while others 'shouted about the degradation of music for the sake of tomfoolery'. Even the enlightened Emperor Joseph II declared Haydn a *Spassmacher* ('jester') whose music was 'just tricks and nonsense'.* For a serious composer to sympathize so naturally and completely with 'unheroic' people – humanity at large – was an unthinkable breach of etiquette.

With Wolfgang Amadeus Mozart (1756–91) the source of

* Despite the label 'Viennese', Haydn met with quicker acceptance in Paris and in London than in Vienna. It was as a 'grand old man' that he was fêted by Viennese society.

inspiration was not so much humanity as individual human beings, which helps to explain why he is more important as an opera composer than as a symphonist. Most of his early Salzburg symphonies are unremarkable in point of form. They are Italianate, *galant* and broadly typical of their period. It is the musical personality that catches one's attention: the refinement of detail, the thematic sense, a natural leaning towards polyphony, and a latent chromaticism. Even in such masterpieces as No. 25 in G minor and No. 29 in A it is the individuality of content, not formal innovation, that gives the music its distinctive quality. Similarly, the marvels of his six truly Viennese symphonies – Nos. 35, 36 and 38 to 41 – are marvels of expression, achieved within a framework already established by Haydn. The last three, composed in 1788, are on a grander scale and richer in content than any previous symphony, a fact which Haydn duly noted when planning his twelve London symphonies; but compared with Haydn's unpredictable designs, their broad formal outlines are almost conventional. It was the piano concerto, not the symphony, that Mozart revolutionized. In the *Jupiter*, however, he created the first 'finale-symphony' – see especially the astonishing *coda* to the finale – and No. 40 in G minor is arguably the greatest of all symphonies before Beethoven.

The classical symphonies of Haydn and Mozart represent the apex of a pyramid whose vast bulk has been discarded and forgotten. Few music-lovers today know the symphonies of Carl Ditters von Dittersdorf (1739–99), Johann Baptist Wanhal (1739–1813), Leopold Kozeluch (1752–1818) or Adalbert Gyrowetz (1763–1850), yet it was composers such as these who were representative of the age. Their music travelled widely and won fulsome praise. A contemporary comment on Kozeluch describes him as 'the most generally popular of all composers now living [*c*. 1790], and that quite rightly. His works are characterized by cheerfulness and grace, the noblest melody combined with the purest harmony and the most pleasing arrangement in respect to rhythm and modulation'. In other words, a purveyor of pleasantries, polished and correct. Dittersdorf, however, was a composer of merit, capable of a spirited invention, and some of his symphonies are well worth hearing.

THE STRING QUARTET

The string quartet has as complex a history as the symphony, and as many composers contributed to its development. For the most part they were the same composers: the two forms tended to develop in double harness, absorbing, transmuting, each evolving its own distinctive character, the one public and orchestral, the other intimate and chamber-musical. This distinction, which reached its climax in the symphonies and string quartets of Beethoven, was largely unknown in the middle of the eighteenth century. The earliest 'string quartets' were not, in fact, quartets at all in the classical sense but virtually Italian symphonies, playable by four instrumentalists or by a small string orchestra. Such are the *quadri* of Giuseppe Tartini (1692–1770), Sammartini and other Italians, composed in the 1740s and even earlier. A related form of music for strings in four parts was cultivated by C. P. E. Bach in Berlin, Gassmann and others in Vienna, and most of all by the Mannheimers. Here, too, the conception was usually orchestral; there was little independence for the viola, which frequently doubled the cello part, and this in turn was labelled *basso* and often figured.

It was in the *divertimento* – that melting-pot of instrumental styles! – that the emerging string quartet underwent its crucial experiences and learned to discard the *basso continuo*. Because this was 'utility' music, often intended for performance out of doors, composers were obliged to write effectively for self-sufficient instrumental groups, without dependence upon the harpsichord. Thus the string quartet, still more than the symphony, owed much to a type of music that earned its living away from the salon and the music room. Most of Haydn's early string quartets (Op. 1 and 2, *c.* 1755–60) were *divertimenti a quattro* suitable for street serenade parties in Vienna. They are in five movements, with two minuets, frequently treat the first violin in a *concertante* manner and are generally popular in style. More striking still, they often resort to a bold kind of texture clearly designed to be effective in the open air. Even a plain two-part harmony, with octave doubling, is not uncommon, especially in the minuets (Ex. 7).

Once again it is Haydn who emerges as the great creative innovator. Just as he transformed the symphony from a *galant* entertainment, a glorified *divertimento*, into a highly organized expression capable of embracing every shade of human emotion, so he gave the string quartet its classical maturity. In this he frequently anticipated his own symphonic development; for what was involved was not only the creation of the true quartet style – a discourse between four equals – but a further working out of the whole sonata principle. Both depended in large measure on the rebirth of polyphony. As early as the Quartets Op. 9 (1769) and Op. 17 (1771) we find attempts to liberate the medium through a blend of polyphonic and homophonic

Haydn *Op. 2, No. 5*

texture. In the *Sun* Quartets, Op. 20 (1772), Haydn explored the possibilities of 'learned' counterpoint, writing three of the six finales in fugal style; but the problem was scarcely to be solved in terms of the baroque, and this experiment was not repeated (Ex. 8). Fugue, however, is only one of the directions tried out in Op. 20. Haydn was consciously enlarging his resources, on every side, and these quartets contain the germ of almost everything that later proved so fruitful, even the kind of thematic development which constitutes the 'entirely new and special manner' the composer claimed for Op. 33.

It is with Haydn's Op. 33 (1781) that the classical string quartet may be said to have arrived. In form and expression, as well as in the absolute mastery of the medium, these quartets –

another set of six – are one of the principal landmarks in the sonata period. Richness and variety of expression, a consistent thematic development with a wealth of interplay between the parts, a command of large-scale organization in every type of movement – these are the outstanding qualities, and they are matched in very few of the symphonies which Haydn had written by this date. One interesting point is the use of the term

scherzo in place of menuetto. Haydn's minuets had long shown scant respect for courtly manners, but here we find a vigorous type of allegro, sometimes capricious to a degree (Ex. 9). Although he reverted to menuetto, Haydn went on developing this scherzando vein, in quick tempo – in his last quartets (from Op. 76) the marking is presto! – and often with great wit and rhythmic ingenuity.

Nowhere is the intensity and drive of Haydn's mature imagination more strikingly revealed than in his later string

quartets. Many features are almost Beethovenian: the unpredictable forms, the sudden plunges into remote keys, the
boisterous humour of the 'minuets' – even, perhaps, the interpretation of *adagio*. But always the voice is Haydn's; and always
there is that wonderful feeling for development which gives
significance to the tiniest of details without any hint of earnest-
ness or lack of spontaneity. As Goethe wrote, 'His works are an
ideal language of truth, *connected in all their parts by necessity*,
and full of life. They may perhaps be outmoded, but never
surpassed'. And Goethe has been called 'unmusical'!

Probably nothing had a profounder influence on Mozart than
Haydn's Op. 33. The six quartets which he dedicated to
Haydn (K. 387, 421, 428, 458, 464 and 465, published in 1785
as Op. 10) were not imitations in the superficial sense; they
were the outcome of an exhaustive study and, as Mozart wrote
in his dedication, 'of a long and wearisome labour'. Their debt
to Haydn is mainly twofold, an enlarged concept of the medium
and a grasp of thematic development, but equally impressive is
the distinctiveness of Mozart's imagination. There are few
surprises in formal organization: Haydn's 'false reprise' and

the unexpected twists in his recapitulations are largely foreign
to Mozart, and neither the *scherzo* nor the popular, 'Croatian'
finale has any place. But the harmony is often more adventurous
than Haydn's, the polyphony more subtle, and a characteristic
chromaticism gives the music a disturbing inner tension. Most
of all, perhaps, it is the interplay of joy and sorrow – at times an
almost kaleidoscopic, shot-silk effect – that distinguishes these
quartets from Haydn's Op. 33. No wonder the courtly-minded
critics disapproved! Mozart had presumed to explore his own
subjective experience and to address himself not to the fashionable public but to the enlightened individual. 'He goes too
far in his attempt to be new, so that feeling and sentiment are
little cared for . . .' The battle between Mozartian individualism
and social propriety as defended by the critics had begun.

In some respects these six quartets are purer chamber music
than almost anything that Haydn wrote. There is no hint of the
open air and nothing of Haydn's tendency, especially in slow
movements, to treat the first violin in a *concertante* manner. But
Mozart's 'purity' lies deeper than that and has much to do with
his feeling for the viola. If this reflects his instinct for polyphony, it is also related to his practical experience: in Vienna
he played the viola in quartets with Haydn, Dittersdorf and
Wanhal, and the dullness of his part must often have dismayed
him. Again, the warm viola tone is the key to Mozart's quintets
for strings, of which at least three (K. 516, 593 and 614) are
among his greatest masterpieces. That they are, in the deepest
sense, chamber music, each part maintaining its independence
and individuality, is in itself notable historically. Mozart did
not 'invent' the medium – Boccherini did that – but was the
first to reveal its inner voice, unforgettably (Ex. 10).

Though hardly an artist of the first rank, Luigi Boccherini
(1743–1805) deserves a special mention. He was essentially a
composer of chamber music (over a hundred each of quartets
and quintets) and unusual in his interest in a variety of instrumental groups. In him we meet the lightness and directness of
the Italian style, as distinct from the richness and complexity of
the Viennese: many of his string quintets give predominance to
one violin and one viola (or cello) in a *concertante* manner, and

their general effect has much in common with the *divertimento* and serenade.

The *concertante* style is also found in chamber music which employs a solo instrument. This is a category more or less distinct from 'pure' chamber music, and was so regarded by the classical masters. Here again the exception, not surprisingly,

is Mozart. His Quintet for clarinet and strings (K. 581) is a rare example of *concertante* chamber music in which the soloist and the accompaniment participate on equal terms, in what Einstein called 'fraternal rivalry'.

'Fraternal rivalry' also characterizes Mozart's treatment of the sonata for violin and piano, a form which he virtually created: his only models were keyboard sonatas *with violin accompaniment*. Once again we meet the basic principle of the new chamber music, that of 'sensible people conversing with each other'.

THE ENLIGHTENMENT AND THE CHURCH

When every aspect of the baroque state was subjected to the test of reason, religious obscurantism came under a withering and sustained attack. Dogma was rejected; only reason, science and experience were held to be valid. Here was an intellectual confrontation of immense historical importance. As yet, however, there was little pure scepticism, leading to atheism. It is very striking that the two conflicting streams of thought *within* the Enlightenment – the strictly rational (Voltaire) and that of 'sensibility' (Rousseau) – alike propounded the idea of 'natural religion': on the one hand a vague deism, with God cast as the 'supreme geometrician', and on the other an equally vague pantheism.

Apart from the assumption that the universe was divinely constructed, natural religion was entirely open to individual judgment and, more subtly, individual temperament. As M. S. Anderson has said, it 'cut at the roots of orthodoxy, both Catholic and Protestant. God's continual manifestation of himself through a universe which science could describe and measure seemed to reduce, even to destroy, the significance of any special act of revelation. Natural religion was therefore by implication hostile to revealed religion, and even to the idea of a personal God'.* Inevitably, this way of thinking penetrated the church itself, and it came to light in some very remarkable quarters. In France, for instance, it is reflected in the writings of a number of Jesuit scholars. In a textbook published in 1769, the Jesuit Abbé Camier even argued that 'moral principles impose obligations independently of the existence of God'. Any ethical humanist would agree.

Natural religion and ethical humanism formed the basis of Freemasonry. If we are looking for an institutional expression of the Enlightenment, surely this is it. Founded, in its modern form, in England early in the century, Masonry spread extensively throughout the continent – despite opposition from the papacy and, intermittently, from kings and princes (including

* *Europe in the Eighteenth Century, 1713–83* (Longmans, 1961): an excellent general history, warmly recommended.

the Empress Maria Theresa and the Duke Carl Theodor, Elector Palatine – see p. 51). With its stress on reason, virtue and human brotherhood, the movement attracted many artists and intellectuals, as well as progressive-minded aristocrats and even rulers. In the second half of the century many musicians became involved, though few, perhaps, with the fervour that was Mozart's. Haydn, who entered the order during his last years in Vienna and never wrote an avowedly Masonic work, may well have been more typical. Both Haydn and Mozart reconciled Masonry with Roman Catholicism.

Such, then, was the intellectual climate, and this profoundly influenced some of the best church music of the classical period (from *c.* 1780). Of this – the best, that is – there is not a great deal. After leaving Salzburg and the Archbishop's service, Mozart composed only two major works to liturgical texts – the C minor Mass (K. 427) and the *Requiem* (K. 626) – and it is almost symbolical that he completed neither of them. The former is a highly individual re-creation of the baroque – Bachian counterpoint and the Neapolitan cantata – in a way that is dramatic and symphonic. The *Requiem*, his last composition, is as much Masonic in inspiration as it is Catholic and uses the liturgy as a framework for the expression of a personal belief. Like the *Maurerische Trauermusik* (*Masonic Funeral Music*, K. 477), the *Requiem* contains all the features of Mozart's Masonic style: the dark-toned orchestration using basset-horns, bassoons and trombones; the simple, hymn-like setting of 'Hostias', in the 'Masonic' key of E flat major – and so on. As Einstein has emphasized, Mozart's 'consciousness of his membership in the order permeates his entire [later] work. Not only *Die Zauberflöte* [see 'Mozart and the Opera'] but many others of his works are Masonic, even though they reveal nothing of this quality to the uninitiated'.* The exquisite little motet *Ave verum corpus* is one example; another, we are told, is the Symphony No. 39 in E flat. Even the coronation opera *La Clemenza di Tito* has a claim to be considered a Masonic work.

Haydn, too, interpreted the liturgy in a personal way, though less consciously, less defiantly than Mozart. He remained, as

* Alfred Einstein, *Mozart, His Character, His Work* (Cassell, 1946).

he said, 'a pious Catholic'; yet the Masses which he wrote between 1796 and 1802, notably the *Nelson*, *Theresa* and *Wind-band* Masses, are rich in the humanism of the London symphonies. The 'religion of humanity', so fundamental to the Enlightenment, is as inescapable here as in the operas of Mozart. Beethoven's *Missa Solemnis* is much indebted to Haydn's great achievement: compare, for instance, the '*Agnus Dei*' with that in Haydn's *Missa in tempore belli* (or *Kettledrum* Mass); consider, too, the powerful sonata treatment of the '*Kyrie*' in the *Nelson* and *Wind-band* Masses, and indeed the use of the wind band itself, which is strikingly prophetic. These are wonderful works, the very climax of Haydn's development, yet shamefully neglected. Haydn's independence is no less evident in *The Creation*, a 'Viennese' oratorio very different from the established German and Italian models. After experiencing the great Handel Festival in London, Haydn composed 'for a whole nation' much as Handel had done, and used a text which, in the words of Wilfrid Mellers, 'turned God into a working mechanic, the story of the Creation into a Masonic parable'.

It is interesting to compare these works with earlier religious music by the same composers. As a young man Haydn identified God with joy-in-living, and the Mass in F major, his first, conveys this feeling in a bright rococo manner typical of the early 1750s. Though convention demanded that certain texts be treated in the 'strict' or 'learned' style (fugal counterpoint), the baroque age was melting away. The church's ceremonial continued to witness to the glory of God and the splendour of princes, but it did so, both musically and architecturally, in a way that was lighter and more sensuously appealing. The awe and majesty of the baroque were yielding to a spirit of diversion; a delight in *coloratura* became an end in itself, in church as at the opera. Mozart's early church music, composed in the service of the Archbishop of Salzburg, is the exact equivalent of the gay, rococo churches of Austria and southern Germany. In mixing the *galant* and the 'learned', Mozart followed the accepted practice of an older generation but invariably rose above the mere routine which both styles invited: see, for instance, the *Dominicus* Mass (K. 66), or the *Litaniae Laure-tanae* (K. 195).

One of Mozart's early models was Haydn's younger brother, Michael Haydn (1737–1806). Another Salzburg musician, he was later associated with the 'reformed' church music demanded by Count Hieronymus Colloredo, who became Archbishop in 1772. A minor figure among the enlightened despots, Colloredo to some extent anticipated the musical reforms of the Emperor Joseph II, who in 1783 restricted the use of musical instruments in church and urged simplicity and dignity in settings of the liturgy. Michael Haydn's Masses, Litanies and Graduals set a standard for the new ecclesiastical style. Inevitably, this was in fact a modification of the old, 'strict' style, modest in its resources and free from ornamentation. Michael Haydn is usually more interesting in his earlier music. He developed more quickly than his brother and his contribution to the classical style, especially in his symphonies and serenades, has yet to be properly assessed. As H. C. Robbins Landon has shown, the *Requiem* composed for Archbishop Sigismund Schrattenbach – Colloredo's predecessor – was undoubtedly the model used by Mozart twenty years later.

The most notable composer of Protestant church music in this period is C. P. E. Bach. His ardent subjectivity belongs to a tradition quite different from the Roman Catholicism of Salzburg or Vienna, yet he provides an important link between the Passions of J. S. Bach and the Masses of Mozart and Haydn. The early *Magnificat* (1749), which shows him both indebted to his father's setting and deliberately turning from it, and the oratorio *Die Auferstehung und Himmelfahrt Jesu* (*The Resurrection and Ascension of Jesus*), published in 1787, are, for different reasons, his most interesting works in this field. The oratorio, to words by Ramler, is perhaps the finest between the works of Handel and Haydn. Though Mozart conducted a performance in Vienna, in 1788, this is not a classical composition: some of the best things in it remind us of the *Sturm und Drang* equating of religion with intense personal experience; it is also deeply Handelian. Once again a clear distinction between the north German and Viennese cultures is impressed upon us.

MOZART AND THE OPERA

The distinctive contribution of the Viennese classical school was instrumental and orchestral. Nonetheless, opera, and especially *opera buffa*, remained the centre of attraction, socially if not artistically. This is easily forgotten, for the most successful opera composers are little more than names now: Anfossi, Cimarosa, Dittersdorf, Gazzaniga, Martín, Paisiello, Salieri, Sarti – the list is a long one, and they were all well thought of in their day. But of their operas, only Cimarosa's *Il Matrimonio segreto* and Dittersdorf's *Doktor und Apotheker* can claim even a modest place on the twentieth-century stage. If many of the others would seem quite intolerable, Dent's remarks on Gazzaniga's *Don Giovanni*, which preceded Mozart's by a few months, help to show us why: 'Every figure, vocal and instrumental, is a stock pattern, a dummy with neither life nor originality. Compared with Mozart's, it suggests a rehearsal at which the actors walk through their parts in their ordinary clothes, on an empty stage in daylight'.* In other words, Mozart's *Don Giovanni* has an added dimension, both musically and dramatically; and the same is true of *Figaro* when compared with *Il Matrimonio segreto* – a comparison which is even more revealing, for Cimarosa's masterpiece stands closer to Mozart than does any other work.

It is not simply that Mozart could do everything better than the most gifted of his contemporaries. If he were simply the greatest of the *buffo* composers, he would be the darling of the Italians, which he is not and has never been. That a difference in kind is also involved was widely recognized at the time. While the average *opera buffa* was conventional in plot and musically thin, Mozart used the form to explore human character and behaviour and gave it a Shakespearian blend of tragedy and comedy; he replaced the well-worn types with living individuals, and mere tunefulness with musical expression, portraiture,

* Edward J. Dent, *Mozart's Operas* (2nd ed., O.U.P., 1947; Oxford Paperbacks, 1960): a most illuminating study, not only of the operas but of Mozart in relation to his age.

characterization. So *Figaro* was said to have 'too many notes' and *Don Giovanni* to be a work of 'whim, caprice, ambition, but not feeling'! For us, Mozart *is* late eighteenth-century opera. In 1793, however, the *Allgemeine Musikalische Zeitung* declared him to have had 'no real taste, and little or perhaps no cultivated taste. He missed, of course, any effect* in his original operas'.†
In resisting Mozart's influence and sticking to the accepted *buffo* style, Cimarosa knew what he was doing!

Mozart's first great achievement as a dramatic composer was *Idomeneo*, an *opera seria* written at the age of twenty-five. Influenced by Gluck's ideals, this combines the French and Italian traditions with extraordinary mastery. Even so, the old heroic values were fundamentally alien to Mozart's experience, and the point is underlined, paradoxically enough, by one of the work's supreme moments, the quartet in the final act. This is the first of those great Mozartian ensembles in which the principal characters are brought together, on their own musical terms, to illuminate a shared experience. The kind of sympathy and psychological insight which this technique conveys is at the root of Mozart's 'modernity'; and it presupposes a complex view of human emotion which can scarcely be reconciled with the baroque world of absolutes.

In *Die Entführung aus dem Serail*, a *Singspiel* written for the short-lived *Nationalsingspiel* promoted by the Emperor Joseph II, Mozart began to open up the possibilities of the 'comic' genres which hitherto he had tended to consider trivial. 'The whole work', says Einstein, 'marks the complete emergence of Mozart's personality as a dramatic composer'. The expressive use of the orchestra is epoch-making, and Mozart's mastery of the ensemble is once again revealed. Despite much fine music, however, *Die Entführung* lacks unity of style and even clarity of purpose. This is only too faithful a reflection of the confusion which existed in the Viennese *Singspiel*: outside northern Germany this supposedly national art-form seldom avoided

---

*'Effect' is surely a loose rendering of *Affekt*, which means, roughly, emotional expression – of a rather rigid, 'cultivated' kind.

† For this and other pearls, see Max Graf, *Composer and Critic* (Chapman & Hall, 1947).

Italian domination, and its 'popular' libretti had an incurable leaning towards the whimsical and fantastic. Certainly Mozart never set a worse libretto; his elaborate, Italianate treatment is often on too grand a scale, and Osmin alone emerges as a genuine character.

It is precisely in the richness and interplay of character that *Le Nozze di Figaro* is truly great. In *opera buffa* Mozart found a more viable convention. Also he had encountered the librettist Lorenzo da Ponte and dramatic material that fired his whole being. *Figaro* is of Mozart's own world. The play by Beaumarchais on which it is based was given in Paris in 1784, after three years of political suppression. When the opera appeared in Vienna, only two years later, the play was still banned there! Mozart and da Ponte took a calculated risk, cutting and adapting, and pulling every string within their reach. It would be mistaken, however, to attribute the difference in tone entirely to the censorship. Unlike Beaumarchais, Mozart was not concerned simply with lampooning the aristocracy. The Countess is a deeply human and sympathetic study, the Count something more than a villain to be mocked; as human beings, they too are seen as victims of an unjust society, albeit a society which sustains their power and privilege. As social satire the opera may well be less inflammatory than the play, but its implications are no less revolutionary. In the 'democracy' of *Figaro* the essential humanity of each individual, whether nobleman or servingmaid, receives the same thoughtful scrutiny.

From *Figaro* to *Don Giovanni* is a major step, though one of only a few months in the composer's life. As in his third, and last, collaboration with da Ponte – *Così fan Tutte* – Mozart created a distinctive world of sound: gone is the rough-and-tumble of workaday *opera buffa* in which much of the music, because it was merely tuneful, could conceivably be switched from one work to another. And yet the *buffo* conventions are still observed. What transforms them is the substance of Mozart's composition, especially his orchestral writing and the prominence given to dramatic conversation. This last is shown magnificently in his act finales, but by no means there alone. In Act I of *Figaro*, for example, we come to know Susanna through her part in three duets and a trio; not until she disguises Cherubino (Act II) does she have an aria of her own, and even then she busily addresses Cherubino and the Countess. The same principle is applied in *Don Giovanni*; the formal aria, treated as a soliloquy, has nothing like its traditional importance. With each successive opera Mozart achieved a greater degree of continuity and conversational interplay; in *Die Zauberflöte*, composed in the last year of his life, he gave the hero and heroine only one solo aria apiece.

Don Giovanni has always worried its critics. Beethoven considered it immoral; Hoffmann and his successors, determined to romanticize the Don, could not accept the *buffo* ending, which seemed to mock their tragic hero. Often, those who have distorted *Don Giovanni* by imposing upon it their own romantic 'meaning' have tried to make *Così fan Tutte* more acceptable by denying that it has any meaning at all: it is just a bit of nonsense, too improbable to be taken seriously. Such a view completely overlooks – or is it shuns? – the core of truth which 'a bit of nonsense' may contain. *Così fan Tutte* in fact reveals Mozart's psychological realism at its sharpest and most uncomfortable, though even here (especially here) the music embodies a tender sympathy for human frailty. As Donald Mitchell has remarked, 'it *is* a shocking opera, not because of its frivolity but because of its ruthlessly rational exposure of the instinctive irrationality of human behaviour'. A less romantic opera is hard to imagine; only by treating it as fantasy, or by substituting an entirely different libretto, could nineteenth-century sensibilities come to terms with it. Such was Mozart's originality within a received and fashionable convention!

Die Zauberflöte belongs to quite another world, that of Emanuel Schikaneder's humble theatre on the outskirts of Vienna. After the failure of the *Nationalsingspiel*, it was the actor-manager Schikaneder who provided opera in German – for a very different audience. Particularly popular was the fantastic, fairy-tale opera, with plenty of colourful stage effects. Such an entertainment *Die Zauberflöte* purports to be; but also it is a Masonic allegory, undoubtedly 'subversive' in its meaning. Of the principal characters, Tamino is Joseph II, Pamina the Austrian people, Sarastro the distinguished scientist and Masonic thinker Ignaz von Born, the Queen of the Night the Empress Maria Theresa – and so on; both story and music are full of Masonic symbolism, and the ideals of liberty, equality and fraternity are only thinly veiled. The year was 1791: in France the *ancien régime* had already fallen. Unlike Mozart's *buffo* works, *Die Zauberflöte* was much admired by Beethoven. Certainly it stands closer to *Fidelio* than to *Così fan Tutte*, and some facets of the music are prophetic of Beethoven's 'middle period'. The musical style is extraordinarily comprehensive, ranging from the popular tunes for Papageno to passages of grave Bachian counterpoint, and the whole is unified with a deceptive simplicity that is peculiarly Mozartian. A profoundly humanistic work, *Die Zauberflöte* is at once the first serious German opera and, as Dent remarks, 'the first and perhaps the only great masterpiece of music ever created deliberately for "the masses"'.

MOZART AND THE PIANO CONCERTO

In origin the solo concerto was a re-creation of the operatic aria in instrumental terms. It is therefore useful to turn from the greatest operas of the Enlightenment to the greatest concertos, especially as they were written by one and the same composer. Moreover, the piano concerto as developed by Mozart is so much a synthesis of the main creative principles of the classical period – the symphonic, the *concertante*, the operatic, and at times even the chamber-musical – that it provides a fitting '*coda*' to any chapter on this subject.

First, however, the background. The typical *galant* concerto was a slight, three-movement work in which soloist and orchestra – often only strings – were very loosely brought together. The solo part was elegant and stylish, with scope for technical display; the orchestra was strictly accompanimental. Concertos were written for a wide range of instruments, from the flute to the baryton, but already the keyboard was establishing its preeminence. The age that created sonata dualism was bound to make a more dualistic approach to *concertante* style and to find that keyboard instruments – first the harpsichord, then the fortepiano – possessed a unique ability to combine with the orchestra on equal terms. Even so, the pre-classical concerto – or rather, its audience – resisted the development of a more symphonic texture: the fashionable public, to whom a concerto was just another form of diversion, put display and surface charm before all else. Thus the solo element was reinforced in its most superficial aspects. The vanity of performers doubtless played its part, but here one has to remember that composer and performer were often the same person. Not until the nineteenth century did instrumental virtuosi wield anything like the power and influence enjoyed by eighteenth-century opera-singers. Even Mozart had to pacify his singers; in his piano concertos, mostly written for himself, his only concessions were to the Viennese public.

Among pre-classical composers, it was C. P. E. Bach, that great despiser of all things dilettantish, who made the most serious contribution. In his many harpsichord concertos one finds a varied, and often an exploratory, use of the medium; the orchestra has its own important role, and expression is seldom sacrificed to mere display. Such works would certainly have made an impact on Mozart, but it seems unlikely that he knew them. The role of 'precursor' is more clearly filled by Bach's younger brother, Johann Christian, and by lesser men like Johann Samuel Schröter (1750–88), both of whom Mozart met in London during the travels of his boyhood.

J. C. Bach's concertos are *galant* social music, distinguished by a mastery of melody. His first movements are transitional in form, a mixture of the old *ritornello* form fashioned by Vivaldi and the new sonata. Most of the material is presented in an opening *tutti*, after which the soloist and orchestra have alternating sections embodying development and recapitulation: the developments are, of course, rudimentary – in the case of Schröter, freely constructed solos. The slow movements are instrumental arias, the finales invariably rondos. Such were Mozart's early models, and he followed them closely. Soon, however, he felt the need to bring soloist and orchestra into a closer relationship, to replace alternation with interaction, and to make the essential dualism altogether richer and more meaningful: the classical concerto was about to be created.

One can put it in this way because Mozart's achievement stands almost alone. Haydn's contribution was slight indeed. Kozeluch, who as pianist and composer was much admired, merely gave his listeners what they wanted – 'cheerfulness and grace', with plenty of bravura. The greatest violinist of the age, Giovanni Battista Viotti (1753–1824) did serious work in concertos for his own instrument – the piano, too, to a lesser extent – but he is chiefly remembered for his technical accomplishment. Only Mozart lifted the concerto to the highest level of symphonic expression. His first great landmark – Mozart's *Eroica* it has been called – is the Piano Concerto in E flat (K. 271), composed at Salzburg in 1777: nothing like it had been heard before; the piano part is of commanding stature, there are remarkable formal innovations and the whole intention is spaciously symphonic. After this, hardly any of Mozart's piano concertos can be lightly passed over. There is an immense variety of treatment and of mood: even Beethoven, by comparison, seems to have confined himself to one broad type.* Immediately impressive is the structural freedom and originality of the opening movements. Mozart consolidated the 'double exposition' – (i) an orchestral prelude, (ii) a sonata exposition for soloist and orchestra – and gave it point by varying the sequence of ideas and allotting new material to the soloist: see, for instance, No. 19 in F (K. 459) and, supremely, No. 24 in C minor, (K. 491). He used a wealth of themes, and their treatment is often comparable with the interplay of character in his operas: whoever first described these movements as 'voiceless dramas' had a sure insight into Mozart's imagination. Bravura is not neglected, but invariably it is an organic part of the composition. The dualism of piano and orchestra never becomes an irreconcilable conflict; even in the two concertos in minor keys – No. 20 in D minor (K. 466) and No. 24 in C minor – the underlying unity is threatened and disrupted only to be reaffirmed. This

* Except, perhaps, for No. 4 in G – always the exception! The piano concertos of Beethoven are more dramatic, more imposing and monumental, but hardly greater than Mozart's.

technique is analogous to the use of key and the ever-widening range of dramatic modulation.

Mozart remained fundamentally a composer of the Enlightenment: the classical 'equilibrium' – the balance between assertion and acceptance, the individual and society – is nowhere more subtly expressed than in his piano concertos, of which the last, No. 27 in B flat (K. 595), is perhaps the most revealing of them all. Where else has such sadness been transmuted into 'gaiety' and 'entertainment'? But in the Concerto in C minor, as in certain other late works, classicism is strained almost to breaking-point by the emotional content: the Enlightenment reaches out to embrace the Revolution. In the comparatively simple slow movement, the eighteenth century is very much with us; in the passionate outer movements, both in C minor, a new world – Beethoven's world – is struggling to be born.

6. The Age of Beethoven

I T is easy to see the Revolution as the inevitable outcome of the Enlightenment – the Enlightenment in action, stripped of its 'Fabian' illusions – and easier still, perhaps, to think of Beethoven as the natural successor to Haydn and even Mozart. The natural and the inevitable: familiarity breeds them both. But did there *have* to be a Beethoven? The question seems absurd, because to us Beethoven *is* the Revolution; no other period is so clearly dominated by one composer. Nevertheless, it is a salutary exercise to try to put him out of mind and to see what then emerges. One of the first results is sure to be a shift of interest from Vienna to Paris and a belated recognition that Rouget de Lisle's *La Marseillaise* was not the only music composed in Revolutionary France.

The almost total eclipse of the Parisian school by the Viennese is a striking example of the way posterity punishes even the brilliantly second-rate. François Joseph Gossec (1734–1829) pioneered the symphony in France and later anticipated Beethoven in his daring use of the orchestra, yet very few readers will have heard a note of his music. True, the French tradition is operatic, not symphonic, which might account for it. But what do we know, in performance, of the operas of Nicolas Dalayrac (1753–1809), Étienne Nicolas Méhul (1763–1817) or Jean François Lesueur (1760–1837) – or even Gasparo Spontini (1774–1851), the 'musician laureate' of the Empire? The honest answer is virtually nothing. These were all highly talented composers, and some of the work of Gossec, Méhul and Lesueur is, in the most immediate and literal sense, the music of the Revolution: occasional music for public celebrations, written for performance by enormous forces in the open air.

A truly original use of colour, popular melody in abundance and a strong ethical seriousness are typical of the French school in the last decade of the century. So is a feeling for the spectacular: Méhul's dream of a festival opera that would involve the entire population of Paris – nothing less! – may well have been fantastic, but it reflected the noblest aspirations of the age. The heroic ideal was to be re-created in the spirit of fraternity and given expression on the grandest possible scale: see, for example, Robespierre's Festival of the Supreme Being (1794), in which music played an indispensable role. All too often, though, the merely theatrical – or massively trivial – was mistaken for the sublime. As Grétry wryly remarked, every operatic perform-ance seemed to re-enact the storming of the Bastille. A romantic taste for the gruesome and horrific – the classic example is Lesueur's *La Caverne* – was another prominent feature. Under the Empire, theatricality was duly enthroned and nineteenth-century 'grand opera' came into being.

Méhul's ardour and extravagance make him a tempting sub-ject for further comment: his masterpiece is *Joseph* (1807), an impressive extension of *opéra comique* in the light of Gluck and of his own stylistic innovations. However, the one composer who really demands closer attention is Luigi Cherubini (1760–1842), another Italian of primary importance in French musical history.

CHERUBINI AND BEETHOVEN

When Cherubini settled in Paris on the eve of the Revolution, his Italian style had already been modified by the music of Gluck. In many ways he was peculiarly un-Italian: there was in his nature a gravity, even severity, that found expression in both a frigid classicism – something far removed from Mozart's Hellenic warmth – and a dramatic intensity that is almost Beethovenian. If his music is often dry and academic, it is never merely theatrical. Many, including Beethoven, considered Cherubini the greatest dramatic composer of his time: *Médée* (1797) is a notable landmark in musical tragedy, *Les Deux Journées* (1800) an outstanding example of the 'rescue opera' so popular during the Revolution. Without the latter, *Fidelio* would not have been composed; and without the C minor

Requiem, Beethoven's *Missa Solemnis* would have been a different work. The relationship with Beethoven is particularly striking in Cherubini's operatic overtures: the strong rhythmic motivation, the acute dynamic contrasts and many features of the scoring reveal the elements of Beethoven's symphonic style. Yet Cherubini had neither Beethoven's stupendous imagination nor his passionate sense of involvement. So we are back at the beginning: the one composer in Revolutionary France who might have achieved lasting stature is dwarfed by a comparison which he is powerless to prevent.

From Cherubini's point of view, such a comparison may well be invidious, but it is also instructive. Beethoven emerges not only as a greater artist but as a very different kind of man – a man of the Revolution in a far deeper sense than Cherubini or any of the composers mentioned above. This has everything to do with his attitude to experience. Though he respected the achievements of his predecessors, and indeed built upon them, Beethoven relied on his own inner resources to an unprecedented degree. His often quoted remark about taking Fate by the throat is really very revealing; no composer of the Enlightenment would have spoken like that. It is the total absence of *acceptance*, and a corresponding assertion of his own creative *will*, that marks out Beethoven – 'middle-period' Beethoven – from even the most gifted of his contemporaries. This does not make him a 'subjective' artist in the romantic sense. As A. K. Holland has rightly stressed, 'he was neither a classicist nor a romanticist, but a realist, and truth of expression was his constant aim'. The 'subject' of the *Eroica* Symphony is Beethoven himself; it is also Napoleon, but more than either it is the human spirit, reborn in the light – or rather, the fire – of one man's inner conflict. It is surely no mere accident that the 'Prometheus' theme (Ex. 11), which dominates the finale, assumed a lasting significance in Beethoven's mind. For he is nothing if not a Promethean figure, reaffirming the power of man to shape his own destiny. This view of the world had been the gospel of the Enlightenment, but often as little more than a speculative proposition. Beethoven gave it the immediacy of a manifesto; much of his work was both a practical demonstration and a call to action. Like Robespierre, he sought to *remake* the world in the image of his own transcendant vision.

BEETHOVEN'S MIDDLE PERIOD

Until 1792, Ludwig van Beethoven (1770–1827) lived at Bonn, in the Rhineland, where he served the Elector of Cologne and was chiefly known as a brilliant pianist with a flair for improvisation. He became acquainted with some of the music of Revolutionary France, which helped to form his own orchestral style – see, for instance, the finale of the Fifth Symphony (1805–8). But that lay in the future; the key to early Beethoven is his writing for the piano.

When he settled in Vienna, in his twenty-second year, his principal models were Haydn and C. P. E. Bach. To say that Beethoven began where Haydn left off is not quite as silly as it seems: the three sonatas of Op. 2 (1795) are on the scale of Haydn's more extended structures, and two of them take for granted his daring use of modulation. The personality is clearly Beethoven's. Listen to the finale of the Sonata in F minor (Op. 2 No. 1): the initial chords and arpeggios are full of a Beethovenian tension, and the *cantabile* second subject is equally revealing (Ex. 12). Even here one feels an underlying ferment, and the treatment of the piano remains percussive.

The link with C. P. E. Bach can best be illustrated by reference to Ex. 13, the opening of the Sonata in C minor, Op. 13

(*Pathétique*). Note the use of dynamic contrasts and expressive silences: these dramatic sighs are an extension of the style that Bach had made his own (see pp. 57–8).

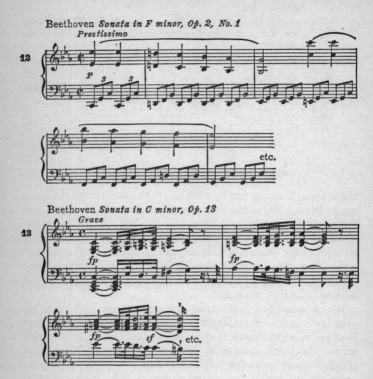

Beethoven *Sonata in F minor, Op. 2, No. 1*
Prestissimo

Beethoven *Sonata in C minor, Op. 13*
Grave

From the outset, Beethoven's desire for a freer, more impulsive mode of expression began to undermine the principles of classicism. Soon the established sequence of movements proved dispensable. Of the four sonatas which date from 1801, only one adheres to the conventional pattern; two are described as *quasi una fantasia*, in recognition of their unusual nature. One of these is the so-called *Moonlight* Sonata in C sharp minor, which is so familiar that its originality is easily forgotten: the opening *Adagio* is a unique expression of suffering, as insistent as it is outwardly calm; the finale is a conflict movement of unprecedented vehemence, and the intervening *Allegretto* is no idle homage to the minuet and trio. The emotional experience which the work embodies has dictated both the substance and the shape. Such music can scarcely be discussed in terms of Haydn, Bach or any other predecessor; it takes us into Beethoven's 'middle period'.

The added power and independence that enters into Beethoven's music at this time has much to do with the onset of deafness. The harrowing personal crisis of 1802, of which we catch a glimpse in the 'Heiligenstadt Testament', was almost bound to result in silence or renewal: the *Eroica* Symphony (1803–4) was the astonishing outcome. Not only is this an infinitely more ambitious work than anything Beethoven had previously attempted; it is also a profoundly truthful work, in a way that the Piano Sonata in C sharp minor is almost certainly not. For the *Eroica* is wholly free from romantic exaggeration; huge it is, yet nothing is falsified or rendered larger than life. And it provides overwhelming evidence of Beethoven's powers of organization – the sheer force of his musical mind.

The immense span of the opening movement is sustained by a most carefully planned succession of keys: the fact that Beethoven worked out the tonal drama first and only then decided on the final shape of the themes is itself significant; so is the much extended *coda*, which begins like a further development section – and lasts for 140 bars! Here, and subsequently in the Fifth, Seventh and Ninth Symphonies – the *Pastoral* too in a different way – Beethoven raised the sonata principle to a new plane of expression, at once more public and more personal. The music addresses, even harangues, the whole of mankind; the last vestige of the courtly, deferential manner has been scornfully discarded.* At the same time, the sonata's character

---

* One thinks of Beethoven's words to Prince Lichnowsky: 'Prince, what you are, you are by accident of birth; what I am, I am of myself. There are and there will be thousands of princes. There is only one Beethoven'.

is transformed, repeatedly, by the force of personal experience.

The *Eroica*'s Funeral March, at once ceremonial and introspective, is something quite new in slow movements: it is instructive to compare the opening with that of the *Andante*, also in C minor, from Haydn's Symphony No. 103. The Promethean *scherzo*, the first that can be so described, is only remotely anticipated in one or two of the piano sonatas. In the typical classical symphony, the final movement is a generalized expression of optimism; it reaffirms the perspective (of reason and enlightenment) in which experience should be evaluated. In the *Eroica*, the finale is itself the climax of experience and is fully intelligible only in relation to the other three movements. Still more obviously climactic is the finale of the Fifth: the change of key from C minor to C major, the march-like themes, the added weight of three trombones (their first appearance in this or any symphony) – together these convey an overwhelming sense of triumph. So, of course, does the choral finale of the Ninth, that great affirmation in which the whole world is felt to share.

Triumph over adversity is the central theme of Beethoven's 'middle period': most of the symphonies, the later piano concertos, the Violin Concerto, *Fidelio*, the *Rasoumovsky* Quartets – all are in some sense 'about' this theme or have it embedded in their background. An indomitable rhythmic energy, epitomized in the symphonic *scherzi*, and a colossal use of key-conflict are the essence of the new heroic style. To adapt Beethoven's words, this is the heroism of those whose nobility is of the heart and the head: Beethoven's republicanism and his 'struggle against Fate' were of exactly the same order.

The heart and the head! Writers on Beethoven have often stressed the one at the expense of the other. The music's emotional impact has proved so enduring that the power of organization underlying it is all too easily taken for granted. A number of Beethoven's contemporaries, especially in France, called new musical forces into being, but the use they made of these was invariably rhetorical and grandiose. Only Beethoven himself both called into being and effectively subdued: his innovations, far from being mere rhetorical gestures, are ultimately inseparable from the structural systems they inspired. There is no more striking example than the Seventh Symphony, which, properly understood, is as much a new beginning as the *Eroica* or the Fifth, and perhaps even more so. In the massive introduction Beethoven established an unprecedented relationship between the key of A major and the (remote) keys of C and F. He then worked this out, consciously and consistently, throughout the symphony; and he matched this enlarged sense of key-relations with a new approach to modulation. No wonder the Seventh so bewildered its first audiences! Passing histrionics, in an otherwise conventional structure, or 'superheated' surface values would have presented few problems; but Beethoven was offering a further transformation of the entire classical system – nothing less. Such powerful headwork daunted even the young Weber, who declared that Beethoven was 'ripe for the madhouse'.

THE LATE QUARTETS

The music of Beethoven's last years is not only profoundly different from anything attempted by his contemporaries – and, indeed, from the achievements of his own 'middle period' – but has never been successfully followed up. Other composers have found ways of reconciling sonata and fugue, dramatic conflict and thematic growth: this, however, means little in itself. Few have even approached the kind of experience embodied in the five string quartets – in E flat (Op. 127), A minor (Op. 132), B flat (Op. 130), C sharp minor (Op. 131) and F (Op. 135) – composed by Beethoven between 1824 and 1826.

The *Grosse Fuge* (Op. 133), intended as the finale of the B flat Quartet, sums up what is perhaps the most crucial aspect of these works, 'the reconciliation of assertion and submission'. Essentially monothematic, it achieves a synthesis of experience very different from that associated with the sonata principle. The composer had discovered that the key to life was not to be found entirely in struggle and resistance. In his increasing loneliness he had learnt the need for submission. This is expressed already in the first movement of the Ninth Symphony – in some respects a transitional work – and it underlies the gaiety of the finale of the Quartet in F, a movement inscribed '*Muss es sein? Es muss sein!*' ('Must it be? It must be!'). The late quartets reveal a new level of consciousness at which the whole range of experience can be reappraised. The struggle is no longer with some external power called Fate; it is a struggle to resolve the conflicting elements *within*, a striving for unity and understanding. Repeatedly in the works from Beethoven's last years a sense of striving becomes a condition of the music's very performance: the *Missa Solemnis* and the finale of the Ninth Symphony, the *Grosse Fuge* and the fugue from the *Hammerklavier* Sonata (Op. 106) – all impose upon their performers a physical stress inseparable from the quality of expression. And if a new sense of striving is communicated, so is a new serenity.

In the finest string quartet, the C sharp minor, the established four-movement scheme, which Beethoven had generally found adaptable to his purpose, is completely superseded. There are seven movements, beginning with a fugue and ending with a 'sonata'; the sequence is unique, determined solely by the imaginative conception. To call this music 'other-worldly' or 'metaphysical', as is commonly done, is to block the understanding with mystification. Truly, there are few works in any medium that so powerfully sustain the claims of art to be a vehicle for an almost superhuman revelation; yet what Beethoven reveals is not some 'heavenly vision' but a higher level of reality which, as J. W. N. Sullivan remarks, 'we recognize both as fundamental and as in advance of anything we have hitherto known'.

The composer of the late quartets has been depicted as a spiritual hermit who withdrew from the world to create for himself and posterity. Is this the complete picture? Clearly, Beethoven was no longer addressing the mass audience implied by his symphonies. But in a sense that audience no longer existed; the conditions which created and sustained it had passed with the defeat of Napoleon. Far from inaugurating an era of freedom and democracy, the War of Liberation had brought in its wake a crushing political reaction. Almost everywhere the old dynasties had been restored; Vienna was the centre of a widespread attempt to stamp out liberal aspirations,

in art as in life. Objectively, this is the world from which
Beethoven 'withdrew'. Some may say that the drastic change
in social climate merely coincided with a new phase in Beethoven's inner development, but such a view ignores two important points. Deaf and lonely as he was, the man who composed
the finale of the Ninth Symphony can hardly have been indiffer-
ent to the tide of reaction. Moreover, Beethoven's writing for
the few – the new élite who in their own private circles would
keep alive the human spirit – is not an isolated case. The work
of Schubert and his friends, so different in substance, forms a
very close parallel.

BEETHOVEN'S CONTEMPORARIES

We tend to forget that Beethoven's later years were also the
period of Schubert, of Weber and, in part, of Spohr. This is,
perhaps, a further reflection of Beethoven's unique dominance
– for us, that is – but it must also be attributed to the younger
composers' very different orientation. Louis Spohr (1784–1859)
was a post-Mozartian, of talent rather than genius, whose
'romanticized classicism' forms a link between Mozart and
Mendelssohn. Carl Maria von Weber (1786–1826) pioneered
German romantic opera; taking as his starting point the sentimental *Singspiel* and the popular fairy opera, he created a world
of chivalry and folk myth which foreshadows Wagner's
Lohengrin. Of the three, only Franz Schubert (1797–1828) was
in any sense a disciple of Beethoven, and his Beethovenian
aspect – his handling of sonata conflict – is generally less remarkable than his feeling for the *Lied*. These composers represent
important strands in the early history of Romanticism and will
be discussed in that context (see Section II).

Of Beethoven's older contemporaries not already mentioned,
the Italian pianist-composer Muzio Clementi (1752–1832) must
be given first place. In both performance and composition,
Clementi did more than anyone to establish an authentic piano
style: his numerous sonatas, composed throughout a long working life, reflect the changing outlook of the period; the first are
galante, the last 'early romantic', and at each stage something

distinctive emerges. He belongs to that valuable category of artists who sum up, even typify, their age. His many distinguished pupils, including Cramer, Czerny, Field, Hummel, Meyerbeer and Moscheles, take us well into the romantic era. The Hungarian, Johann Nepomuk Hummel (1778–1837), and the Irishman, John Field (1782–1837), are indispensable links between the classical piano style and that of Chopin, Liszt and Schumann. Field's nocturnes and the poetic piano pieces of the Czech composer Václav Jaromir Tomášek (1774–1850) are highly prophetic; they belong to the dreamy, idyllic world of the nineteenth-century drawing-room. Tomášek is significant in other respects besides: even his earlier pieces show unmistakable national traits – pointers to Smetana – and a conscious allying of music to literature.

Further intimations of the romantic era abound in the music of Prince Louis Ferdinand of Prussia (1772–1806). A pupil of the Czech classical master Jan Ladislav Dussek (1760–1812), Louis Ferdinand composed mainly for chamber groups with piano, in a manner that much impressed Schumann: the subtly varied inflexion of his themes and his individual handling of established forms mark him out as an early exponent of 'romanticized classicism'. Another worthy composer of chamber music is Emanuel Aloys Förster (1748–1823). Of the same generation as Mozart and Clementi, Förster anticipated early Beethoven in his writing for string quartet, especially in his spontaneous expansion of ideas. A notable 'might-have-been' is Juan Arriaga (1806–26), a gifted young Spaniard whose string quartets, composed in Paris, prompt comparisons with Haydn.

Artists such as these enable us to form a fuller picture of the period. For even in an age of revolution, when aesthetic values and the artist's social function are undergoing far-reaching changes, much is achieved that is clearly evolutionary in character. This is further underlined by the continuing development of Italian opera. It is salutary to recall that Rossini's international triumph and the last five string quartets of Beethoven belong to the same decade: on the one hand the ultimate climax of eighteenth-century *opera buffa*, and on the other the profoundest searching of the individual consciousness.

II . THE NINETEENTH CENTURY

A. J. B. Hutchings

1. The Romantic Era

STENDHAL, wishing to extol imaginative artists who lived before the nineteenth century, declared that all art was romantic in its own day. Moved by Bach's St Peter or by Handel's Cleopatra, we understand the aphorism; yet if evocative power makes any artist a romantic, the romantic era becomes extended back indefinitely. From Plato to Pepys men have been as strongly moved by music as were Wagner's devotees. The fact need not prevent our using 'romantic' to distinguish in this opening phrase of a Schubert song a subtle shade of feeling which we do not recall in previous songs, nor, for all their wonderful range of emotions, in Mozart's operas:

Schubert *Die Winterreise, No. 11 (Frühlingsträume)*

14

How does its tenderness differ from that of previous music? To call it 'vernal' is not enough, for so (by name) is one of Beethoven's violin sonatas and so is Vivaldi's concerto *La Primavera*! It is of the utmost importance to see the futility of any attempt to answer that 'How?' Sensibility recognizes from Schubert what cannot be defined verbally – a turn of expression associated with Schumann and Chopin rather than Haydn and Mozart.

Though the romantic era offers music inspired by nature, literature, historical characters and events, its composers would have practised a purely ancillary art if they had done no more than symbolize visual ideas and express emotions that can be named, such as victory, anger, longing: even their most programmatic work, like any music worth hearing, conveys ideas and emotions which cannot be named. If we found in

Berlioz's *Symphonie fantastique* no more than is suggested by the sub-titles we should suppose it a feeble piece. Who would feel terror during the '*Marche au supplice*' if its title were not known? Fortunately the piece offers ample compensations for terror.

The aesthetics of the romantic era are usually explained by amplifications of Hugo's 'artistic freedom' or Lessing's and Schiller's opposing of 'classical' and 'romantic'. 'Classical art had to express only the finite . . . romantic art had to represent the infinite and the spiritual': so wrote Heine, who added that the classical artist could use definite and usually symmetrical forms. This statement can be challenged, even if we translate 'forms' as 'inherited designs' – fugue, French overture, rondo, sonata. As for 'the beauty of classical art is objective, that of romantic art is subjective', or 'the classical artist is more concerned with form than expression', or 'the romantic artist is catholic, not restricted in his tastes' – these are propagandist oversimplifications.

Nineteenth-century composers were not more versatile and powerful than Bach or Mozart, and none was as consummate a craftsman, but almost every one of them had opportunity for a wider general culture. Free from the obligation to perform and compose for church, city or prince, looking to wide audiences from the increasingly enfranchised middle classes (many capital cities quadrupled their population between 1800 and 1860), gifted musicians were welcome in literary and artistic circles. Beethoven's patrons paid the piper but did not presume to call the tune; their successors were ready to regard artists as critics and prophets. The baroque and classical composer was hardly aware that he belonged to a school or period, that he had any choice of style except between what showed 'taste' (a favourite eighteenth-century word) and what did not. The romantic artist, on the other hand, was conscious of being a romantic, of kinship with the young and with writers and painters, and of living in an age of enormous material expansion and adventure. 'The Artist' not 'The Musician' was Wagner's self-description, but others less bold, such as Schumann, so described themselves. Were they not themselves poets and essayists? Was Berlioz, composer and author, an inferior artist to E. T. A. Hoffmann, author and composer? He would have been so in the previous century.

From thousands of exegeses of the romantic movement perhaps the most valuable brief comment was Sir W. A. Raleigh's, that to the romantics distance in space or time often lends enchantment. Distant hills are romantic; so is any horizon of adventure or yearning: so are legends and conceptions of historical scenes and events, as were the people and land of Scott's novels to Europeans who had never seen Scotland. Opera has always favoured the legendary past and has 'romanticized' settings purporting to be contemporary and realistic. No wonder, therefore, that the romantic movement found its greatest musical triumphs in the lyric theatre.

GERMAN OPERA AND SONG

Weber and German Romantic Opera

The ascendance of the romantic movement during the classic era is evident when we note, maybe with surprise, that the career of Carl Maria von Weber (1786–1826) falls within Beethoven's. His father was Austrian, and related to Mozart's wife, but the dramatic company with which he toured for some years frequented north and central German towns. The composer was born near Lübeck, and this fact, together with a youthful period of service as secretary to the Duke of Württemberg may have made him feel himself a German appealing to Germans who aspired to the unification of a nation.

Though 'born to the theatre', and a natural judge of stage effect (Beethoven, having seen some of his songs and piano pieces, said 'Weber should compose operas, many operas'), Weber succeeded in opera thanks to his intelligence, wide reading and refined tastes as much as to his stage upbringing and his being born at the right time to appeal to Germans and romantics. The company's migrations prevented his staying long with one music teacher, but he acknowledged debt to the earlier, stricter and more conservative lessons under Heuschkel and Michael Haydn as well as to those later taken under the charlatan but liberal Vogler, who claims another distinguished operatic pupil in Meyerbeer. Whatever Weber's natural talents, he must have studied playing and composing techniques more seriously than is often acknowledged in order to become a concert pianist and the composer of those works for piano and orchestra or clarinet and orchestra which still brighten the repertory. He would be honoured if we knew only his instrumental music, yet to the historian the most significant of his non-stage works is the collection of songs for male chorus or solo voice with piano called *Lyre and Sword*, not so much prefiguring the huntsmen's choruses in his operas as arousing fervid enthusiasm all over Germany, especially among students and devotees of the growing national movement.

The rise of consciously 'nationalist' music later in the century, while acknowledged to be part of the romantic movement, is also often explained as the reaction of such composers as Glinka, Smetana and Debussy against German hegemony. This view sees in German music a recognizable 'central' technique of composition derived from an apostolic succession of German-speaking musicians from Bach and Handel, through the Viennese 'Big Four' to Schumann, Mendelssohn, Brahms and Wagner. Yet a German nationalist movement of which Weber is a clear example preceded these others. It is less distinctive to the ear than the Russian or Czech movement because it does not seem consciously fertilized by folk song and dance. This is because the characteristics of German *Volkslied* were already absorbed in German 'art' music from Luther's time to Weber's. Consequently, though Wagner appealed to a picturesque national past by the story and scenery of *Die Meistersinger*, his medieval 'master themes' brought nothing archaic or folksy into the music.

Yet Weber, like Wagner, was a deliberate nationalist. In Weber's boyhood Mozart (who himself wrote and spoke of 'Us Germans' who would eclipse 'these Italians') had raised to magnificence the only kind of opera to German words – the *Singspiel* of the fairgrounds. Along with the rich trombone scoring for the priestly scenes and the brilliant Italianate arias for the Queen of the Night are Papageno's songs which come

most nearly to German *Volkslied*. Mozart's delighted response
for Schikaneder's popular theatre may not have been consciously
nationalist, but it inspired those who jettisoned classical myths
for Teutonic folk and fairy tales and continued the elevation of
Singspiel into German opera even before it had shed its spoken
dialogue. Links in the chain between Mozart's German masterpiece and *Der Freischütz*, include continuations of *Die Zauberflöte*, plays about Danube nymphs, an opera called *The Swiss
Family* (Robinson to us) and Schubert's unsuccessful *Rosamunde* music as well as his other wasted *Singspiele*. The nearest
approach to *Freischütz* in theme, mood and music, however, was
E. T. A. Hoffman's *Undine*, produced in 1816 in Berlin.

Despite the romantic verve and colour of other Weber operas,
popularly known by their brilliant overtures (*Preciosa, Rubezahl,
Abu Hassan, Euryanthe*), none had quite the impact of *Der
Freischütz* and even its composer cannot have foreseen its
enormous appeal to German audiences. It comes from communal rather than political symbols – the *Lindenbaum* in the
village square, *Der Wald* which symbolizes much more than
'the forest', the shooting contest, the very clothes of the forest-
ers. In a German theatre there is almost a religious atmosphere
in productions of this opera: elsewhere we relish the evocative
power of orchestral effects used as older composers used
melodic themes, e.g. the tensely quiet 'bullet' pizzicato under
a shuddering string tremolo, first found in the Overture at the
end of the slow introduction. Beethoven seems to have recognized Weber's command of adroit transitions and telling effects.
His harmony is limited, but so imaginatively used that we
wonder how malevolence and eeriness can gather tension and
still make us feel terror during the casting of the bullets in the
Wolf's Glen when later composers have so enriched resources.
Weber's last German opera, *Euryanthe*, judged purely as music
– especially in its choruses and scenas – was his best. There is
more deliberate recourse to recurrent ideas or leitmotive and
for the first time in a *Singspiel* the music is continuous between
rise and fall of curtain.

Thus Weber's operas point us to *Der fliegende Holländer,
Lohengrin* and *Tannhäuser*. With Weber's early death, as with

Schubert's, music lost 'still fairer hopes' for German operas until Wagner's were ready. Heinrich Marschner (1795–1861) bridged the gap with romantic folk lore and eerie evocation of the supernatural in *Der Vampyr* (1828) and in his masterpiece *Hans Heiling* (1833), works which influenced Wagner in *Der fliegende Holländer*. Not all German-speaking romantics were consciously nationalist. Some were Viennese; some like

Weber *Wolf's Glen music from Der Freischütz*

Marschner were much influenced by Italian *opera buffa* and French *opéra comique*. (Operas by Hérold and Adam were so popular in Germany from 1830 to 1840 that Italian music seemed to have been banished only to give place to French.) Finally due tribute must be paid to some attractive light and humorous German operas of the romantic epoch. The best known of the somewhat Viennese operettas of Albert Lortzing (1801–1851) are *Zar und Zimmermann*, *Der Wildschütz* and *Der Waffenschmied*, all using leitmotive and evoking the supernatural. His *Hans Sachs* naturally interested Wagner. Robustly comic without supernatural elements are *The Merry Wives of Windsor* by the Viennese conductor-composer Otto Nicolai (1810–49) and the lyrically beautiful *Barber of Baghdad* by Peter Cornelius (1824–74), a poet-composer who championed Liszt and Wagner.

Schubert and German Song

Franz Peter Schubert (1797–1828), the 'last of the giants' and the only one of the four born Viennese, had no fame beyond his native city during his tragically short life. His instrumental masterpieces are held in such affection that to discuss them here would merely defer to the belief that history should apportion pages in ratio to esteem and merit, writing more about some universally admired sonata than about its provocative fellow. These classical works represent the Schubert for whom the designs of Haydn, Mozart and Beethoven were so beloved an inheritance that 'heavenly length' presented no problems. He could be both magniloquent and relaxed, tragic and tender in symphony and sonata. He could weave 'magic casements' of harmonic colour and texture in such works as the C major Quintet, the A minor, D minor and G major Quartets within spreading movements which rarely lose classical proportion and sense of purpose. The last and most magnificent of his symphonies, the C major of 1828, was discovered by Schumann, and its more sombre and pathetic rival in B minor, begun six years earlier, remained unfinished but offers two of the most sublime movements in the whole repertory.

Schubert the symphonist is a luxury inessential to the tracing of history: not so the Schubert who *did* enjoy unremunerative popularity with friends in and around Vienna. One does not underplay his poverty and occasional unhappiness by noting that at the Imperial Seminary (Konvict) where, as one of the cathedral choristers, his education was free he formed lasting friendships with well-to-do and intelligent boys, that his bohemian life was his own choice, since he detested teaching, and that if he had lived a little longer he would probably have reaped the material reward of genius. Moreover he must have been happier at a 'Schubertiad' or musical party in the family home of one of his friends than are many musicians during their acclaim in concert hall or theatre, for he was the centre of affection as well as admiration. This opinion is not negated by our recognizing, among his many sociable duets, marches, waltzes and piano pieces, such impressive evidences of his forward-looking genius as the Grand Duo and the *Wanderer* Fantasy.

Schubert *Die Winterreise, No. 20 (Der Wegweiser)*

If Schubert had written only his 603 songs, or if we knew him only by the cycles *Die schöne Müllerin* and *Die Winterreise* and the collection called *Schwanengesang*, he would be a first-rate artist of inestimable historical importance. The songs embody not only the lyrical Schubert but also Beethoven's musical legatee. The nature and dimension of such a favourite song as *Der Wegweiser* is not far from that of the *Andante* in the great C major Symphony; and one has but to imagine the terrifying *Erlkönig* as an operatic *scena* (the main accompanimental figure is an unconscious reminiscence of the dungeon scene in *Fidelio*), with the horns in octaves occasionally joining the ominous triplets, to recognize the Schubert whose romantic operas might have rivalled *Freischütz*.

These tragic and more complex songs, or the settings of Goethe's *Ganymed* and *Prometheus*, are not more wonderful than those which, in Capell's words, express 'the rapture and poignancy of first sensations'. Nor should such spontaneous popular favourites as *Das Wandern* and *Heidenröslein* be dismissed as 'Biedermeier' trifles after the simple happy character in a humorous Viennese periodical whose name now designates the cosy-romantic sentiment of his period. They give us the obverse of *Der Leiermann* and *Der Doppelgänger* which express a pathos too deep for tears.

The songs are above Müller's literary level. There was a time when critics marvelled that the great Schubert was attracted to so light a versifier as Müller: we now recognize his wisdom in taking from Müller as from Goethe just what elicited music and in rejecting what did not. Schubert's songs are not mere word-setting (occasionally he could be rough with verbal accent) but a marriage in which music comes first, the romantic piano with its expressive figurations and telling modulations playing a part comparable with that of Weber's orchestra. Goethe supplied him with poems for seventy-one songs and Schiller with forty-two, but we have no proof that minor versifiers would not have inspired some of his greatest songs even if there had been more Goethe lyrics of appealing rhythm and imagery.

Like Berlioz and Weber, Robert Schumann (1810–56) had refined tastes and wrote well himself. From his articles in his periodical, the *Neue Zeitschrift für Musik*, we know the names of many minor contemporaries of Schubert who were fired by the new flow of lyric verse but whose songs are now almost forgotten. Many of Schumann's songs continue to be held in high esteem, including those written in 1840 after twelve years during which he had composed only for the piano, believing that the romantic 'inexpressible' could not be tied down by words. This articulate knowledge of his expressive desires together with his own and his wife's training as pianists led to distinguishing features between his songs and Schubert's. So far from tying 'the inexpressible' to the singing of words, many of Schumann's songs convey their riches and subtleties of sentiment if played as piano solos or duets or with an instrument replacing the voice. Beethoven's sonatas can be regarded as the epics of the instrument, their rhetoric contrasted with lyricism, whereas Schumann's characteristic piano pieces are the equivalents of short lyrics published in collections containing odes. His songs, with the same finely judged figurations, spacing of chords, use of the sustaining pedal and *cantabile* melodies, are a proliferation rather than an interruption in their output. There are exceptions. The well-known *Die beiden Grenadiere* culminating in the melody of *La Marseillaise* is a Schubertian ballad, and the piano provides only simple accompaniment in miniatures like *Die Rose, die Lilie* and certain songs to Burns lyrics.

In general, however, Schumann belongs to the full flush of romantic fever, no longer picturesque and hearty but personal and heart-felt if not (as has been said of the Chamisso cycle *Frauenliebe und Leben*) near-psychotic. 1840 was the year of Schumann's rapturously happy marriage, and his chosen poets often spoke of the intense yearning and suffering which preceded that cruelly opposed union. He loved to compose song cycles, as he did suites of genre pieces for piano, for within either of the *Liederkreis* cycles (the first Heine, the second Eichendorff) or *Dichterliebe* (Heine) the piano often carries the drama, the atmosphere and the imagery. His choice of poets implies international connoisseurship and a cultivated taste. A few Heine lyrics came Schubert's way but he missed Eichendorff: for Schumann these poets 'gave a very echo to the seat where love sits throned'.

Carl Loewe (1796–1869) was actually a year older than Schubert and could claim honour if only for the fact that his *Erlkönig*, composed soon after Schubert's marvellous setting but before he knew it, is still valued as showing an effective and integrated contrast, and proving that not even Schubert exhausted the possibilities of a stimulating poem. Loewe was born in Bach's district, Thuringia, and became a cantor. His was a manly, happy temperament, as he reveals in an enjoyable autobiography which tells us how the King of Westphalia, admiring his self-accompanied singing, gave him a small annuity which enabled him to devote himself to music. His songs cover an international galaxy of poets and he travelled much in Germany, Scandinavia and France as his own interpreter. Always a hard worker, Loewe composed operas, oratorios, symphonies, piano pieces and an enormous number of songs which seem a little too fluent and 'artless' simply because we judge him by Schubert and Schumann. Many are in a style rightly or wrongly called *Volkslied*, more suited to domestic than concert performance. He is cultivated, especially in Germany, for the two veins in which he is distinctive – the dramatic ballad, as exemplified by *Edward* and *Prinz Eugen*, and humorous songs, such as *Hinkende Jamben*.

The songs of Robert Franz (1815–92) were admired by Schumann, Mendelssohn and Liszt. He, too, was a cantor (which by his time meant simply organist-choirmaster) and became a university musician in his native Halle. He wilfully eschewed the dramatic and passionate yet achieved without affectation an admirable reflective simplicity in such songs as *Schlummerlied*, *Im Rhein* and *Die Widmung*. His is the art that conceals art for he was less the visionary than the highly skilled professional musician and teacher.

Johannes Brahms (1833–97) belongs to a generation later than Schumann's. His lyrical blooms are of summer and autumn rather than spring, being less impulsive. This contrast is attributable partly to the passing of the first flush of the romantic movement, partly to Brahms's temperament.

He was an industrious professional musician, not a romantic bohemian. After boyhood in the squalor of Hamburg's waterfront he seemed a taciturn youth except in his brilliant piano playing and compositions which made conservative critics regard him as one of 'the rabid Liszt school' – a fact too easily forgotten as we admire the powerful restraint of his mature music and his tributes to classical designs. His father, a horn and double-bass player in local bands, understood the child's musical yearnings and generously secured as teacher Hamburg's best pianist-composer, Marxen. Brahms's first considerable earnings were as an accompanist first to Remenyi, a Hungarian virtuoso violinist, and then to Joachim. Admired by Joachim, Liszt and the Schumanns, he secured from his mid thirties onwards an esteem which few composers enjoy until later years, and but for his love of Hamburg he might have remained the musical lion of Vienna. The reserved and industrious young man grew to a stout, bearded and often sarcastic bachelor – an exterior which hid a passionately warm nature.

Despite the impressive orchestral and chamber works, many musicians regard Brahms's songs as containing the quintessence of his art, and his instrumental works from the violin sonatas to the last symphony as most rewarding in the song-like passages that glow more richly for being offset by classical rhetoric. Neither their lyricism nor that of the songs can be fully enjoyed by those totally inattentive to the shape of his spreading melodies, the fine fashioning of their extensions and overlappings, their punctuation and paragraphing. He was more inspired by musical 'architecture' (especially in Bach or Beethoven) than were other romantic pianists. Even when verses required swift movement, vigour, or bluff humour (e.g. *Das Mädchen spricht*, *Der Schmied*, *Vergebliches Ständchen*) his effects were carefully studied and the piano subordinated to a finely balanced vocal melody, for he insisted upon an unequivocal polarity of melody and bass in all textures.

There are no sudden vintage years in Brahms's continuous and consistent output of songs, and his only cycle is *Die schöne Magelone* to verses from Tieck's 'medieval' tale. His last *Vier ernste Gesänge* from the Bible are hardly a cycle. Though they reflect on life and death they do not reach their climaxes in philosophic declamation, magnificent though it is, but in lyricism. St Paul's *Agape* or *Caritas* was perforce translated by Luther as *Liebe*, at which word Brahms's monody takes phrase-shapes as in his love songs; and the finest song of the four is that in which the stark harmonies of 'O Death how bitter . . .' serve but to offset the lyrical rapture of 'O Death how welcome . . .'. Sequences or rhetorical repetitions sometimes make Brahms's phrases not unlike Wagner's (Ex. 17A), but Brahms's melody is more subtle and less direct, especially in rhythm. (See

Ex. 17B – a hemiola extension in a superficially simple song.)
Brahms's songs are not for lazy ears content to enjoy first sensations nor for weak minds disturbed by their fully adult emotion.
The sexuality in some of Brahms's (and Schumann's) best songs
is unlike the idyllic hope or despair – 'in love with love' – of
Schubert's. Giving outlet to the 'inexpressibles' of the sub-
conscious, some of the romantics elicited not merely self-
revelation but shame, and led to harsh words about artists who,

like George Sand or Wagner, could be accused of marital incon-
stancy. But such critics missed in Schumann's Piano Quintet
and Brahms's Clarinet Quintet as rich an expression of sexual
longing as is found in any Wagner drama except *Tristan*. Being
post-Freud we can recognize it as much in the pathos of '*O
wüsst ich doch . . .*' ('O that I knew the path back to childhood')
– which is possibly Brahms's loveliest song – as in the overt
libido of *Sapphische Ode* and *Die Mainacht*. Their ideal voice is
a rich contralto, and we recall that Brahms loved the alto
register in such instruments as clarinet, horn and viola.

FRANCE (1800–1850)

During the French as during the Russian Revolutionary years, the theatres were crowded and the taste of the citizens was for the operatic splendour formerly enjoyed by their rulers. With Napoleon's conquests and plunderings Paris became rich, and English travellers commented upon new prosperity in the countryside. Paris, not Vienna, was an international Mecca for composers and performers even before Napoleon's downfall, and Napoleon's reign witnessed the first stages in the erection of the grandest opera-house in Europe. (He could not erect native genius. During the first half of the century we look in vain for any great French musician except Berlioz to equal the energy or calibre of settlers – Spontini, Cherubini, Rossini, Meyerbeer, Liszt, Chopin, Wagner.) By the 1830s new buildings, squares and gardens, above all the new gas-lighting, had made Paris *la ville lumière*, and she was to be further transformed into 'Great Exhibition' Paris by Haussmann's boulevards, the new water supply and the still famous sewers! To the musician, 'France 1800–1850' suggests 'grand' opera, Berlioz, and Chopin.

'Grand Opera' in Paris

Before the Revolution Paris had been the scene of Gluck's triumphs, partly because there the Lully–Rameau lyric tragedy had never permitted the abuses which he attacked in his *Alceste* preface, and from which *Alceste* itself was so conspicuously free. It was in the native language: the string-accompanied *récit* respected the verse, the *airs* tended towards brevity rather than prolix concerto style, and the chorus enjoyed a ritual and ceremonial participation in the drama. This reconstituted ('re-formed' is a tendentious mistranslation) *opera seria* is often supposed to have had little influence, since *opera seria* as a genre was ousted by romantic opera in the vernacular of its country, and in Italy by the unstilted vernacular of *opera buffa*. But the spectacular operas of the Revolutionary and Napoleonic period were often like highly aggrandized and decorated Gluck tragedies, especially when their setting was classical. Gluck's basic recipe is present from Cherubini's *Médée* (1797) to Berlioz's *Les Troyens*, finished in 1858, but these are among the few operas of their place and time which maintain any marked dignity.

Most of the opera composers competing for popularity in Paris took note of the triumph of Spontini's *La Vestale* in 1807. Like many grandiose works to follow, this masterpiece by Napoleon's favourite composer contains fine items, solo and ensemble, and fewer *longueurs* than many works by greater artists, so shrewdly did the purveyors in Paris understand 'good stage'. Many have derided what Wagner called 'effects without causes' without noting Wagner's own recourse to them in *Rienzi* and *Lohengrin*. If the heaven-sent streak of lightning which kindled the vestal fire and established Julia's innocence in *La Vestale* is a 'gimmick', then so is the coming to life of Diana's statue in Gluck's *Iphigénie en Tauride*. It is sometimes forgotten that the chief attractions of the old lyric tragedy were the *divertissements* which used choruses, ballets and scenic effects. They are acceptable by the sternest critic if they spring from the dramatic situation; hence the favourite pastoral-rejoicing, sacrificial, funeral, council and ceremonial scenes. The spectacular crowds and noisy marches in *La Vestale* or its successors – Spontini's *Fernand Cortez* (1817) and *Olympie* (1819), Auber's *La Muette de Portici* (1828), Rossini's *Guillaume Tell* (1829), Meyerbeer's *Robert le Diable* (1831), and Halévy's *La Juive* (1835) – would seem no less plausible than the *divertissements* in the Lully–Rameau tragedy or the ritual choruses and ballets used by Gluck but for the simple fact that, except for Rossini, these are third-rate composers: their harmonies and rhythms are stodgily limited and cannot meet the diversity of emotions demanded by the story.

Rossini and Meyerbeer
The magnetism of Paris needs no stronger testimony than its attraction of Gioacchino Rossini (1792–1868), whose thirty-five or so operas were all produced in the nineteen years following his own eighteenth, when he began his meteoric rise to fame

in Italy. One does not minimize his talents by noting contributory factors to his popularity – his indolent good humour, his opportunism in dealing with managers, performers and possible rivals, and his commercial alliance with Barbaja, formerly a café waiter, who from the profits of gaming tables and theatres secured a controlling interest in the most famous Italian operahouses, and later in Vienna during the Congress period.

It is by his comic operas, especially *Il Barbiere di Siviglia*, *La Cenerentola*, *Il Turco in Italia* and *Le Comte Ory*, as well as the overtures to several others that Rossini has maintained his popularity. We think of him chiefly as a wit, his beloved Mozart's successor in *opera buffa* since he inherited some of Mozart's skills. The principal skill is one of illusion, making the story seem to move at speed, arias coming either at moments of lyrical repose or when the characters advance the audience's complicity in the intrigue. His use of tension is also skilful, extending finales of acts by cumulative ensembles of leading characters. The 'Rossini *crescendo*', especially when it engages a whole cast in an act-finale *imbroglio strepitoso*, is both an effect to 'bring down the house' and also a symbol of his dramatic acumen. His vivacious comic operas are less 'real-life' even than Mozart's *Così fan Tutte* and lack the quivering, passionate undercurrents of *Figaro* and *Don Giovanni*; but what comic opera until Verdi's *Falstaff* restores them? The slander song in *Il Barbiere* represents the abundance and the limitation of Rossini's humour.

At this point it is well worth recalling the fact that Schubert, Weber and Rossini were contemporaries, and also noting how Rossini outshone the others in light, catchy melodies. Three samples are reduced in Ex. 18 to a common key and time-signature.

Paris lured Rossini in 1828. His advent piece was *Le Comte Ory*, tailored to French taste, more a burlesque than a classical *opera buffa*, and the model for French comic operettas of the mid century. In the following year came his tribute to Parisian grand opera, *Guillaume Tell*, and then Rossini wrote no more operas. Instead he enjoyed forty years as a bon vivant who entertained artists and other friends to dinners which he helped to cook, treating them also to the songs and piano pieces he called 'the sins of my old age'. He felt himself 'born to *opera buffa*', belonging, like its classical harmony, to the eighteenth century; yet merely to play over the second act of *Guillaume Tell* or the *Agnus Dei* in his *Petite Messe solenelle* (1864) – the meiosis of the title is typically Rossinian, maliciously flicked towards many a flatulent and sanctimonious *Grande Messe solenelle* – is to understand the veneration of other musicians and to wonder if his merry shade should be reproached for declining the effort which could have revealed greater depths of expression.

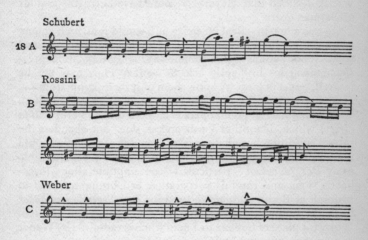

Like its predecessors, *opera seria* and *tragédie lyrique*, 'grand opera' still implied a contrast with *opéra comique*, *Singspiel* and ballad opera in which there might be spoken dialogue, but it ceased to show distinctions in the source of its stories. Both types of opera might use one of Scott's enormously popular Waverley Novels. The term 'grand opera' became popular during the reign of its high priests – Louis Véron, director of the Paris opera, Eugène Scribe, its most influential librettist, and Giacomo Meyerbeer (1791–1864), conductor and composer.

Meyerbeer, born Jakob Beer, son of a Jewish banker in Berlin, took the 'Meyer' from a wealthy relative who left him a legacy.

After his debut as a brilliant young pianist he studied with Zelter, then Vogler, forming a lasting friendship with Weber, his junior among Vogler's pupils. Salieri encouraged him when his first operas were unsuccessful in Berlin and Vienna; following the advice to be less 'scholastic' and to study the voice, he went to Venice during the triumph of Rossini's *Tancredi* and secured a triumph himself with *Il Crociato in Egitto*. Invited in 1826 to see it produced in Paris he soon became a Francophile and Parisian, though he passed a good deal of time in Berlin. Weber declared that Meyerbeer could have been 'the saviour of German opera'.

He was a fine practical musician and would rank high among opera composers if he had commanded an integrated, personal style. Nobody seems able to point to any highly idiomatic expression among his brilliantly eclectic works. They may yet be revived, but at present we know them only by excerpts from *Les Huguenots* (1836), *Le Prophète* (1849) and *L'Africaine* (1865). The date of his last grand opera is close to that of Verdi's *Aida* (1871) which, like other Verdi operas, does not abandon the 'grand' tradition but vitalizes it by dramatic genius. We should not disparage Meyerbeer because of Wagner's contemptible essay *Das Judentum* – particularly contemptible after Meyerbeer's 'long and careful' preparation had brought *Rienzi* to triumph at Berlin and had secured for *Der fliegende Holländer* its Berlin production after failure in Paris, Leipzig and Munich. We owe a place of honour to a man who was admired by Weber and lived to influence both Verdi and Wagner.

Yet our giving of due honour cannot lead us to call much internationally purveyed opera 'great' instead of merely 'grand'. As if to expose false evaluation Providence allowed just one native French composer – spurned as an opera composer by Paris – to be recognized by posterity as a genius.

Berlioz

Hector Berlioz (1803–69) came from the Grenoble district where his father practised medicine. He himself was sent to Paris for medical training and abandoned it to study at the Conservatoire which Napoleon had established. The director,

Cherubini, was conservative; so were Lesueur the opera composer and Fétis the historian of music, yet Berlioz was grateful to them for friendly teaching and encouraging press notices. After two failures he won the Prix de Rome with *Sardanapale*, adding the conflagration scene after the prize had been secured and causing a sensation by flinging the score into the orchestra during the muddled performance. Several desks were overturned.

If by 'imaginative' we mean 'intensely excited by experiences which most people enjoy or suffer as normal to humanity' then Berlioz was abnormally imaginative. Virgil's *Aeneid*, for other schoolboys a discipline to be accepted or enjoyed, affected young Berlioz as Chapman's translation of Homer did young Keats. His first taste of opera opened another illuminated world and his first hearing of Beethoven excited him to sleeplessness. Yet it was Shakespeare, as revealed by Kemble's company, who provided the most radiant of his mental revelations, coupled with a wild passion for the Ophelia and Juliet of the company, Harriet Smithson. He had to prove his own artistry by arranging concerts of his works of which she knew nothing; and when she returned to England he endured the phantasmagoria which he supplied as the 'programme' of his *Symphonie fantastique* (composed when he was twenty-six). All these statements must be qualified by 'if we are to take him at his word', for he was a forgivably imaginative liar. Did he 'flee' at the first sight of the dissecting room? Then he soon returned, for his success in the first medical degree is a recorded fact. In 1840 he was 'miserably underpaid' for his *Symphonie funèbre et triomphale* commissioned by the Ministry of Fine Arts, yet the official payment was 10,000 francs. He 'burnt' his overture to *Rob Roy*! Tovey writes: 'In Berlioz's vocabulary "burnt" means "carefully preserved" . . . a large part of Berlioz's charm consists in his earnest aspirations to achieve the glamour of desperate wickedness against the background of his inveterate and easily shockable respectability'. Berlioz's *Memoirs* are in places as fictitious as his amusing *Evenings in the Orchestra*, yet the *wish* to be thought an extreme romantic and his communication to friends of his real or imagined states of mind aligned him with *avant-garde* rebellion, for which there was justification in the musical

France of his day. He was no liar about his love for Virgil, Shakespeare and Gluck, and it is a matter for gratitude that the most romantic of French composers shows in his art an idealization of certain classical values – for instance an emotional chastity, wild passion without erotic desire, the Gluckian dignity which restrains and makes potent the burning emotions of Cassandra or Dido.

His biography after youth was not directly mirrored in his works. He married Harriet. Her charms soon faded: she was at first a suspicious termagant and heavy drinker, later a querulous invalid. When she died in 1854 he wrote of 'two poor artists loving and lacerating one another'. His second marriage, to the singer Marie Recio, lasted only eight years. It seems to have been happy, and she insisted on travelling with him in Germany where his music was enthusiastically received not only by Liszt's friends but by the Leipzig conservatives and the Prussian court. Unfortunately she also insisted on singing, and she was not of the first class. During tours in Germany and Russia he was thrilled by excellent orchestras and gratified by receipts which enabled him to discharge debts at home. He was less successful in England, thanks to Jullien's rascality. He spent money on extra players and rehearsals when he directed his works in Paris and he was rarely affluent. He supplemented his small stipend as librarian of the Paris Conservatoire by musical journalism, for which we are grateful but which he detested – he may even have disliked writing the *Treatise on Orchestration*. His life and temperament played havoc with his health, and from middle age he suffered much physical pain. He was stoically reticent about his disappointment in Harriet, his failure with the opera directors, or the creative pains of *Les Troyens* which must have equalled Wagner's during the composition of *Der Ring*. One of the harshest blows struck him when he was no longer young. In 1867 his son Louis died of yellow fever in Havana. He loved this son dearly and was proud of his rise to the captaincy of a large ship. Berlioz's real sufferings would have deranged many an unromantic mind and it is therefore hard not to share Mendelssohn's cynicism – 'he tries to make us believe that he is mad'. The real Berlioz must have been as tough as most provincial Frenchmen, and the striking contours of his portrait correspond with noble traits in his character.

In no generation has Berlioz's music failed to engage factions, but his orchestral scoring has never been questioned: its brilliant clarity is still uniquely personal, enjoyed by those who dislike the *ampleur* of much German scoring and by those who are unprejudiced but relish Berlioz's dazzlingly insubstantial textures by contrast. The insubstantiality becomes a virtue in the accompaniments of Berlioz's operas and the many splendid songs which he scored for orchestra and are still, to our shame, infrequently heard at symphony concerts. We have advertised chiefly his most ambitious conceptions, some of which like the *Te Deum* contain poor music, and have rarely reminded ourselves, except by Christmas performances of *L'Enfance du Christ*, that his originality can be manifest in delicate charm.

The overtures *Benvenuto Cellini*, *Le Carnaval Romain* (for the second act of *Cellini*), *Le Corsair*, *Les Francs-juges* and *King Lear* amply reveal the limitations of a racer who would not have run at all if he had not tried to run before he could walk correctly from chord to chord, a student whose affectionate home had no piano, who could not play that instrument, who lacked professional musical ancestry, and who matured where there was no symphonic tradition like Vienna's. Since, however, audiences acclaim those of Berlioz's orchestral works which musicians know to be faulty, their faults do not greatly handicap their expressive purport. It is foolish to deny the cracks in his structures as wholes and in their harmonic progressions, or to say that musicians are prejudiced in favour of German structures (very sensibly if they are better structures) or that Berlioz 'constructs by growth of melody'. So did Schubert; so did the un-German Verdi. Berlioz himself could have recognized in, say, the overture to Verdi's *Luisa Miller* something of his own ardour and brilliance, along with constructive and harmonic competence to rival any German's. Berlioz adored Beethoven for the dramatic content of his symphonies, but did he learn from their architecture? Meeting solecism in student exercise, Parry would ask: 'Inexperience or something characteristic?' No great musician more often poses this question than Berlioz.

Let any musician who would rashly answer it be sure, first that he has not judged Berlioz by trial at the piano, and second that he has witnessed a first-rate performance of *Les Troyens* and then discovered the futility of trying to recapture the experience from a piano score.

We take a great artist's expression as a whole, unable to know the extent to which his limitations were a stimulus or a handicap to his invention. By one unique masterpiece Berlioz is enrolled among the great as surely as is Mussorgsky by *Boris Godunov*. The comparison is not far-fetched, for Mussorgsky was not a symphonist and his great opera, like Berlioz's, achieves its effect by the total impact of what he called 'pictures'. Like Berlioz he provided too many of them for a normal evening's performance; like Berlioz he further jeopardized easy success by the size and variety of cast. Berlioz's scene-complexes and crowds, the ballet, the effects – for instance the appearance of Mercury or of the ghosts of Priam and Hector – are all utterly convincing and dignified. *Les Troyens* is the grandest of French grand operas yet its grandeur makes grandiosity seem tawdry. Berlioz translated Virgil's world as he knew it into music for such souls as shared it, so that he could select his words without supplying a connected story. He possessed by birthright the traditions of *tragédie lyrique* wherein the very *divertissements* – marches, choruses, spectacles and ballet – suit the dimensions of the protagonists. Gluck himself is either transcended or apotheosized in this one great French 'grand opera', not by the Berlioz who would dazzle or shock the bourgeoisie but by an artist working only for his noble ideal. His election to an academy chair in 1856 improved his income and so gave him time to devote to this masterpiece. Not until 1863 did it secure a much cut performance of its second part, *Les Troyens à Carthage*, and then not at the Opéra. (The first part is a vast prologue, *La Prise de Troie*; most modern performances select from both parts.)

Berlioz had also selected his scenes and written his words for *La Damnation de Faust* (1846), a 'concert opera' or dramatic oratorio which, it is true, has been staged, though it is impossible to make what is seen and done match the composer's imagination. It is an unequal work based on an earlier *Huit Scènes de Faust* and the impact of its parts does not combine, like those of *Les Troyens*, to suggest a tragedy greater than the whole. It might well be subtitled 'characteristic romantic pieces inspired by Goethe's *Faust*'. Along with weaker pieces like the chorus of demons and the chorus of soldiers are the wonderful *Ride to the Abyss*, the deeply moving *Marguerite's Romance* and the enchanting *Dance of the Sylphs*. Should anyone doubt claims made for Berlioz purely as a composer, let the popular *Hungarian March* be compared with Liszt's commonplace treatment of the *Rákóczi March*.

Berlioz's two-act *opéra comique Béatrice et Bénédict*, after Shakespeare's *Much Ado About Nothing*, seems more conventional. The spoken dialogue allows music to have its effect at opportune points. (It was commissioned for a new theatre at Baden but first performed in Weimar in 1862.) Even this work, however, is a mine of 'Hectorisms' (as Peter Warlock called them) including as it does a scene in which the rehearsal of wedding music gives scope for a burlesque upon conductors' and chorus-masters' vanities. The duet *Nuit paisible et sereine* is so exquisitely scored as to suggest a concert *scena* in its own right. This work has justified revival and one hopes there will be opportunity to compare it with its rivals such as Boïeldieu's *Le Petit Chaperon Rouge* (1818) and *La Dame blanche* (1825), which takes it settings from Scott's *Guy Mannering*, Auber's *Fra Diavolo* (1830), *Le Domino noir* (1837) and *Les Diamants de la Couronne* (1841), Hérold's *Zampa* (1831) and *Le Pré aux clercs*. These gay French pieces and the operettas of Adolphe Adam (1803–56) seem to have sprung from admiration of Rossini's *Le Comte Ory*, for they have a more urbane flavour than the comic and pastoral pieces of the eighteenth-century Paris fairgrounds.

POST-BEETHOVEN INSTRUMENTAL MUSIC

Hearing Berlioz's *Symphonie fantastique*, how do we understand his declaration 'I begin where Beethoven leaves off'? Berlioz recognized in Beethoven's symphonies what he called drama, and he continued from this point to make his own music express action and emotion beyond the capabilities of words or a theatre; but the drama in Beethoven amounts to more than this: he did not write symphonies that merely sounded like excerpts from operas, and his music would be dramatic even if it were all jovial or pastoral. A drama, as distinct from a poem or novel, does not show its characters fully at the opening; it sets them in dialogue and opposition, revealing what they are by what they do and say in the total of situations. Thus does Beethoven with his themes, and to be dramatic in a Beethovenian sense a symphony, quartet or sonata needs either Beethovenian motivic development or some equally close-knit means of integration. Spohr, Schumann and Mendelssohn in their more ambitious instrumental pieces and chamber music *did* learn from Beethoven's method, and Wagner did so in *The Ride of the Valkyries*, in the prelude to any act in his music-dramas, and even when voices and instruments make one vast symphony called an Act. That Berlioz did *not* do so ought to be equally apparent. (Lest this be thought a pejorative comment it may be well to declare a temperamental preference for the unequal, uncosy, non-sensual, non-pseudo-religious and often incompetent Berlioz over any German-speaking composer of the century.)

Berlioz's admirers warn us not to expect a classical economy in which motivic development may hide seams and allow pedestrian work to 'get by'. Instead, they say, Berlioz constructs in great spans of melody (not Wagner's 'endless melody' which is but the superfice of his 'endless harmony') and we are asked to note that Berlioz's line may expand into a polyphony of lines. (*Harold en Italie* is often quoted because the solo viola takes one of these lines.) This opinion is acceptable only if it is not offered as a generalization. After enjoying the *Trojan March* several times one may be able to play some of its harmonies without being able to whistle its melody. Moreover Berlioz's melody is not an entity: at times it seems partly remembered from Cherubini, Lesueur, Rossini or Weber, yet its progress is always unpredictable. Sometimes its unpredictability is unsatisfactory for, as Constant Lambert once said, 'I can compose a five-bar or six-bar melody merely by letting a four-bar conception dither to its end'. Yet at its best Berlioz's long-reaching melody is even more wonderful than his dazzling, impetuous passages for full orchestra. Such a melody as Ex. 19, from the *Orgy of Brigands* (finale of *Harold en Italie*), is still as unique and wonderful as it was in 1834.

How then is it integrated? Analysts are probably correct in declaring that all coherent music proceeds from motives and their 'expanding variation', and no doubt conscious or unconscious ur-motives can be revealed in this Berlioz melody, in the

movement and in the whole symphony. Their demonstration should not alter our judgement of the work. Whether we are dealing with Berlioz or Brahms, our satisfaction with long movements depends upon the *length* of music which the composer can conceive at full heat of imagination. The impulsive Berlioz, who did not cover his cracks with a passable 'busyness' of classical development, easily shows his moments of exhaustion. The marvel is that they are shown so rarely that he could integrate such large stretches of music by the torrent of his imagination.

One must protest at the fallacy that 'romanticism with its programmes burst the symphony'. There is no sign of bursting in Berlioz's symphonies. Neither Berlioz nor any subsequent romantic composer was fool enough to think that music could *grow in its own way* while taking its form from a chain of verbal images, from the lines, distances and volumes of a picture, or from the action of a story. It cannot do so even in opera, where the rival arts continuously give and take. The danger of hugging a programme is not that the growth of ideas will burst a symphony but that growth will be stifled or cut off, one idea having no room to develop before the programme demands another. But there is no more reason why self-sufficient symphonic music should not illustrate a programme than that an opera should not reveal much of its musical excellence where its language is not understood. Declared programmes are almost as old as the symphony, and certainly older than Haydn's or Dittersdorf's titled works. Extra-musical ideas inspire Beethoven's *Eroica*; his Fifth would suggest such ideas even without its unimportant *idée fixe*; his Sixth has a declared programme which we feel to have existed *ab initio*, not put like Berlioz's to music previously composed for other purposes; and his Ninth, before bringing in words and chorus, includes a thematic review of past movements.

The belief that Berlioz and later composers 'burst the symphony' comes from expecting symphonies like Beethoven's. To the question 'Why is there no Beethovenian symphony after Beethoven?' the answer is 'Why should there be?' The symphony changed like all growths, and was not disintegrated by romanticism except where the composer lacked command of symphonic dimensions. We can hardly mistake natural change for malady when we see looming ahead the figures of Wagner, Brahms, Strauss and Sibelius. Healthy change comes chiefly from fertilization and so the symphony continued to be influenced by the theatre. Beethoven had brought in piccolos and trombones for more than 'Turkish' and 'military' ideas, and had fertilized symphony with cantata. How natural for his followers to do so! Before Beethoven, minuets and marches were introduced to the symphony, but he himself did not greatly speed an invasion of pieces formerly belonging to the suite. Berlioz did.

The three works by Berlioz actually called symphonies are *Symphonie fantastique* (1830), *Harold en Italie* (1834) and

Roméo et Juliette (with chorus, 1839). Their more exacting movements (especially first and last) justify the generic title: others are like 'Pictures from an Exhibition'. The Queen Mab movements are no more essential to the symphony than Mercutio's speech about Mab is essential to Shakespeare's play. Berlioz's determination to follow a programme too closely made a slight blemish in his first symphony. He salvaged an excellent march from the *Francs-juges* opera and gave it an adipose coda merely to evoke the comical and utterly unterrifying fall of the guillotine; yet we may well marvel that all these symphonies were composed before Berlioz was past his mid thirties, and that they use materials from earlier works, written when he could have heard no such music from Beethoven or anyone else.

German-speaking symphonists of the nineteenth century paid more respect to the classical designs. Louis Spohr (1784–1859) himself belonged to Vienna, had particular reverence for Mozart, and was the inheritor of that vein of Mozart's chameleon-like talent which makes pathetic use of chromatic melody and harmony. He was famous as a violinist and it is not surprising that he is now better known by discerning chamber-music players than by concert-goers. He has been even more harshly judged than Mendelssohn whom he equals in skill though not in imagination. His operas do not survive, but we sometimes hear his violin concertos and his chamber works for mixed string and wind ensembles. No student who has examined his 'double' quartets is likely to disparage his craftsmanship. He disliked Beethoven's extremes of emotion, yet as a symphonist he is aligned with the romantics. His fourth symphony is based on a poem called *The Consecration of Sounds*, with movements evoking the sounds of wild nature, of martial, nursery, dance and funeral music; his fifth is called *Historical* Symphony, purporting to recall musical expression of four periods between 1720 and 1840; a later work is a 'symphony for double orchestra', *The Earthly and Divine in Man's Life* – the distinction symbolized by interplay of orchestral tutti and a concertino of eleven soloists; in 1850 he produced a symphony of *The Seasons*.

Respect for the classical symphonists has been mistakenly regarded as a weakness of the well-educated composers called 'the Leipzig School', meaning chiefly Schumann and Mendelssohn. They were as sensible as Spohr to be guided by their forebears in composing long movements and the fact that Schumann is at his most characteristic in epigrammatic, short pieces and in songs should not make us regret his symphonic ambition. It made articulate much fine romantic expression which needed room to spread. His first two symphonies (Nos. 1 and 4) have no declared programme, though Schumann is said to have called the enclosing movements of No. 1 'Spring's awakening' and 'Spring's farewell'. Certainly the popular title 'Spring Symphony' is apt for this ardently vernal work in B flat. The D minor Symphony is more complex. Its predecessor had thematic links between movements but Schumann wished the movements of the D minor to follow without break, and the chief of its themes, announced in a slow introduction, assumes differing forms in succeeding movements. His next symphony, No. 2 in C, has a link-theme too, but this work is more grandiose and less romantically tender than its fellows. It illustrates Schumann's chief handicap in long pieces – a loss of taut thread between sections. The cadences mark the sectionalism by heavy punctuation, and though there is much fine music we may wish that there were less of C major and fewer full closes, especially in the otherwise vigorous finale. Schumann's last symphony, No. 3 in E flat (1850), would reveal its rich beauties even if we were unaware of any programme. It opens with one of the best and most original movements between Beethoven and Brahms. The name 'Rhenish Symphony' stemmed from the slow introduction to the finale in which solemn trombone chords recall ceremonies witnessed in Cologne Cathedral; but the finale itself, like the first movement, suggests the exhilaration of open-air adventure. The broad tune of the second movement might also be associated with a big river. Schumann's Overture, Scherzo and Finale, contemporary with his first two symphonies, lacks only a slow movement in order to swell the number of his symphonies to five.

Stylistic resemblances between Schumann and Felix Mendelssohn-Bartholdy (1809–47) are obvious but superficial, for these men differed greatly in temperament. Mendelssohn, son of a Hamburg–Berlin banking family, was richly endowed materially, mentally and morally. His grandfather, Moses Mendelssohn, was the philosopher and friend of Lessing, and family friends included Schlegel, Heine, Spohr, Kalkbrenner and Moscheles. The Mendelssohns were Christian Jews with high humanitarian principles. The parents lovingly educated the children and instilled into them the duty of hard work not only in school subjects but also in the fine arts. One must draw, paint, practise music and compose regularly. This may have helped to make Felix a musical child prodigy, and formed the hard-working conductor and fulfiller of engagements; but it may also have led him to bridle romantic impulses in order to produce cantatas and oratorios to elevating texts which failed to elicit a high proportion of invigorating music.

This fact does not warrant indiscriminate sneers at Mendelssohn's best offerings to choral societies and church choirs. The popularity of *Lobgesang*, of psalm settings inspired by the musical revival in the Prussian court chapel, and of *Elijah* is a tribute to the good sense of unpretentious provincial music lovers. It is as right that this music should sound Victorian as that Handel's should sound Augustan. Most of it can claim a consummate congruence of form and design. To recognize this we need not take a whole dramatic *scena* from *Elijah* (parts of which might have been written for a Gluckian opera) but merely a little gem-like trio for sopranos and altos, 'Lift thine eyes', its craftsmanship unparalleled since *Die Zauberflöte*.

Snobbery has foolishly disparaged Mendelssohn for limitations which are the obverse of virtues. His weaknesses included a distaste for opera, for panache, for Chopin's disturbing eroticism, and too great a reliance on the opinions of his family and friends. He composed only 'early' work, for he died at thirty-five, and since his Violin Concerto dates from his thirty-third and his magnificent F minor Quartet from his last year it is nonsense to say that his genius deserted him after a prodigious childhood. A new phase, perhaps influenced by Bach studies, even a turning to opera, might have distinguished a

Mendelssohn aged forty, for it must be remembered that his contemporaries called 'passionate' several of his works which we are now rediscovering, for example his D minor Quartet. If we blame him for publishing much facile music, let us be fair and put Handel, Haydn and other giants into the dock by his side.

Facility and fine features are suffused by the glow of vitality whenever Mendelssohn's artistry is fertilized by romantic imagination, as in the Octet composed when he was only sixteen, the *Midsummer Night's Dream* Overture of the following year, the overtures *Die schöne Melusine* and *The Hebrides*, and the *Italian* Symphony. It is curious that local colour fails to make the later *Scottish* Symphony as appealing as the *Italian*, and somewhat strange that Mendelssohn's symphonies are less appealing than Schumann's despite the feeling for orchestral instruments in which Schumann was deficient.

Mendelssohn's first symphony, in C minor, was written for performance in London when he was fifteen and has little more tension than a staidly expanded serenade. Six years later, in 1830, he composed the so-called '*Reformation* Symphony' for the tercentenary of the Augsburg Confession. It is mentioned because it is still performed and because of the romantic idea of symbolizing the Papal–Lutheran antagonism by opposed motives – the *Dresden Amen* and the chorale *Ein' feste Burg*; yet there is little strong conflict in the music. The last of Mendelssohn's symphonies, the *Scottish* of 1842, is mildly exhilarating though more leisurely than its evocative purpose and themes lead us to expect. It is unfortunate that the best of this work comes first.

The comparisons between Mendelssohn and Schumann are worth pursuing a little further. Mendelssohn had so few technical limitations that every movement in his amazing boyhood Octet employs classical sonata form with the effortless stride of an athlete; but is not its delicious *scherzo* very similar to subsequent delicious *scherzi* from the same hand? By contrast the *scherzi* in Schumann's symphonies seem to be by different hands – those of Eusebius, Florestan, Harlequin – and they often have two trios so that we can enjoy epigrams in contrasting styles. Schumann's rhythmic wit, not only in *scherzi*, is often recalcitrant to classical growth and design, but the average listener prefers Schumann's freshness to Mendelssohn's perfection. This is one reason why the best of Schumann's piano pieces, not only those in the various 'ballroom' suites, are more widely esteemed than most of Mendelssohn's piano works outside the D minor *Variations sérieuses* and some of the *Songs Without Words*. The comparison is hardly fair since the piano was to Schumann what instrumental ensemble was to Mendelssohn. Schumann was an exploratory and sometimes visionary poet at the piano whereas Mendelssohn merely wrote sensitively and idiomatically for the piano as for other media. His *Songs Without Words* have great documentary value, some of them high musical value, the evergreens among them showing some concession to the home-player's display and to domestic love of the picturesque. The contrast between the two composers is also illustrated in their works for the organ. Mendelssohn's Preludes and Fugues, together with his Six Sonatas, provided organists with the first considerable augmentation of their repertory after Bach. The design of their best movements is not only satisfying but original. Although Schumann honoured the organ with Six Fugues on B–A–C–H which are more than good essays, they are less personal than Mendelssohn's Sonatas, and to savour Schumann's distinctive authorship we turn to the very attractive Six Canons and the Four Sketches, usually heard as organ pieces or in a piano-duet arrangement though they were composed for solo piano with pedalier.

THE PIANO: CHOPIN AND LISZT

Has the reader ever heard of harpsichord recitals given by such great players as Couperin, Handel, Bach or Scarlatti? One hears only of so-and-so (a prince, traveller or connoisseur) witnessing their fine playing, usually of their own work, prepared or extempore. Performance is private or semi-private, but it may occur as do piano and organ solos within a promenade concert. Even the great players earned by teaching rather than performing. Sonatas were published as 'Lessons' and the greatest of all harpsichord music – Bach's – as 'Keyboard Practice' (*Clavier-übung*). The rise of the keyboard concerto gave opportunity for the performer-composer to include solos in the programme, but until Beethoven had composed most of his sonatas the public piano recital was not common; and despite the literary and musical culture of Schumann, Liszt and other pianist-composers the contrasting of many periods and styles was scarcely known in recitals during the first half of the nineteenth century. Public performers did not think of drawing upon previous composers, such as Bach, but since Beethoven had used the piano to suggest the colour and range of the orchestra, from horn calls and drum rolls to the shimmer of *tremolando* strings, they did introduce arrangements and programme pieces such as storm and battle fantasies, evocations of lightning, explosions, groans, prayers, popular songs and moonlight with nightingales.

No excuse is needed for such pieces, from Mozart's variations on popular airs to Schumann's *Scenes of Childhood* and Mendelssohn's *Songs Without Words*. Intended for domestic performers, these are neither pretentious nor, at their best, 'written down'. The upright piano became part of the furniture of nineteenth-century homes, whereas to have owned a harpsichord was to have been unusually musical, for it needed frequent 'servicing' and its owner was normally able to quill and tune it. From Clementi onwards pianists drew their income chiefly from teaching the womenfolk whose families regarded piano playing along with singing, drawing, embroidery and elementary French as a qualification towards 'eligibility', social or matrimonial. One might have distinguished 'musical' from musical ladies by discovering which of them played or wished to play Mozart and Beethoven.

Gyrowetz, Herz, Steibelt, Thalberg and other 'Paganinis of the keyboard' rarely did so. Even programmes by Hummel, Weber, Czerny, Cramer, Kalkbrenner and other genuinely musical virtuosi included transcriptions from Meyerbeer's or Rossini's popular operas, variations on popular tunes, dances, rondos, caprices and carefully prepared 'improvisations' with more glitter than substance. Still more showy were the louder and faster arrangements for two or more pianos made fashion-

able by Kalkbrenner who, in 1838, played a twelve-handed
arrangement of the *Zauberflöte* Overture with five other performers including Liszt – music far removed from Mozart's
own four-handed works or from Schubert's sociable or impres-
sively 'orchestral' duets. Yet genius was to transform the
pianist's appeal to popular taste into by no means empty
creations – the best paraphrases, études, nocturnes and concert
waltzes. Paraphrases (i.e. passages from operas partly trans-
scribed and partly set within improvisations) were the first to
attain distinction through young Liszt's *fantaisies* and
réminiscences on dozens of operas and orchestral works. Some
are admirable only for a skill in arrangement which provided
virtuosic translations of Berlioz's overtures; others, such as the
fantasies on *Don Giovanni* and *Norma*, are as highly original as
symphonic poems. They represent Liszt's art as validly as a
fugue on a subject by Corelli does Bach's. They also performed
a service to Berlioz, Donizetti and others in days before mechani-
cal reproduction gave listeners opportunity to judge their works
in the theatre, and before quick travel enabled most listeners to
visit the capital and return on the same evening.

Though a year younger than Chopin, Franz Liszt (1811–86)
captured Paris first. He delighted or scandalized sophisticated
society as an international Byronic figure whose private thoughts
and life were public. Taught to regard with distaste a character
lacking *gravitas* and *probitas* Englishmen saw little more in the
man or music than attitudinizing and display. Mendelssohn
was the musical idol of a London in which Liszt was hailed only
by connoisseurs, whereas Liszt's visits to most European cities
rivalled those of modern stars of disk and television.

Liszt was the son of a steward on the Esterhazy estate in a
Hungary which still remembered Haydn, and he was a public
performer from the age of nine, befriended by several Hungarian
noblemen. By the age of eleven he had played in Vienna and
been publicly kissed by Beethoven, and there he studied under
Czerny and Salieri. He went to Paris in 1823 hoping to enter the
Conservatoire, but Cherubini would not relax the rule to exclude
foreigners and Liszt began his '*années de pèlerinage*' – tours to
various countries from England to Turkey, Spain to Russia –

returning to Paris for long periods. His circle included Hugo, Lamartine, Berlioz, Chopin, George Sand and another female author, 'Daniel Stern' – the Comtesse d'Agoult – who was the mother of his daughter Cosima, married first to Bülow and then to Wagner. Even as a child Liszt's appearance was striking, and it became even more so during his Paris period. His public concerts towards the end of his stay in Paris (1848) witnessed the climax of his lionization as a performer and probably of his superb virtuosity.

Like Berlioz, Liszt has been as ridiculously extolled as ridiculously disparaged. It is foolish to deny that during his years in Paris (and from time to time later) he liked to dazzle the ladies, that his posing, extravagance and gusto better became a gipsy (he probably possessed Hungarian gipsy blood) than a great artist (which he was), or that enough display can be found in what he published to tell us that he indulged in it during his performances. Yet Alfred Einstein tells us that 'Schumann, Liszt and Chopin are the three musicians who saved piano composition from the shallowness into which it ... had already fallen', and those who wonder that Liszt is thus linked with Schumann and Chopin should ask how much of Liszt's music they know. Because little of it can be managed by the average pianist and because concert promoters rarely give us any of the orchestral works except the two concertos (thus avoiding the cost of chorus and organ) its enormous variety must be imagined by scanning the list of his compositions in *Grove*.

The difference between Liszt and the other showmen may be recognized in the least likely of his piano publications to reveal it, the fruits of his first ten years as a public virtuoso – the *Grandes Études* which defied other pianists. These differ from other men's in their poetic content, for their titles come from romantic poems and scenes. *Mazeppa*, from Hugo or Byron, is the first version of Liszt's symphonic poem of that title. Similarly the scenes in the first sets of *Années de Pèlerinage* are often viewed through the eyes of a writer or painter; the *Vallée d'Obermann* was a setting in a novel by Senancour, the *Sposalizio* a picture by Raphael; Liszt's own songs to sonnets of Petrarch are made into piano pieces. Sometimes the title is no clue without a literary quotation, and sometimes we need a historical clue. Thus *Funérailles* (a very fine piece) is not a 'dead march' but the equivalent of a public speech in honour of the Hungarians who died in the 1848 revolution.

Liszt was more than a musical speech-maker or a payer of compliments by transcriptions and variations. He was probably the most generous creature among famous musicians, giving lavishly to the distressed and helping not merely artists of genius like Wagner, but sculptors, poets and musicians of more promise than achievement. We hear of no depreciatory comments upon other artists by Liszt himself. It is well sometimes to forget Liszt the public performer, the restless traveller, the idol of romantic women, and remember the composer who must have done much solitary hard work, comforted but not compensated for by coffee drinking and cigar smoking. When he tired of the strain of Paris and public recitals and seized the opportunity of the Weimar Kapellmeistership (meaning simply 'conductorship') in 1842, he championed progressive and unknown composers to an extent which brought more conflict than he could tolerate after 1861, and he also deepened his own musical studies.

He is known to have taken the appointment so seriously as to make a very thorough study of orchestral instruments, but this included a study of classical and romantic symphonies, concertos and overtures. Whether the great B minor Piano Sonata of 1853 was directly affected by this preoccupation with structure or not, between 1850 and 1860 there appeared the twelve symphonic poems which constitute Liszt's chief claim to historical importance since they are held to establish a new genre as well as a new name:

> *Ce qu'on entend sur la montagne* (Hugo), 1848–9
> *Tasso, Lamento e trionfo* (Byron), 1849–54
> *Les Préludes* (Lamartine), 1848
> *Orpheus* (Introduction to Gluck's opera), 1853–4
> *Prometheus* (Herder), 1850
> *Mazeppa* (Hugo), 1851
> *Festklänge*, 1853
> *Héroïde funèbre* (From a *Revolution* Symphony), 1848

Hungaria, 1854
Hamlet (Shakespeare), 1858
Hunnenschlacht (painting by Kaulbach), 1856–7
Die Ideale (Schiller), 1857
Von der Wiege bis zum Grabe, 1881–2

Those marked with an asterisk were used as overtures in the theatre; *Hungaria* and *Héroïde funèbre* ('Heroic Elegy') are patriotic tributes incorporating characteristics of Hungarian music; but the rest purport to express in music the matter of poems, or in one case a picture. They are not just programme pieces of varying length worthy to form the main movement of an ambitious symphony; they belong to a distinct *type* of programme piece. Secondly they are characterized by 'representative themes' and 'the transformation of themes', both of which can be illustrated from baroque composers and from Berlioz. Theme transformation is nowhere more happily used than in Schubert's *Wanderer* Fantasy which Liszt edited, and Liszt used the principle in his *Faust* Symphony (regarded as his orchestral masterpiece), *Dante* Symphony, and B minor Piano Sonata. The symphonic poems are not Liszt's very best orchestral works, yet it is a pity that a long and inferior one like *Les Préludes* should be heard more often than a short and magnificent one like *Prometheus*.

At Weimar Liszt exerted tremendous influence by the performance of new operas, especially Wagner's, and by the 'seminars' at his home in which his piano pupils heard each other play. (They included Bülow, Tausig, Busoni and the brilliant Reubke who died while almost a boy.) Curiously enough it was the first performance of one of modern Germany's most popular operas, Cornelius's *Barber of Baghdad*, that elicited so much opposition that Liszt, already weary, resigned his official appointment. The last part of his life (from about 1860) was spent between Weimar, Rome and Budapest, for the Magyars greatly honoured their compatriot and founded their National Academy of Music with Liszt as its president. For Budapest he composed his *Legend of St Elizabeth* and *Christus*. Another of his best choral works is the Mass for the consecration of a basilica at Gran. Liszt was much concerned with religious and devotional subjects during his last years when he took minor orders. His religious sincerity has not been doubted, and some of his later compositions are quite without flamboyant gestures even when we should expect them, as in the piano pieces about the Villa d'Este and the second *Mephisto* Waltz. Many of them anticipate harmony and texture associated with composers like Debussy who lived into the twentieth century – augmented and diminished triads, whole-tone scale effects, parallel fourths and fifths, enharmonic modulations and elliptical phrases.

Wagner, who was not disposed to acknowledge any debt to living composers, wrote to Bülow: 'Since coming to know Liszt's music, I have become a very different harmonist than I was formerly' (even the famous opening progression of *Tristan* comes from Liszt); yet Liszt rarely receives the tributes as a composer that he does as an artist. This is because, despite his easily identified mannerisms, his harmonic style does not strike one as closely integrated. It is cosmopolitan, so that at different places in the same work we may be reminded of Berlioz, Chopin, Schumann, Wagner, Franck, Smetana, Verdi or Puccini; yet the truth is that most of these composers formed their style by cultivating what appealed to them in the large and rankly fertile garden of Liszt. He suffers heavily in the age of Stravinsky which exalts neat construction, and it must be admitted that his inequalities are evident within many of his best works. The habit of rhetorical repetition even mars the *Faust* Symphony, and the transformation of a fine theme is often for the poorer unless mockery is intended. In a work by Liszt expressing his reaction to poem, picture or *genius loci*, we may think poorly of a musical idea because, as presented to us, it will not communicate all that it meant to him; consequently one listener, catching what Liszt wished to communicate, may be enraptured by a passage which seems sterile to another listener. It is one thing to be inspired by an idea and another to have the mind of a Schubert so that one's reaction emerges spontaneously as music.

To survey Liszt's work we have passed into the age of Wagner and travelled far from the Paris in which he met Frédéric

Chopin (1810–49), virtually a Parisian though born on an estate near Warsaw. His father was a French *émigré* teacher, and French was the polite language in a Russian-dominated society which Chopin left at the age of eighteen. Reliable accounts of his playing show that physical frailty prevented his rivalling other virtuosi in loud brilliance, yet he achieved or suggested within his quieter scale a greater range of dynamic than any player except Liszt, and if 'original' meant 'uniquely personal' or 'idiomatic in expression and style' Chopin would be the most original of wholly nineteenth-century musicians. We are as responsible for this assessment as were his closest friends, for we give the place allowed to Chopin to no other composer who left valuable music only for one instrument and whose total output can be printed in two volumes.

The extremes of Chopin's expression – disturbingly intro-spective 'accidia', wilful passion, tearful longing and ethereal radiance – cannot be diagnosed summarily. His being an exile? So was Liszt, and so had been dozens of musicians before him: Chopin was distressed by the fate of his native country but had no intention of leaving the high society of Paris which had set him up so elegantly. The tuberculosis which caused his early death and which George Sand hoped to combat by their settling in Majorca? But there is no parallel between Chopin's expres-sion and that of other consumptive composers, and it is recorded that, though delicate in appearance and small-built, the young Chopin was vigorous and passionate. The trials of a crowded life? No, Chopin's existence was far removed from Liszt's except in the adoration he elicited from society women, from the Rothschilds to countesses with pre-Revolution titles. He gave lessons at the topmost fees (placed on the mantelpiece, not vulgarly noticed or handled) to an exclusive clientele which sometimes left his house in tears. He rarely gave a recital, and then it was but a large salon-soirée to the same clientele, its relatives and friends, sometimes for a charity but always at a price per ticket which would even today be thought high.

In Chopin's art we find much that Berlioz and Liszt claimed to express, but there is no reference to poems, scenes and pictures. This does not mean that Majorca produced no *Années de Pèlerinage* but that Chopin's catalysts became amalgamated with his specifically musical imagination and so ceased to be catalysts. His expression of romantic feelings engendered by poem, place or person welled up in his mind as completed music, not as a representative theme or harmonic progression which might *begin* a musical translation. It may thus be contended that this most 'poetic' of musicians, whose every published *prélude*, *nocturne* and *étude* had a romantic title in early editions, is more a musician than Liszt or Schumann. None of the titles was written by him. He is not known to have taken great interest in any art than music; this, and his lack of Byronic flamboyance, his aristocratic reclusiveness, make him exceptional among romantics of the first half of the nineteenth century.

After the age of twenty-one he made no excursion into any medium but the pianoforte and no attempt at a large-scale work. Instead he achieved near-perfection in pieces of simple general design but subtle and complex cell-structure. The subtlety and complexity are less evident in the *Valses* and *Nocturnes*, however fascinating their occasional turns of harmony, than in the *Préludes*, *Études* and *Scherzos* which are his finest works, if we except certain of the *Mazurkas* which are not 'nationalist' tributes like the *Polonaises* but intimate and personal. This may explain why so many young people have found their first overwhelming musical experience from Chopin.

The name 'Nocturne' for a reverie-like piece resembling a cavatina or tender operatic melody was established by the Irish-born John Field (1782–1837), who studied with Clementi and later became a virtuoso pianist. He was employed to demonstrate pianos by the London firm bearing Clementi's name. His half-starved appearance may have come from his recourse to drink rather than food, for he seems to have been a melancholy creature. One of his tours took him to Russia, where he remained until his death 'of dissipation and despair'. We still occasionally hear Field's concertos and those movements from his sonatas which recall the facile concert rondos of Hummel and Weber and had some effect upon Chopin's earlier pieces; but Field's nocturnes claim permanent honour despite the excellence of Chopin's. Their vocal nuance, exquisite chromatics, ornaments, modulations and evocations of Bellini's style make some of them mistakable for Chopin's own (Ex. 20).

One more Parisian pianist-composer, C. V. Alkan (1813–88), is not even mentioned in several largish histories of music and his work is played only by a small band of enthusiasts. These

Field *Nocturne No. 14*

20

facts are baffling. The explanation cannot be anti-Semitic prejudice (his real name was Charles Henri Valentin Morhange) for Einstein, generous with his praise for Mendelssohn and Mahler, is reserved towards Alkan. His music 'horrified' Schumann: it was 'a desert of wood and sticks and hangman's rope – borrowed from Beethoven or Berlioz at that. We would guard the errant genius if there were only some music discoverable'. These words may be forgiven as the harshest notice of a generous reviewer, and applied to Alkan's three *études* called *Aime-moi*, *Le Vent* and *Morte*; they are less harsh than the neglect which seems tacitly to apply them to some eighty other pieces. Alkan has been called a 'pianistic Berlioz' because he combines superficial clarity and brilliance with a love of the macabre, diabolical and romantically bizarre, but he is more elusive and restrained than Berlioz. One sometimes hears his more easily relished genre pieces like *The Fire in the Neighbouring Village* and *The Railway*, and also *Le Festin d'Ésope*, a set of variations widely regarded as his masterpiece. His champion was Liszt and his neglect is particularly noticeable since the deaths of Liszt's pupil, Busoni, and his pupil, Egon Petri.

Alkan's transcriptions and arrangements could be taken for Liszt's, and he also composed for solo piano a remarkable 'symphony' reproducing orchestral effects, and a 'concerto' with solo-tutti effects as in Bach's. (He was very keen about the pedal-piano.) Yet these were not for his recitals, which he abandoned at the age of twenty-one after being launched as a prodigy at fourteen and enjoying success as a virtuoso performer. He returned from a visit to London, settled in Paris and was friendly with Chopin and his circle and also with Hugo and other writers, yet more and more he lived a reclusive, almost monastic life. At first, like Chopin, he played occasionally to a select audience and was regularly visited by Liszt, but an account of the romantic movement would be incomplete if it dealt only with the Byronic public figures and failed to point out those of whom Morhange is typical – the eccentrics and solitaries who wished to live in the world of their own imagination and found urban society irrelevant, cruel or intolerable. The opposite type is that of the conqueror, the self-conceived prophet, leader (and bleeder) of society, supremely represented by the revered and detested, admirable and despicable man who bestrides the nineteenth century like a colossus.

2. Wagner

IN early life Richard Wagner (1813–83) wrote plays and verse, and hoped to be a dramatist. Apart from *A Faust Overture* and the *Siegfried Idyll* all his significant music is for the theatre and it is linked with texts carefully composed by himself. A list of his operas and music dramas shows that the works which place him with the greatest artists all date from after 1850:

> *Die Feen*, 1833
> *Rienzi*, 1840
> *Der fliegende Holländer*, 1842
> *Tannhäuser*, 1845
> *Lohengrin*, 1847
> *Das Rheingold* (No. 1 of *Der Ring des Nibelungen*), 1854
> *Die Walküre* (No. 2 of *Der Ring*), 1856
> *Tristan und Isolde*, 1859
> *Siegfried* (No. 3 of *Der Ring*), 1865
> *Die Meistersinger von Nürnberg*, 1867
> *Götterdämmerung* (No. 4 of *Der Ring*), 1874
> *Parsifal*, 1882

At Leipzig University Wagner neglected his studies but haunted the theatre and the concert hall. With abnormal self-confidence he composed ambitiously, using the skill he had picked up from the Leipzig cantor, Weinlig. *Das Liebesverbot* ('The Love Ban') was based on *Measure for Measure* and its music was somewhat Italianate; but by the age of twenty, when he had secured work as chorus master at Würzburg, excerpts from the first opera in our list strongly revealed the influence of Weber. In 1834 Wagner's appointment as conductor at Königsberg enabled him to marry the actress Minna Planer. Greater resources and remuneration soon enticed him to the opera house at Riga where he almost completed *Rienzi*. On expiration of his contract in 1839 he set out for London, narrowly escaped shipwreck in a storm and, while taking refuge in a Norwegian harbour, heard from sailors the legend of the Flying Dutchman. From London he moved via Boulogne to Paris where, to keep himself and Minna from starvation, he was forced to copy parts and arrange music; but *Rienzi* was sent to Dresden, secured performance in 1842, and proved a tremendous success. Bulwer Lytton's novel set in fourteenth-century Rome, with vast crowd scenes culminating in the firing of the Capitol, was suited to this *grande opéra à la* Meyerbeer; yet Wagner waited in vain for a production in Paris, and since Dresden eagerly sought another opera from him, *Der fliegende Holländer* was produced there in 1843 and Wagner himself was appointed 'for life' to the Saxon royal Kapellmeistership where Weber had been his most distinguished predecessor.

Der fliegende Holländer is worth more frequent performance than the two operas which followed it, *Tannhäuser* and *Lohengrin*, both of which contain more advanced and, in places, more admirable music; but they do not maintain their level of excellence. Moreover the plot of *Der fliegende Holländer* is well suited to the consistent shaping of music-drama, Wagner's name for a form of art which he distinguished from opera and thought superior to it. To understand music-drama (always to be spelt here with a hyphen) we must distinguish it from a musical drama. This last term can be applied loosely since most Italian operas have been published under the title *dramma per musica*. Although '*dramma*' simply means 'play', we normally apply the term 'musical drama' only to operas which tell a straight tale and delineate human characters. We apply it to Purcell's *Dido and Aeneas*, but not readily to a mixture of masque and spoken poetry like his *King Arthur*, nor to a delicious fantasy like Rimsky-Korsakov's *Snow Maiden*. Our discrimination is harmless unless we suppose that the works just mentioned are necessarily poorer operas than those we call musical dramas. *Così fan Tutte* is Mozart's best operatic full score and his neatest plot, but in *Figaro* the music subtly reveals 'real-life' complexity in the characters and we are more inclined to call it a drama. That fact alone does not warrant our calling it the better work. Sometimes part of an opera rises to musical drama while another part fails to meet the demands of the drama.

What concerned Wagner was *whether the music contained the drama* or whether it was just an addition to the drama, no doubt heightening certain situations and emotions, or a diversion. According to his theory the *Ride of the Valkyries* is unnecessary, for without it the drama would lose nothing essential however great our musical loss. Many beautiful items in *Der Ring, Die Meistersinger* and other works make us glad that Wagner's practice did not always take his theory to an extreme, yet he is among the very few composers whose work can be enjoyed the more for *knowing* his theory. He declared that Beethoven's symphonies inspired the conception of his music-drama ideal. The section on 'Post-Beethoven Instrumental Music' (p. 121) gives reasons for calling much of Beethoven's music dramatic when it does not suggest the theatre and is neither heroic nor tragic. How much it meant to Wagner will be apparent in the following conditions which he laid down for the existence of music-drama:

1. A music-drama is not the work of a mere musician who makes his contribution after someone else (at best a Goethe, at worst a hack) has supplied the stimuli to which he must rise. A music-drama is the work of THE ARTIST. When a musician such as Beethoven is a greater artist than any living poet or playwright or scene designer it is intolerable that he should merely respond to others.

2. A music-drama is an amalgam of the arts (*Gesamtkunstwerk*) such as was implicit in Beethoven's Ninth Symphony although it used only music and words: but since music is the most powerful of the arts, the great art-work of the future would stem from music and THE ARTIST would be primarily a composer of music. At first music-drama would be the communal expression of the German race, the ritual of a nation as was ancient Greek tragedy, until the new culture spread beyond Germany.

3. In music-drama music should not sound for music's sake. Though music-drama was achieved in *passages* of operas by Gluck, Mozart, Weber and Beethoven, these works of musicians were marred by 'set pieces' designed to show the calibre of composer or performer as musicians. 'The error in opera has been that a means (music) has been made an end, while the

end (drama) has been made the means'. (Let the reader measure this judgement against *Tristan* and be glad that Wagner was primarily a musician.)

4. A music-drama proceeds on a scale like that of Beethoven's symphonies; it is not interrupted to accommodate choruses, ballets, airs, processions and marches. Instead there is endless melody, which is maintained by the orchestra when the contribution of the actors must be speech-like or declamatory.

5. A music-drama, like a Beethoven symphony, is integrated by themes or motives. The chief among them (*Leitmotive*) bind not only music to music but also music to drama, for they are associated with persons, things and ideas, e.g. Siegfried, gold, jealousy. As each act of a music-drama resembles a vast symphonic movement the motives undergo transformation to suit succeeding moods and situations.

We see, therefore, that Wagner's Dresden operas reached towards his ideal in different ways. *Tannhäuser* and *Lohengrin* present fine lengths of the new *arioso*, greatly extend the motive technique, and in some scenes betray no initial division into 'numbers' before the welding into continuous music: but *Der fliegende Holländer* has fewer 'romantic grand opera' scenic and choral effects and it tells a more relentlessly purposeful tale. The sea and its marvellous music enwrap and integrate it as the forest does *Der Freischütz*; and though the motive technique is not elaborate, themes stand out as in a dramatic symphony, especially the stormy Dutchman theme, first heard at the opening of the Overture, and the theme of Senta's love. Then, too, the supernatural element, in the tradition of *Hans Heiling*, *Der Vampyr* and *Der Freischütz*, imbues the work with a fatal inexorability well suited to music-drama. It is noteworthy that Senta's ballad, which epitomizes the dramatic conflict, was composed first, and the rest built around it.

We cannot tell how Wagner's music-dramas would have advanced if he had gone on to triumph in his Dresden post. A period of meditation and planning, a short retreat 'in the wilderness' often precedes an idealist's missionary ministry, and we cannot easily imagine how Wagner would have secured any retreat other than short summer holidays to recuperate from the labour of rehearsal and production in a royal opera-house.

But the retreat was forced upon him. During the political disturbances of 1848 he fled to Weimar where Liszt was preparing *Tannhäuser*, and it was Liszt who secured him a passport when news came of a warrant for his arrest. In Paris and in Zurich Wagner wrote first his *Opera and Drama* and then the words and music of his greatest music-dramas.

We imagine composers as they were after their victories. It is important to remember that Wagner was exiled in his midthirties, the age just before most artists realize their finest conceptions, and that his twelve years of banishment from Germany were decisive for his ministry to convert his countrymen. The chief means by which his cause was won were: (*a*) Championship by the already converted, especially Liszt and Bülow, whose performances of the Dresden operas contained enough of the 'art-work of the future' to whet the appetite of young aesthetes and ardent futurists. Without familiarization with 'the new music' would they have been ready for *Das Rheingold*? Would the *Ring* dramas have been an overwhelming success in the early 1850s? (*b*) The securing by these performances in Germany of his most powerful ally, the young King Ludwig of Bavaria, without whom he could not have founded the Wagner Festival Theatre at Bayreuth; (*c*) Letters, pamphlets, essays and articles. Wagner's literary verbiage fills ten volumes; it did not waste his time even if it would now waste ours. Its unbroken self-justification seems to have been psychologically necessary, for almost every literary or musical product of his pen is egocentric to such a degree that even people who disliked him personally were fascinated by his expression of their own unfulfilled desire for power, sexual freedom, acclaim and heroic leadership. Ultimately he and they, without conscious chicanery, could incorporate within this expression an interpretation of Christianity. Wagner could even regard himself, and be regarded, as a mystic.

Unless 'mystic' is to be defined as 'one who uses symbols to communicate the otherwise incommunicable', and is thus to be applied to so many artists as to lose its value, then Wagner was nothing of the sort: he was very much a humanist – not in the meaning of the word adopted by those of us who should properly call ourselves rationalists. An orthodox Christian can be a humanist for all his distrust of unassisted humanity. He must 'keep himself unspotted from the world', yet he is guilty of the Manichean heresy if, like the Hindu, he seeks non-attachment to the world or if, like Wagner's heroes, he renounces worldly pleasure for power, self-improvement or the love of a woman. He may renounce only for the greater love and enjoyment of God. Consequently it is possible for many people other than church-goers to find some of Wagner's works – *Lohengrin, Tristan*, above all the pseudo-Christian *Parsifal* – more distasteful than overtly lustful or cruel plays.

Every work by Wagner presents us with a personal struggle and the victory of some human aspiration, the conflict and triumph being so closely identified with Wagner's own that he interrupted work on the *Ring* dramas to compose *Tristan* in the fever of his relations with Otto and Mathilde van Wesendonck. Today we do not concede a great artist's right to give unbridled reign to Will (as enthroned by Nietzsche, who at first supported Wagner but was as revolted by *Parsifal* as by the bourgeois atmosphere of Bayreuth festivals), but we shall not understand Wagner unless we see why Wagner's age was disposed to make this concession, to bow to the romantic conception of the Artist as Prophet and Priest, not as public or private servant. It was an age that gloried in size – admired a big territorial empire, a great exhibition, a Crystal Palace, Eiffel Tower or other huge feat of engineering, vast industrial expansion; even the domineering, parvenu profiteer was admired by his underpaid workfolk since his success was the means of prosperity and encouraged their own dream of the luck and self-help by which they might re-place or rival him. In such an age the Artist could be maltreated at school and despised in society unless he was recognized for a conqueror; and there was plainly in Wagner's personality what subjected men as well as women – some of them highly intelli-gent. The *successful* artist, especially the grandiose artist, was revered. Beethoven had written the biggest-yet symphony and was the first composer with a determined *conquistador* spirit: his words speak of joy in brotherhood but the music is that of struggle and triumphant will. Wagner's was so in the biggest-

yet music-drama, taking four evenings. It is difficult to understand how anybody swallowed the doctrine of a sinful man's
'redemption' by a good woman's love, but easier to understand
the longing for death as a fulfilment of will.

This idea is not of death as the way to new life (even *Parsifal*,
though wishing to express that Christian idea, fails to do so) but
of death as already implicit if desire is fulfilled. If a human
longing or emotion is fulfilled it ceases. If I kill my enemy I kill
my desire to kill him and my anger may even turn to remorse
and pity. If a life is epitomized in one desire, its fulfilment ends
that life: therefore the all-giving, all-taking, all-consuming
desire between Tristan and Isolde craved the end expressed in
Keats's poem – 'To cease upon the midnight without pain'.
This is no more wicked than Macbeth perishing with the fulfilment of ambition, but it was deliciously shocking in 1865
when people were afraid at self-revelation and the knowledge,
before Freud, that their sexuality accounted for approved
vitality ('high animal spirits'), aggressiveness, the desire for
creative achievement and even religious fervour. *Die Meistersinger* is not a tragedy: it begins in a church and ends in a marriage, and the only desire that is fulfilled and killed, the only
struggle, is an artistic one – the acceptance of Walther's (i.e.
Wagner's) new music, said with true romantic tushery to have
been fertilized by the freedom of Nature (the capital 'N' has
often stood for Nonsense as well) and bird-song. The wedding
finale of comedy implies 'So they lived happily ever after',
because it does not show fulfilment of the lovers' desires.

We need not wonder that there exist perfect Wagnerites,
imperfect Wagnerites who admire parts or features of all
Wagner's works, people who admire *Die Meistersinger* most,
and people for whom the supreme work is *Tristan*. Certainly
Tristan, more even than *Der Ring* was 'the art-work of the
future', the greatest influence on composers in other countries
including that of Wagner's fiercest critics, France. Gounod,
Saint-Saëns, Fauré, Chabrier, Debussy – all made the pilgrimage to Bayreuth. Perfection is not easily achieved when the
medium is vast, rich and complex. Mozart could write a near-
perfect string quartet; Verdi a near-perfect scene in *Falstaff*:

the marvel is that Wagner achieved near-perfection for at least long stretches of music-drama, chiefly because of his wonderful progress in the capacity he disowned, that is to say as professional musician and composer. Lacking space to deal thoroughly with the subject we may profitably cover some of it by examining adverse criticism solely by reference to *Der Ring*.

First, the traditional gibe of the more unintelligent 'Brahmins' – that Wagner could not have composed a great symphony. This can be countered by recalling the years in which England had few opportunities to see music-drama, for even Covent Garden gave only 'seasons'. Before the coming of radio and recordings audiences thronged the Queen's Hall for Wood's Promenade Concerts on Monday nights to hear 'bleeding chunks' – sometimes whole acts – of Wagner's dramas, many of the voice parts cued in by instruments to save great expense.

Listening to the magnificent introductions to the first act of *Die Walküre* (or to the succeeding acts) or the Prelude to *Siegfried* (which one has heard, in isolation, compared with the beginning of Sibelius's Fourth Symphony) one cannot doubt Wagner's capacity to compose purely instrumental music on the scale of huge symphonic movements, and so to have made Bruckner's tribute to him otiose. Yet quite rightly, as was pointed out by the comparison with Sibelius, we are made aware that this symphonic development is vastly preludial; as there was no will to compose a symphony it is useless to ask if the imagination *could* have conceived one. (The very early Wagner Symphony in C is enjoyable but of little more than documentary interest.) We cannot use even the *Siegfried Idyll* as a complete rejoinder to criticism since its themes are the product of imagination applied to drama.

Once his imagination was set to his dramatic end Wagner had no need to rely upon his pre-composed motives. No composer was ever more fertile. His texture can be likened to tropical vegetation wherein one plant is at spring while another sheds its fruit or leaves. In the middle of an act which we do not happen to know by heart we cannot guess which strand of the polyphony will burgeon into a subsidiary motive or some variant of a main one. Let the point be shown from that exhilarating opening of a symphony-scherzo called *Siegfried's Journey down the Rhine*. It opens with a horn-call motive (Ex. 21A) which is then put in the bass (Ex. 21B), but development of the counter-

motive specially put to this bass and used only for this piece is what carries the movement forward to the 'Rhine' motive. The *Siegfried Idyll* also refutes the opinion that Wagner was a megalomaniac. Wagner's scoring is sensitive and at times exquisitely delicate.

More reasonable are charges against his treatment of voices, though not the one that he required from them extremes of range and volume. For the supermen and superwomen of *Der Ring* tremendous voices are needed, allied to minds willing to give years to the study of one man's unprecedented demands and often to become thereby solely Wagnerian artists; but such artists have been and are forthcoming. The questionable treatment of voices comes from conceiving music-drama as a symphony 'carrying' the drama. When successful, this maintains intense dramatic interest even at times of little stage action, for, as Ernest Newman pointed out, if we were shown everything that 'happened' in the music of *Tristan*, its performance would be banned; but the symphony-drama incurs the accommodating of voices as if they were solo clarinets or horns. When the symphony carries the drama so well that it must not be spoilt, a voice may have to sing whatever notes suit the orchestral texture. It may repeat a note where the words call for inflexion, leap an interval to suit the instrumental harmony, or take such a length of time between change of syllables that even German listeners do not catch the words. In some of Wotan's homilies, or when a few characters declaim without stage action 'in slow turns like councillors at a meeting', Wagner loses by keeping the *a priori* conventions of music-drama. They were so far relaxed in *Die Meistersinger* as to allow the beautiful but wholly 'operatic' quintet in Act III. Yet at its average excellence how splendid is the declamatory *arioso* of the *Ring*! How ridiculous to say that it depends upon the pre-designed motives! With what fertility it is integrated, so that its secure sweep forward is felt by those of us who think it profitless to analyse it into sequences, half-sequences and germinal *articula*! The sample quoted as Ex. 22 was copied from the page at which the score fell open during a search for Ex. 21 in *Götterdämmerung*.

Tristan is Wagner's most marvellously integrated symphony because of its unity of mood and technique. The concert symphony is regarded as a supreme test because the composer submits three or four essays, belonging to each other yet disparate in design and style, thus proving his 'universality', but erotic desire and its longing for the consummation which is its death suffuses all *Tristan*; and since all its acts use the main motives,

Wagner *Götterdämmerung*

the work can be compared with one vast movement. In the concert room we are content to hear its end joined to its beginning as 'Prelude and *Liebestod*', perhaps with an item from the middle, *Liebesträume*. The harmony brought from Wagner at the bidding of *Tristan* (its leading-note and other chromatic discords which are not 'resolved' any more than their yearning is satisfied until the last chord of all) had the greatest effect on subsequent composers and led Schoenberg and others to believe that classical harmony was 'played out'.

It is to Wagner's credit that he rarely boasted about his prowess as a composer, but he did say, with justice, that he had learnt 'the art of transition'. The theatre composer is not free to pass from one musical idea to any other which it suggests by kinship or contrast: the 'next idea' must be right for the next stage situation or the next words, and this compulsion favours either the composer-librettist or the co-operation of composer and librettist. Wagner needs space for his symphony to unfold gloriously, and that is probably why, despite much that is enjoyable in *Das Rheingold*, most of us would choose one of its successors as our favourite *Ring* drama. It was necessary to Wagner's design to show the systematic allotment of motives in the first drama of the tetralogy. His unwillingness to forgo a motive at the appearance or mention of its corresponding person, idea or thing was relaxed as the cycle proceeded, and the heavy concentration of motives at the end of *Götterdämmerung* belongs to music-drama rather than symphony. To judge it as concert music is a foolish habit in which listeners could rarely indulge before the coming of radio and gramophone. In the theatre we are caught in Wagner's spell as the motives are piling towards climax, responding to their associations and therefore to the gathering of dramatic threads.

The end of the *Meistersinger* Prelude, which we are forced to hear purely as music, shows the crudeness of Wagner's over-contrived effects. The simultaneous sounding of motives is helped by a plaster of added harmonies. It lacks the thrust of well-timed discord, which is the main purpose of counterpoint. Its vulgar forcing of an effect after so much spontaneous-sounding music illustrates the point that Wagner is best when driven by impulse, not contrivance; and it is the absence of too-obvious contrivance combined with the replacement of personified ideas by warm human characters that makes *Die Meistersinger* so attractive.

Its harmony, being as 'classical' as Brahms's, has not elicited specific admiration as has that of *Tristan*, yet it is just as personal. Indeed it is unique. Can one switch on the radio in the middle of *Die Meistersinger* and mistake it for any other work? It is marred only by Wagner's loutish attempts at humour. As tailors are supposed to be funny in Germany we may pardon his glance to the gallery with the overwhelming joke of a whole chorus of tailors. But how could so great a man make Beckmesser, after all a qualified member of the guild, into a congenital idiot? Were Wagnerians too unmusical to recognize an uninspired, stiff and formal song? Would a Mastersinger make hash of scansion, sing *'Bleich wie ein Kraut'* instead of *'Gleich einer Braut'*, and produce such incompetent work that the whole of Nuremberg was ready to beat him up? Though Wagner does not shine as a humorist, the man who produced such a diversity as *Der Ring*, *Tristan* and *Die Meistersinger* had no rival in versatility since Mozart: and the man who advanced from *Rienzi* to these dramas travelled farther than any predecessor except Beethoven.

GERMAN OPERA AFTER WAGNER

Music-drama fulfilling all Wagner's conditions has not been successfully attempted since *Der Ring* and *Tristan* but the recurrence of musical ideas for dramatic point was so effectively extended by Wagner that few composers since have completely disregarded it. Without drawing upon mythology or symbolism, composers could share Wagner's ideas of *Gesamtkunstwerk* and 'endless melody'. Thus Cornelius's excellent *The Barber of Baghdad* owes as much to Wagner as does his almost forgotten epic *Le Cid*. A number of operas between 1880 and 1900 unsuccessfully attempted to explore heroic mythology – Greek, Hindu, Celtic – some even spreading into cycles. (Strauss attempted mythology in his early

Guntram of 1894.) The result was to cause a popular reaction in favour of 'human' stories or fairy tales.

The most Wagnerian of post-Wagner operas is *Hänsel und Gretel* (1893) by Wagner's friend Engelbert Humperdinck, who taught several composers, including Wagner's son Siegfried. One emphasizes the inspired accomplishment of *Hänsel und Gretel* lest its association with children and Christmas performances should lead anybody to suppose it a light achievement. Against the background of some hundred German comic operas performed between Wagner's death and Lehár's Viennese operettas (which date from the first decade of the twentieth century), Humperdinck's masterpiece is outstanding, far more so than Pfitzner's *Palestrina* of 1917 which romanticizes the legend of Palestrina's dealings with the Council of Trent to make it resemble Walther's with the Mastersingers. Pfitzner even wrote his own libretto and devised a set of association-motives. Strauss's *Feuersnot* ('Fire-famine') of 1901 is decidedly Wagnerian in general style: but the famous Strauss operas which were to follow owe only a general debt. Hugo Wolf was an ardent enough Wagnerian, and his *Corregidor* (1896) is a non-philosophizing comedy deserving more frequent performances than it receives. It would have been still finer if Wolf had paid less respect to Wagner and more to Mozart, letting this work rollick along as a series of excellent songs and ensembles. Instead he bothered too much with the impedimenta of motives and too little with effective movement and characterization.

Between 1850 and 1900 a very large number of new German operas appeared, and some of the comic pieces may prove worth translation and revival; but few approached in vitality the best operas forthcoming from composers of Latin and Slav ancestry.

ITALIAN OPERA

By 'Italian Opera' we mean opera produced in Italy as distinct from the operas by Italians who had been attracted to Paris. Before Garibaldi, Cavour, and others succeeded in their struggle to make a unified nation, Italy was a land of decadent feudal

states, her labouring folk and most of her citizens poor and
untravelled compared with the frequenters of opera-houses
in Vienna and Paris. The successful native composer had to
cater for audiences who loved fine voices, and wished to hear
them displayed in *bravura*, *coloratura* or *bel canto* arias, cavatinas and duets, during which the function of the instruments
was to accompany, not to begin a symphony gathering in the
voices; audiences also demanded what are called 'strong situations' in tragedy, and intrigue and caricature in comedy. Few
Italian opera-houses could afford elaborate scenic effects or
large orchestras, and the great singers of the nineteenth century
– Pasta, Mario, Malibran, and so on – were international stars,
not to be held by this or that Italian theatre. Yet, with this
background and from banal beginnings one native composer,
Verdi, reached in his old age a zenith of musicianship and dramatic genius greater than Wagner's.

If for the sake of study we wished to date the romantic movement in Italian opera we could use 1801, when Florence saw
the production of *Ginevra di Scozia* by Simon Mayr, a Bavarian
priest who was organist and director of the Liceo at Bergamo.
He wrote nearly seventy operas. His best-known pupils, Merca-
dente and Donizetti, became hardly less popular in Italy than
their master had been between 1810 and 1820. Mayr familiar-
ized Italy with romantic-historical libretti, chiefly of French
origin.

Gaetano Donizetti (1797–1848) began composing operas a
few years after Rossini, whom he seemed to imitate; but just
when Rossini settled to semi-retirement in Paris, Donizetti
showed a distinct personality, less classical and predictable than
Rossini's and also more sentimental, despite the vivacity of
L'Elisir d'amore (1832), *La Fille du régiment* (1840) and *Don
Pasquale* (1843). The French title of the second-mentioned
opera is given because it is less a Rossinian *opera buffa* than a
French *opéra comique*, composed for Paris. *Lucia di Lammer-
moor* (1835) is his only well-known serious opera, but there have
recently been richly deserved revivals of *Anna Bolena* and
Lucrezia Borgia. It is true that if one wished to show the most
'corny' features of popular Italian opera one could not easily

find better material than Donizetti's melodramas, yet despite his unblushing alliance of violent situations with catchy tunes, stock harmonies and ensembles or choruses that echo a protagonist's phrases in unison there are challenges to great singers like those in *Lucia* and also unexpected dramatic thrills – tense climactic scenes which brought the composer through melodrama to drama.

Donizetti's operas give an overall impression of bathos which is reinforced by the ineptitude of classical harmony in meeting the demands of romantic melodrama; but in the operas of Vincenzo Bellini (1801–35) the cavatina with florid cadenza (followed by the faster coloratura-laden *cabaletta*) is genuine romantic music, elegant and tender rather than violent. Bellini was scarcely interested in comic opera or in grand effects. Donald J. Grout calls him 'the aristocrat of opera as Chopin is of the piano' and it is probable that he not only influenced Chopin but was in return influenced by him. Bellini's exquisitely formed melodies with their sequenced phrases could not be mistaken for any other composer's unless Chopin's were set to words with orchestra. Bellini supplied impassioned music where it was demanded, as in *Norma* (1831), which presents the intrusion of carnal love into religious vocation, and in *I Puritani* (1835). The latter unsuccessfully emulates grand opera with crowd scenes, but might have been more effective if Bellini had possessed Chopin's forceful and sinister expression.

One could not easily enjoy Bellini on all nights of a week, yet it is remarkable that many of his contemporaries did so. He was admired even by Wagner, probably because of a literary sensitivity not shown by other Italian composers. The libretti of most of his eight operas were by Felice Romani, from whom he often required alterations. His simple arpeggio accompaniments with infrequent changes of chord have been disparaged as equivalent to a popular guitarist's, yet they are deftly arranged and timed so that any change of harmony, even by the chromatic alteration of a note, sounds highly effective. In less sensitive hands the libretto of *La Sonnambula*, dealing with the embarrassments into which sleep-walking leads the heroine, could be comically banal.

Despite the number of minor composers competing to supply Italian theatres with melodrama or with lyric comedy, the figure of Giuseppe Verdi (1813–1901) seems to dominate Italy, as Wagner's did northern Europe, from soon after 1842 until the end of the century – almost exactly from the time when Donizetti finished composing. Verdi's chief works are as follows:

Nabucco, 1842
I Lombardi alla Prima Crociata, 1843
Ernani, 1844 (libretto by Piave from Hugo's drama)
I Due Foscari, 1844 (Piave from Byron)
Giovanna d'Arco, 1845
Macbeth, 1847 (Piave from Shakespeare)
I Masnadieri, 1847 (Maffei from Schiller's *Die Räuber*)
La Battaglia di Legnano, 1849
Luisa Miller, 1849 (from Schiller's *Kabale und Liebe*)
Rigoletto (orig. *The Curse*), 1851 (Piave from Hugo's *Le Roi s'amuse*)
Il Trovatore, 1853
La Traviata, 1853 (Piave from Dumas the Younger's *La Dame aux camélias*)
I Vespri Siciliani, 1855 (Scribe)
Simon Boccanegra, 1857 (Piave)
Un Ballo in maschera, 1859 (from Scribe's *Gustave III*)
La Forza del Destino, 1862 (adaptation by Piave)
Don Carlos, 1867 (from Schiller)
Aida, 1872
String Quartet in E minor, 1873
Requiem for Manzoni, 1874
Otello, 1887 (Boito from Shakespeare)
Te Deum, 1898
Falstaff, 1893 (Boito from Shakespeare)
(Revised versions of *Simon Boccanegra* and *Don Carlos*, the latter by Boito, appeared in 1881 and 1884 respectively.)

The list includes only those Verdi operas which are regularly performed or have been revived in England since the last war. It will be noted that, as with Wagner, mature work dates from roughly 1850, and that its general advance presents no surprises comparable with the dissimilarities of style between *Der Ring*,

Tristan and *Die Meistersinger*. Verdi is not chameleon-like except by response to moods and characters within a story. But he sprang one great surprise, instigated by Boito and kept secret, by the production of *Falstaff* when he was eighty. He had usually set violent, tragic stories, sometimes more sinister than heroic, adapted from historical plays or novels. There could have been no doubt of his reflecting human motives and character as nobody had done since Mozart, but proof was needed that his art extended to humour, other than cruel sarcasm. *Falstaff* provided that proof.

Since no work in all music earns such gratitude that an artist lived long with undiminished powers, let our first quotation from Verdi show comic genius unparalleled in the nineteenth century. It would be misleading to take a snippet from Falstaff's wonderful catechism about honour, from the great phrases of the final scene and its tremendous fugue 'Tutti nel mondo è burla', or from the scandalmongering and mirth of the ladies in the second scene. Better show Verdi's subtle capture of quick-passing situations. Let the first be Mistress Quickly's moment of meeting the fat knight with a profound obeisance. Why should the simple thirds before the gesture so perfectly convey complicity in the plot against Falstaff? (Ex. 23A). And as she tells him how Mistress Ford sighs for him, what is so funny about Falstaff's little punctuations like 'Lo so, continua'? – not just our recognition of his fine conceit of himself, which we know before the opera begins. Indeed since most of us know every point in the story, only Verdi's art can give any interest to its re-telling, and both Boito and Verdi make points not found in Shakespeare. 'This lovely Alice, poor woman . . . has a fiercely jealous husband . . .'; but Falstaff does not seem to hear this important information; one point has stuck in his mind, the date and time when Alice will be at home to him, between two and three o'clock (Ex. 23B).

When the vehemence of *Nabucco* overwhelmed the audience of La Scala even Donizetti's music seemed tame. Verdi's success should not be attributed only to his appeal to partisans of the *Risorgimento*, who during his lifetime came to include almost all Italians. Yet in this story about Nebuchadnezzar's

persecution of the Hebrews and in subsequent libretti set in
various historical periods between 1200 and 1600 he could
hardly avoid the themes of patriotism, hatred between nations
or dynasties, popular leadership against oppression, and con-
spiracies to political ends. Men whose aim was first freedom
from Austrian rule and then the political unification of Italy
identified themselves with the captive Jews in Babylon; having
decided that the composer was their spokesman they found
their emotions uncontrollable after the rousing choruses of the

somewhat crude *I Lombardi*, *Ernani* and so on, until the demon-
strations during *La Battaglia di Legnano* (Rome, 1849) roused
alarm with police and censors. They foolishly supposed they
could draw the sting from *Un Ballo in maschera* by insisting on
puritan Boston instead of Spain as its locale, but after the performance in Naples crowds began shouting 'Viva Verdi' on
discovery that the letters of his name were the initials of
'Vittorio Emanuele Re d'Italia'.

Triviality, melodrama and actual brutality is to be found not
only in early but in mature Verdi. Then why, even when
Nabucco or *Macbeth* were recently revived, were we sure of so
much to admire – not just in passages like the sleep-walking
scene of *Macbeth* but in the more naive sections? Whence the

thrill when it is proposed to revive a Verdi opera? There are two answers. First, Verdi's *natural* musical endowment was of the highest order. Eric Blom,* paying eloquent tribute to the uncanny rightness of Verdi's choice of chord inversions, points out that Ex. 24A, 'this extraordinarily modern passage in Iago's false account of Cassio's dream', is not formed by a chain of parallel chords:

The approaches to his favourite cadences (examine them in the *Requiem*!) are diverse and ingenious; his basses, unlike Donizetti's, even Wagner's, are unorthodox yet secure (Ex. 24B). This is not the product of culture but of an endowed 'ear'.

The second reason for our unexpected satisfaction even with early operas by Verdi comes from the fact that he did not 'write down' to naive taste; his own taste began at the naive level of his audiences. He was the son of a village innkeeper and, though helped by local admirers, was not even admitted to the Liceo when he went to Milan. He said himself that his life was hard until the surprising acceptance of his first opera and the persistent offer of contracts by La Scala. At each stage of his life he wrote the kind of music he knew, which until he was nineteen meant that of brass bands, parish churches, provincial gatherings, and popular, usually banal, operas. By *Macbeth* he had

* In *Music and Letters*, October 1931.

reached Shakespeare and would soon reach the Viennese musical classics and Wagner. Granted genius, the level of taste to which a man advances is less important than the extent to which his genius is exercised. Insincerity cannot produce artistic vitality. Hence the fatuous attempts of serious, educated composers to emulate jazzmen or folk musicians. They do not stretch their creative powers at the popular level, whereas the more naive musician who is not imitating uses all the skill he can command. Verdi's invention, his ransacking of the music he knew, his passionate vigour and his gift of melody were manifest at all stages.

Though we lack proof that Wagner influenced Verdi's work directly we also lack proof that he did not. Verdi was intelligently aware of Wagner's progress but his own might have proceeded to the superb integration of *Otello* if he had never known anything about Wagner. When financial security enabled him to acquire a country estate and pursue the call of literary and musical culture, his main interest was in his Italian predecessors from Palestrina to Piccinni, and one could compile a lengthy list of references to passages in his last eight operas which give incontrovertible proof of his unconscious recollections of works by Beethoven.

Though nearly all of his libretti are historical tragedies suited to his fiery muse, every so often he chose a romantic story 'in modern dress', for instance *Luisa Miller* and *La Traviata*, in which there was little call for heroics and rousing chorus-work, but opportunity for the characterization without which such stories, in novel or opera, can be insipid. To express human passions and emotions in general was no task at all for Verdi: he either did that – his disparagers could say 'inappropriately' in church music – or he remained mute. The admirable characterization in his operas from *Rigoletto* onwards is primarily due to that ability to get inside individual characters which we admire in Shakespeare and Mozart. It has been remarked that if the words were suppressed nobody could mistake a bar of music set for one of the ladies in *Don Giovanni* or *Figaro* for anything associated with another. This could also be said of both male and female characters in Verdi's operas after *Luisa Miller*.

With the growth in Verdi's powers of characterization goes advance in techniques which favour it. Mozart revealed only the broad points of his characters in arias: for the subtle points he needed their interplay with others in ensembles, from two persons to an imbroglio which involved most of a cast. Verdi himself spoke of *Rigoletto* as an opera of duets, and refused to give one of its singers an additional aria or change the title-character to a handsome instead of a deformed man. The famous quartet is 'closer to Mozart than to the quintet in *The Mastersingers*. Wagner's ensemble is a static set-piece: Verdi's is dramatic movement, in which the interlocking passions of the characters create unity from tension. . . . Verdi's imagination has learned, too, how to make even the "hit-number" dramatically relevant'.* That is why in *Aida*, commissioned for the opening of the new opera-house in Cairo, even the banal march tunes in the Act I I finale are dramatically relevant and give room between their noise for development of character. Yet it is difficult to know why special trumpets were needed for this crowd scene or why the scoring should be admired, for the matter tells its authorship while the manner pays tribute to Meyerbeer. Except for this lapse, *Aida* (rightly the 'grand opera' for which Verdi was paid) contains in its solos and duets some of the best lyricism in any work except *Otello*. The astounding loveliness of the final entombment scene seems almost to elevate us to a spiritual plane, despite the ghastly reality which we ought to feel, since we see it happen.

The contrasts and similarities between Verdi's advance and Wagner's could be the subject of a lengthy dissertation. Here one must be content to observe that Verdi had no conscious theories about thematic integration and 'endless melody', that the recurrent motives and (with cutting of tendrils) isolable songs and *scenas* of *Otello* and *Falstaff* are no more embedded in connective recitative than are the more obvious 'numbers' of *Rigoletto*. Like Wagner (but in his own way, which resembles Mozart's in Elvira's '*In quali eccessi*'), Verdi has simply progressed in the arts of transition and integration. That is why we are hurled headlong into *Otello* – an overture or prelude is

* Wilfrid Mellers in *Man and His Music*, Volume 3.

unthinkable. This finest of musical dramas has time and room to present all its richly varied situations, yet no score is more economical in the true sense of the word. We are similarly hurled into *Falstaff*, though even more memorable is the precipitate vigour with which *Falstaff* finishes. After a century during which in place of the musician there had grown a dreary multiplication of 'the Artist', with what refreshment, with what affection one welcomes any work – from a vulgar early opera to the great Manzoni *Requiem* – that was composed for honest money or in honest love by the only great musician who was also a successful farmer!

FRENCH MUSIC AFTER 1850

Grand opera, native or imported, persisted at the Paris Opéra during the Second Empire, which ended after the Franco-Prussian War in 1870; but *opéra comique*, to which the Opéra doors were closed, claimed greater musical vitality and greater respect outside France. During the 1850s and 1860s there was a spate of operettas (including *Le Petit Faust*, Hervé's parody of Gounod's masterpiece) but all were eclipsed by Offenbach's *Orphée aux enfers* (1858), *La Belle Hélène* (1864), *La Vie parisienne* (1866) and *Les Contes d'Hoffmann* (1881). They wear better than the sentimental and often heavy Viennese operettas of Lehár and Johann Strauss, whose *Fledermaus* contains so much excellent music as to make one wish that its story contained humour a little less dull than the return of drunks. Neither can Vienna or Germany show any ballet music as perennially fresh as that of Léo Delibes (1836–91), now known chiefly by *Coppélia* and *Sylvia*.

Ambroise Thomas (1811–96) and Charles Gounod (1818–93) are now being rediscovered after years of silly condemnation for being of their age and reflecting its sentiment. They inherited racial finesse in orchestral scoring and are historically important as marking a reaction against the flatulence of the Meyerbeer hegemony. Thomas's *Hamlet* is still given in France but he is known here chiefly by elegant excerpts from *Mignon* (1866), an opera from Goethe's *Wilhelm Meister*. Gounod's *Faust* (1859) is so much with us that too few people are aware of its excellence. To complain that it does not match up to Goethe, or that it contrives a happy ending, is unintelligent. Berlioz loved it, having the sense to see that it is concerned only with the love story in Goethe's Part I (and is therefore known in Germany as *Margarethe*). The point to emphasize is that it was classed with *opéra comique*,* as were Gounod's *Mireille* (1864) and *Roméo et Juliette* (1867). These represent the other extreme of *opéra comique* from operetta.

People who have explored Gounod's beautiful songs, or participated in his Little Symphony for Wind Instruments cannot doubt his artistry, but if they are old enough to remember the days when his somewhat unctuous oratorios and masses were sung by choirs and choral societies they may discriminate between the Gounod who belongs only to his times and the Gounod whose invention was not equalled by his contemporaries, nor by Jules Massenet (1852–1912), who is his successor in the alluring, tenderly erotic vein. The bloodlessly elegant melody of Massenet's *Manon* (1884) infected his betters among French composers just as Puccini's manner infected Italians.

Only Gounod's oratorios with their *Parsifal*-like harmonies showed any considerable influence of Wagner in France until the arrival in Paris of the Belgian organist, César Franck (1822–90). Those least impressed by Teutonic pseudo-profundity and most impressed by the art that conceals art with the civilized unpretentiousness of a Bizet or a Fauré – that is to say the most Francophile among us – have to admit that the state of music in the middle of the century was nowhere so narrow as in France. Popular taste seemed to be identical with that of the fossilized Conservatoire, and as in pre-Revolutionary years a huge agricultural country saw most artistic activity gravitating to one capital city. To Franck most of its music must have seemed empty, for the interesting feature about all his major works is their concern with structural adventure.

* It was, however, later admitted to the Opéra in a new form with recitatives. It happens to be, according to the number of performances in no less than twenty-four languages, the most popular of all operas.

Fashionable piano recitals did not compensate for the almost total lack of chamber and orchestral concerts at which Paris should have heard music of Greater Germany, Bohemia and Russia. In this respect even London was better. Berlioz tried with little success to remedy the defect. It persisted until in 1861 Pasdeloup founded his Concerts Populaires which spread over each year a repertory comparable with one of Wood's 'Promenade' seasons. The Lamoureux Concerts did not begin until twenty years later. Franck is best known by single instrumental essays – one symphony, one piano concerto called Symphonic Variations, one quartet, and so on, each earnestly tackling an original conception, sometimes with admirable success, as in the recitativo-fantasia and canonic finale of the wholly splendid Violin Sonata, or in the Symphonic Variations with their two alternating, transformed and finally joined themes. How can people who have heard this deservedly popular work talk about Franck's 'organ scoring'? Nothing in it, or in the symphonic poems *Les Éolides*, *Le Chasseur maudit* and *Les Djinns*, is reminiscent of organ registration; yet some of his defects remind us of an improvising organist because his constructive ability did not always rise to the magnitude of his self-imposed task. In this, as well as in his general style, Franck is no French artist but a Walloon who admired the Germans.

No composer is more frequently disparaged for his shortcomings, the chief of which is that he flounders ('*une machine à moduler*') when his developments are still-born; we tolerate the floundering because it may lead to more considerable music than his French contemporaries could have conceived. The *Trois Chorals* are among the most fascinating of romantic organ works; they would stand as the organist's heritage from the symphonic poem or the Schubert *Wanderer* Fantasy if only we dared to rewrite them or play them with omissions; but one cannot take the weeds without snapping the plant.

When Gounod called Franck's D minor Symphony 'the affirmation of incompetence pushed to a dogma', one of its heinous offences was the employment of a cor anglais in the middle movement; another was that the work consisted of only three movements. Had Franck offered it as a symphonic poem

called *Redemption* Gounod's unfamiliarity with the genre might
have led to discreet silence. A cor anglais solo was certainly out
of place in Gounod's conception of a symphony, but his own
Symphony in D major, though worth playing, would have been
a work of art as well as artistry if it implied his awareness that
any other symphonies had been composed since Clementi's in
the same key. The young Belgian came to a Paris in which the
Prix de Rome, followed by success in opera and ballet, was the
ambition of every young composer, and he was noble-minded
enough not to curse his fate as almost entirely a composer for
instruments. He had begun his career as a virtuoso pianist
exploited by his money-greedy father, but commended by
Liszt from whom he derived many points of style. Franck's
turgid yet fine *Prelude, Chorale and Fugue* and the limpidly
beautiful *Prelude, Fugue and Variation* serve well to show how
much he owed to Liszt and Wagner, and how much to a distinct
genius of his own.

When, aged twenty-four, Franck shook off his father's yoke
and came to Paris he had to traverse miles of streets giving
lessons and to compose in the early morning. Soon his originality as a performer, his cosmopolitan knowledge, seriousness of
purpose yet pleasant personality drew disciples round him as
organist of St Clothilde and eventually as organ professor at the
Conservatoire, where the organ department became a cell of
general musical instruction rivalling the official composition
department. Most of Franck's ambitious works were written in
the last decades of this hard life. The nickname '*Pater Seraph-
icus*' applied to him by his devoted pupils (the most notable
were d'Indy, Duparc, Bordes and Chausson) may indicate only
his meek acceptance of opposition and child-like facial expression. Recent research shows that he had none of Gounod's
religious obsessions although he was a sincere Catholic. His
life was like his teaching – sane, balanced, gentle yet vivacious.
For all the hardship his career is enviable in its slow *crescendo* of
happiness, from his successful marriage to a beautiful actress
to the final knowledge that he had not worked in vain.

Only his Quartet was very enthusiastically acclaimed before
he died; but within another few years his disciples had made

his orchestral and organ works almost too popular, and by 1894 had founded a rival and 'Franckist' conservatoire, the Schola Cantorum under d'Indy. Franck's was a timely intrusion into a Paris where music was both complacent and complaisant. The Conservatoire succession – Saint-Saëns, Fauré, Debussy and Ravel – was not Franckist; yet Saint-Saëns and Fauré recognized what was valuable in Franck's personality and influence. Their recognition can be shared now that we no longer regard Franck in the stained glass of d'Indy's biography. Franck would have been a major composer of the second rank if he had left us only his secular works – the symphonic poems and Symphonic Variations. His religious music (with the possible exception of *Les Béatitudes*) is his poorest, belonging to the period in which people confused erotic piety with religious vision.

Vincent d'Indy (1851–1931) should be honoured for his expenditure upon and untiring personal services to public music, especially in the promotion of concerts and opera performances. He was an aristocrat who served with gallantry in the Franco-Prussian War, yet had a burning desire to 'make good' as a working musician. He was most happy when accepted as timpanist at the Théâtre-Italien among men who depended upon their playing for a livelihood. He spent his spare time in his ancestral district of the Cévennes and used its traditional melodies in several of his works, notably the *Symphonie sur un chant montagnard*. His natural dignity and fine command of pictorial effects make one regret that his *Fervaal* is rarely heard outside France. It fulfils Wagner's conditions of music-drama; the words, by the composer, oppose sacred and profane love, the former being symbolized by a plainsong hymn melody. Ardent catholicism made d'Indy cold towards Debussy and Ravel and while during the 1920s the younger musicians tended to identify him as a survivor from the nineteenth century he felt that their 'new music' lacked high seriousness.

Though less versatile than d'Indy, Chausson and Duparc wrote finer works in their limited fields. Ernest Chausson (1855–99) began as a lawyer and did not become Franck's pupil until the 1880s. His noble Symphony in B flat (1890) and some of his songs excel any by Franck in breadth of melody. Henri Duparc (1848–1933) was one of Franck's first Parisian pupils. An excessively self-critical man, Duparc destroyed many ambitious works which his admirers tell us were valuable. Such they were if they were comparable with the fourteen songs on which his reputation rests. Duparc and Fauré were the first composers to bring distinction to the kind of songs called *Mélodies*, sensitive yet strong settings of words from the symbolist poets. A nervous breakdown in 1885 led Duparc to give up composition and retire to Switzerland.

In strong contrast with Franck and his Wagner-influenced pupils is a genius of entirely Latin temperament who would have eclipsed all contemporary French composers except Fauré if he had not died of tuberculosis just after his brilliance was fully revealed. Georges Bizet (1838–75) invites pointed comparison with Gounod, although twenty years younger, because in his quiet singing movements his melody and harmony sound as if Gounod had excelled himself – examples are *La Poupée* in the suite *Jeux d'enfants*, and the *Adagietto*, portraying an aged couple's mutual devotion, in *L'Arlésienne*. In more vigorous movements Bizet's fire and energy are unique. After the vivacious Symphony in C, an amazingly assured work for a youth of seventeen, Bizet spent some years in which nothing from him fulfils the promise of a Conservatoire student who had been praised by Liszt for his piano playing and won the Prix de Rome, let alone the composer of that still valued symphony. A clue may be found in *Roma* and in the opera *Les Pêcheurs de perles* (1863), both of which contain lyricism like that of Gounod (his chief teacher and a personal friend) together with turgid music which suggests that he distrusted his spontaneous ideas. He was also forced to earn money by so much arranging and hack-work for music publishers that his health suffered from the strain.

Neither with *La Jolie Fille de Perth* (1866) nor with *Djamileh* (1872) did Bizet achieve popularity. In both he had a poor libretto, and his fine works all date from after the Franco-Prussian War, beginning in 1871 with the twelve commissioned piano duets *Jeux d'enfants*, now known chiefly by the selection which he so brilliantly arranged for orchestra. Their very nature demanded wit, invention, colour and spontaneity, and with them Bizet found himself. The same qualities pervade the incidental music for Daudet's *L'Arlésienne*, also known to us by orchestral suites. In the following year he began his master-piece, *Carmen*, to a libretto from Prosper Mérimée's story 'toned down' for its first audience. The heroine, a gipsy, is seen coming out of a cigarette factory with other girls who flirt with waiting soldiers: she wantonly throws a flower at José, the one who has *not* made advances. Such was the then-scandalous introductory scene; and the very end of the play, José's stabbing of Carmen during the cheering of his rival by the crowd at a bullfight – this too was a novelty. Bizet witnessed the *succès de scandale* but died within the year that brought him an unqualified triumph.

Carmen can be regarded as the greatest example of what must be called technically *opéra comique* – almost the last to main-tain the distinction, for, without the spoken words (which should be restored), it soon moved to the Opéra. Despite musical ideas which recur for dramatic effect, *Carmen* gives no indica-tion that Wagner had ever existed, yet its sheer vitality proves that the desiderata of music-drama (rather than Wagner's own methods) are the touchstones of greatness in opera. *Carmen* is great opera. No other attempt at *'verismo'* or 'realism' – the romanticizing of socially despised people and scenes – can be so called, not even *Cavalleria Rusticana*, *I Pagliacci* or *La Bohème* (1896). The French prototype of *La Bohème*, though not com-parable with Puccini's full-blooded melodrama, is Charpentier's *Louise* (1900). Set in the poor streets of Paris artisans its sweet music (in the style of the composer's teacher, Massenet) is theatrically effective though it cannot fully rise to tragedy.

If the outstanding talent of Édouard Lalo (1823–92) had equalled Bizet's, which it closely approaches, he would be remembered by more of his many works than the excellent violin concerto, *Symphonie espagnole*, for anybody who is lucky enough to hear his colourful *Le Roi d'Ys* must know that opera-houses outside France have yet to do him justice. One admits that French opera loses more than German or Italian by trans-lation. The Frenchness of all Lalo's known music is remarkable, for he was of Spanish ancestry and, as the leader of a string quartet, worshipped the classical masters of chamber music from Haydn to Schubert and even (exceptionally for a French musician) became fond of Brahms.

Similarly colourful, direct and sensuous were Emmanuel Chabrier (1841–1904) and the much younger Paul Dukas (see p. 205). Chabrier was more important than might be supposed from his *España* and *Marche joyeuse* – two wonderfully imaginative orchestral scores. These works indicate the closeness of ideals shared by impressionist painters and *avant-garde* composers, and Chabrier's harmony as well as his texture had considerable influence on Debussy and Ravel. It was a visit to Germany and the hearing of *Tristan* (which he helped to produce in Paris) that induced Chabrier to turn composer somewhat late in life despite his early promise as a pianist. Unfortunately he was led to forgo his native exuberance in order to pay tribute to Wagner. A mental breakdown silenced him after the 1890s.

GERMANY AFTER 1850

Although Germany as a whole did not share Richard Strauss's pre-eminence in the theatre, she more than made up for it in the concert hall. Vienna, the imperial capital of a feudal federation which came to an end with the unifying of Germany by Prussian domination under Bismarck, Moltke and the Hohenzollerns, retained considerable musical prestige apart from that reflected from Haydn, Mozart, Beethoven and Schubert. But in the later years of the nineteenth century Leipzig was the Mecca for English and other music students, the Bayreuth pilgrimage being part of its full course. Brahms, the greatest instrumental composer of the century, though lionized in Vienna, belonged to the north, and could not for long stay away from his native Hamburg.

Many musicians may be surprised when they first recognize Anton Bruckner (1824–96) as being by nine years Brahms's senior, and just as surprised when they first read that the young Brahms (composer of the remarkable but not wholly satisfying sonatas, ballads and variations for piano of the 1850s) was as much disliked by conservatives as was Wagner. This fact might be coupled with Bruckner's adoption by the Wagnerites and lead us to ask why two symphonists whose music should show similarities differ not merely in their broad conceptions of movements but in style. Comparison is difficult to avoid because Bruckner matured late and did not produce his first symphony until 1868, and though Brahms waited till he was over forty before producing his first, the four symphonies by Brahms and eight* by Bruckner were all heard first between 1868 and 1886.

It is desirable to clear our minds of misconceptions concerning each of these composers. Because of Brahms's admiration for Beethoven and some occasional turns of phrase, his first symphony was foolishly hailed as 'the Tenth'; the first misconception is that Brahms 'modelled himself' on Beethoven or was equipped with the kind of musical genius to shine as a reincarnation of Beethoven. The second misconception is that Bruckner's symphonies are Wagnerian except in superficial points of style.

The truth is that Bruckner, not Brahms, had the inheritance of the Viennese classics in him, though he was not conscious of the fact, for he was even less widely cultured than Schubert. Bruckner was a child when Schubert was still alive, and he eventually studied under Sechter, from whom Schubert had wished to learn counterpoint and composition. He came to Vienna at the age of forty-two having served as organist first at the monastery of St Florian and then at Linz. His large-scale works of this period are comparable in style with Schubert's last Masses. For Brahms, composition on a large scale was a triumph secured by labour, and his wonderful short Intermezzi for piano (along with his best songs) are more perfect works than his most admirable and impressive symphonic movements. For Bruckner's ponderous muse, huge movements were the necessary room to move, and he seems to fill them with no more

* There were more than the eight symphonies actually completed by Bruckner, but for information that cannot be satisfactorily given in a few lines the reader should consult *The Symphony*, Volume 1 (Penguin Books, 1967).

effort than Schubert. He was concerned only to honour God with awareness of the vastness of nature and the divine universe, probably unconscious of being pantheistic since he was meticulous in religious practice.

Sechter revealed to him the later works of Beethoven and a good deal of Bach. The effect was a fertilization of a Viennese-style *Kapellmeistermusik* with Baroque polyphony, for Bruckner saw how Beethoven late in life took a new interest in counterpoint. The 'Cecilian' movement in church music added to this Brucknerian amalgam some archaisms from Gregorian chant and Renaissance polyphony. In 1865 Bruckner saw in Munich a production of *Tristan*, which seemed the most religious music he knew except Beethoven's Ninth Symphony. The psychology by which this naive creature found the glory of heaven in the most humanly sexual work ever composed is not unique, for the sophisticated Heseltine found Delius's music 'religious' and 'mystical'. Suffice it to say that Wagner, though of *Der Ring* rather than of *Tristan*, was the catalyst which joined Bruckner's expressive amalgam and made it the vehicle of symphonies which speak of glory, glory and still more glory. Because of their effect they are unique and wonderful; without it, they would be intolerably boring – except for some of their scherzos in which Viennese *Gemüthlichkeit* is transformed by the size or overlapping of phrases. When Bruckner *scherzi* fail to dance in staid joy they are his most ineffective movements; his slow movements are never so, however long they take to reach ecstasy.

The degree of our liking for Bruckner's music is probably as simple as a preference for living in this or that kind of landscape or country. There can be few musicians who utterly dislike Bruckner's symphonies but many who are not at all surprised at their infrequent performance outside Germany. Viennese audiences may appreciate Bruckner's symphonies no more intelligently than London ones, but they are happy to take an hour or more's music in the language with which they are familiar, since that language grew under Beethoven and Schubert in their own city.

And how that language was enriched by Brahms! In Brahms's expression outside the short piano pieces and songs we find conflict and passion which is sublimated in the great polyphonic spread of Bruckner, a passion which makes false the Brahmins' 'classical' statue of their hero. The clue to the difference in effect between Brahms and his contemporaries is Brahms's deliberate cultivation of the art of restraint, not necessarily by recourse to 'objective' stylization in fugue, passacaglia and chorale prelude. Suppression may suggest smouldering passion in the heavily controlled passage or enhance by contrast the passage in which emotion is released. Examples of the first are the familiar G minor Rhapsody, the *Edward* ballad or the wonderful A flat minor Fugue for organ; of the second there is no better example than the *Tragic* Overture; its opening bare fifths have (for their period) a certain ferocity, but the whole of the 'first group' is somewhat formal, and in places wintry, so that when the trombones and horns lead in the rapturous 'second group' with warm major-key chords it is as though the romantic revival were celebrated in a single piece, or as if the music were programmatic and signified a quick passage from winter to summer. There is something akin to this in the conflict between C minor anger and C major contentment in the first and last movements of Brahms's First Symphony.

No composer has been better rewarded for not rushing into symphonic composition and not composing more than four symphonies; for of no other composer can it be said that professional musicians and general listeners alike must hesitate if asked to name the finest among his symphonies. The final votes might well show four close numbers; and is there a single more admirable post-Beethovenian nineteenth-century piano concerto or violin concerto than Brahms's in B flat and D respectively, or are there any finer violin sonatas than his?

Whether his music is to one's taste or not, one cannot deny his German romantic impulse, his rhythmic subtlety, and his conscientiousness. His less attractive works (or less convincing passages in fine works) are those in which one of these qualities is present without counterbalance. A certain north German cosiness rather than depth goes with the philosophizing of the Alto Rhapsody and parts of the *German Requiem*; paradoxically some of the string quartets come alive in their lyrical sections and are less vital, for all their fever, in the conscientious 'classical development' sections. Occasionally a Brahms work which one knows to be admirable – for instance, the G major Sextet or the A minor Quartet – can sound strangely like an exercise in the classical manner if it is played just after some impassioned chamber work by Beethoven or Bartok. Yet, since Beethoven, is anybody Brahms's peer in the realm of chamber music?

It is a pity that the revival of chaconne structure in the finale of the Fourth Symphony (which still falls into three broad sections and coda) or of chorale preludes have associated Brahms with 'classicism'. The same Brahms, of the *Liebeslieder* Waltzes, admired Johann Strauss and hoped to write a comic opera. The sheer wealth of his ideas, which can be noted merely by counting their number and contrast in the exposition of a sonata or symphony, or the sheer bulk of his songs, chamber and piano works, should testify to a fertility unparalleled in his time except by Wagner. It was a giant who composed both the spirited and ingratiating Horn Trio and the Clarinet Quintet which many would select as the single most searchingly emotional instrumental work of the whole romantic movement.

Brahms's music reflects the conflict in his personality, which is evident even in his mannerisms. Are these piano chords too grumpy and coarse, the lower notes too close? The effect is intentional, for elsewhere Brahms's piano writing can be as gently sonorous as Schumann's or as limpid as Chopin's. Is his orchestral 'doubling', his fondness for woodwind misalliances evidence of a defective ear? Not at all. Brahms wanted the sounds he produced, and if we doubt his ability to secure utter clarity chiefly by primary colours we can turn to such a movement as the *grazioso* variations in his Second Symphony.

His most consistent detractor was Hugo Wolf (1860–1903), who wrote vitriolic judgements of his music in the Vienna *Salonblatt*.* This was an angry young man fighting an inferiority complex because of his sour appearance or humble origins

* Their idiocy may be judged by the description of Brahms's E minor Symphony as illustrating 'the art of composing with no ideas', or the generalization that Brahms's music combined 'emptiness, sterility and hypocrisy'.

(his father was a tanner), an unpleasantly opinionated creature, expelled from several schools, and finally from the Vienna Conservatory after telling the director that its instruction was valueless to him. He could write to friends that his own latest song was 'divinely marvellous'. (The attractive but hardly heaven-scraping *Fussreise* was commended by the words 'when you have heard it you can have only one wish – to die'.) Unsociable egotists are found wherever there are students, and they may later prove highly talented; among them are sometimes fanatical hero-worshippers capable of Wolf's running ahead of Wagner's cab in order to open the door; but judgement on Wolf as a man is impossible. We do not know what mental tortures he suffered before his late thirties when he went to finish life in an asylum. His most merciful days were of grandiose delusion and his most terrible those of such violence that he was kept in a caged bed.

Of the symphonic poem *Penthesilea*, which he said Richter deliberately ruined, we know little; but the *Italian Serenade* (for string quartet or small orchestra) as well as certain songs, such as his settings of Michelangelo, suggest the calibre of a symphonist as well as the wit of a miniaturist. For all his worship of Wagner, only a few songs like the familiar *Lebewohl*, the settings of verses about Calvary in the *Spanisches Liederbuch* and other songs on religious subjects – *Karwoche, Gebet* – reflect Wagnerian harmony; the nimble wit in some of Wolf's best songs is unparalleled in Wagner. No doubt, however, Wagner's symphonic repetitions and sequences influenced Wolf's piano parts and his declamation, for sometimes the texture as a whole provides the 'endless melody' and sometimes the voice holds the melodic thread.

When he was twenty-eight Wolf betook himself with some financial help to an attic study-bedroom in a village twenty miles from Vienna and composed his songs in spasms of enormous energy. Forty-three poems by Mörike were set within less than three months. This spate of composition occurred during the early months of 1888 in the cold, lonely attic. In autumn of the same year he set fifty poems by Goethe in a similar frenzied ecstasy. Later on the poems of his *Span-*

isches Liederbuch and *Italienisches Liederbuch* were set in two similar bouts of incredible high pressure, yet between them Wolf suffered spells of torture and sterility comparable only with those which made Tchaikovsky declare he was finished between the composition of his last and best symphonies and operas. His letters during these fallow periods are distressing. He can imagine neither melody nor harmony and begins to doubt 'whether the compositions bearing my name are really by me'. After the *Italienisches Liederbuch* this loss of power was permanent. Nearly all that we treasure of Wolf's songs were conceived between 1888 and 1896, though there are also at least a dozen very good ones to be picked from the few years before the 1888 spate of fifty-three Mörike songs.

However much we treasure Schubert's music, Wolf's does more justice to the poet's work. Schubert will make one or two of the literary images for ever memorable; Wolf uncannily reflects every image, every turn of irony or pathos, without losing integrity in a mere aggregate. To avoid that fault he sometimes drives accompanimental figures (chosen with uncanny suggestiveness) obsessively, yet this persistence is often the source of most interesting harmonic clashes between voice and piano. How difficult to illustrate Wolf's inspired response to words without extensive quotation! Imagine, therefore, what begins Ex. 25 as the third in a chain of rising sequences – 'Praise God who [1] made the ocean and its wondrous deeps [2] made the vessels that o'er its surface glide [3] made Paradise with its eternal light [4] made beauty and thy countenance'. The song opens with the majestic figure which the extract shows transferred to the bass. The numbers show the sequences: beginning quietly, rising at [3] to crescendo, and then, just as the climax and tonic key are reached with the innocent blasphemy about beauty and the beloved's face, a sudden intense *pianissimo* and *sotto voce*. One of Wolf's remarkable musical gifts is wit.

The extract is from the *Italienisches Liederbuch*, which contains some of his most exquisite aphoristic miniatures, written in response to splendid translations. Recalling the range in Schubert from *Erlkönig* to *Der Leiermann*, we still should not be foolish to say that it was exceeded by Wolf. Consider just five contrasts – for 'types' cannot be isolated; every Wolf song is unique – the exuberant virtuosity of *Der Rattenfänger*, the agonized defiance of another Goethe song, the most tremend-

ous of all settings of *Prometheus*, the moving simplicity of Kerner's *Zur Ruh', zur Ruh'!*, the flirtatious cynicism of *Ich hab' in Penna einen Liebsten* from the *Italienisches Liederbuch*, and the world-weariness of *Alles endet, was entstehet* from the last three songs. Did anyone set these Michaelangelo sonnets before? Dare anyone now attempt their German version? Wolf did not merely show new respect for poetic rhythm and meaning; he found a new kind of music for every new poem he set. His texture and harmonies responded to his poet as totally as did his vocal declamation. He was innocent of cliché or formula and that can hardly be said of a single other composer of so many songs.

At one time he shared a cheap room in Vienna with Gustav Mahler (1860–1911), son of a Jewish shopkeeper who pursued a conductor's career to obtain the time and money for symphonic composition. Beethoven, Berlioz, Liszt and Wagner had all helped to make conducting a specialist's vocation, and Mahler's insight into classical and romantic scores together with his exhausting attention to all details of performance, first at Hamburg and then, after 1897, at the Vienna opera-house, produced standards that proved him one of the greatest conductors. His was a fearsome but utterly dedicated tyranny. Otherwise he would not have endured constant hostility.

Educated both at conservatoire and university and deeply interested in philosophy (in later life he turned towards Catholicism), Mahler reveals his concern with metaphysical and religious ideas, and with the human conditions, especially suffering and death, which invoke speculative and aspiring thought. His most characteristic expression therefore uses words, not only in his songs with orchestra but in most of his symphonies. We mention here only the symphonies finished before 1900, his first four, which are sometimes regarded as representing a sentimental 'first period' belonging to their century. Mahler does not hide his obsession with subjects that excite his pity, dread or affection – for instance the thought of dissolution, personal and universal, or of pain. Thus the minor-key treatment of the *Frère Jacques* tune in Symphony No. 1 in D (1888) is an arresting yet naive stroke; so is the *Ländler*-like *scherzo*; almost all themes in the work suggest childhood. Symphony No. 2 in C minor (1894) is more vehement and includes both a poem from *Des Knaben Wunderhorn* and a choral finale to Klopstock's *Resurrection* ode. No. 3 in G (1895) has seven movements, and requires a contralto soloist as well as women's and boys' choirs, the words being from *Des Knaben*

Wunderhorn and from Nietzsche. The popular No. 4 in G (1900) overtly projects a child's mental imagery, including that of heaven, and reaches another *Wunderhorn* lyric for soprano solo in its final fourth movement.

The distortion of the *Frère Jacques* tune, its nearness to one of Mahler's frequent funeral marches, the making of *Ländler* into vast yearning movements, the mixture of Schubertian lyricism and Brucknerian grandiosity, the horn calls and trumpet fanfares, the Lisztian attitudinizing – these prevent most English musicians from revering Mahler with the near-worship shown by Schoenberg and other Vienna friends. Being the highly educated creature of a decadent city and empire, Mahler loathed the society which he represented. As a Jew he was aware of one form of herd-nastiness, and he suffered from lack of a home among peasantry or Vienna street-folk, just as he lacked one either in synagogue or Catholic church. We shall not respond profitably to his yearning and vision if we are determined to cry 'Vulgar!'; for this honest man could not express exactly what he wished except by commentary upon the child's tune and dream, or by deliberate adoption of the Schubertian lyricism or the Brucknerian expansive vision.

Many historians couple Mahler with Richard Strauss (1864–1949), and justifiably. Strauss also held a series of famous conductorships and as a composer had a marvellous orchestral expertise; but his was a far less complex and more extravert nature. His conducting was no economic necessity for he was related to the biggest of the Munich brewing firms and his vulgarity is of the crude Bavarian type, not like Mahler's scaling the heights and falling. It is not Salome's dance but the supposedly spiritual utterance of Jokanaan that revolts one, as does the metallic evocation of futurity in *Tod und Verklärung*. One mentions this ugly streak not in malice, but in order to be done with it and admire without digression the man who was the chief inspiration of young musicians in Europe and America at the beginning of this century; similarly it is not in malice that one condemns the nickname 'Richard the Second' but because it is ridiculously inept.

Instead of Mahler's speculative straining for expression

beyond his inheritance or technique, Strauss shows us magnificent professional musicianship surpassing inheritance when fired by an idea. The fact that he was not given to Mahler's philosophic musings did not make him less intelligent than Mahler. Intelligence expressed sympathy for, as well as amusement at, Don Quixote, and perceived in a Hofmannsthal libretto what suited music and what risked musical paralysis.

The 'classic' romantics – Schumann, Mendelssohn and Brahms – provided young Strauss with the musical language so ably exploited in youthful works such as the *Festival March*, the jolly Horn Concerto of his teens and the even more admirable Serenade for Woodwind Instruments which attracted Bülow's attention. Because Strauss wrote tone poems and operas he has been considered more romantic than Mahler who wrote symphonies. Our ears endorse no such judgement, for Strauss's most enviable gift (after the necessary one of imagination) was classical security of construction. Imagination could range without fear. For *Ein Heldenleben* ('A Hero's Life') Strauss supplied a vast list of labelled motives which probably brought more money than did copies of the score, but as this was almost the last of his brilliant tone poems we should not imagine that he needed the list himself.

Before he had composed any of his enduring operas and before the century had ended, Strauss claimed international fame for the following:

Don Juan, 1889
Tod und Verklärung, 1890
Macbeth, 1891
Till Eulenspiegels lustige Streiche, 1895
Also sprach Zarathustra and *Don Quixote*, 1896
Ein Heldenleben, 1899

They are called tone poems with no greater significance than that '*Tondichtung*' is shorter and more euphonious than Liszt's '*Symphonische Dichtung*'. They are not cut to any mould, and there is no point in the question solemnly posed on the pocket score of *Till*: 'Is *Till Eulenspiegel* a rondo?' Is the nomenclature important? Are some of Haydn's slow movements rondos or

interrupted variations? Strauss happened to write on his manu-
script that *Till* evoked a *Radau* or uproar, but the 'rondo'
mistake is useful to our recognition of Strauss's methods. His
outstanding achievement in tone poem or opera was delineation
of character, and only a perverse musician would prevent our
associating a character with a recurrent and perhaps varied
theme, contrasting it with musical ideas evoking scenery, events
or other characters; but a recurrent theme and episodes do not
necessarily make a rondo. The question might as well be applied
to Elgar's *Falstaff*, which owes much to Strauss's example and
excels it.

Strauss did himself a disservice by talking widely about
music's power to 'express anything' and declaring that in his
Sinfonia Domestica of 1904 one might recognize a dropping
spoon, a crying baby and so on. This work is no longer held in
great esteem. Strauss's best musical expression is what cannot
be rivalled by words or painting to which spoons or babies
belong. Five of the seven tone poems in the list above are appar-
ently evergreen masterpieces, and five in seven is a wonderfully
high proportion; yet is it coincidental that the other two attempt
obscure symbolism? A four-part texture for double basses is
ponderous and can be accepted as representing the ponderous-
ness of human thought ridiculed by Nietzsche's Zarathustra;
but without verbal explanation how can we tell that a fugue-
subject employing all twelve chromatic notes illustrates the all-
embracing domain of science?

The ascendance of so many great composers in Germany
between Haydn and Mahler was no freak of nature, yet nature
is capricious concerning the bestowal of absolutely supreme
genius. It may appear where it is least deserved. As the nineteenth century drew to its close Germany continued to offer the
most fertile culture for musical talent but Mahler and Strauss
are not head and shoulders above composers of other countries.
Fortunately even in Germany itself there are now musicians
who will not treat with scorn the suggestion that posterity may
regard Fauré or Bartok as Strauss's equals or superiors. Ten
years ago they would scarcely have been classed there with Max
Reger and Hans Pfitzner.

3. Nationalism

SINCE regional characteristics have always existed in human expression, 'nationalist' is a questionable label for a phase in the romantic movement, and calls for certain reservations. First, no 'nationalist' music made more appeal to its races than did operas by Weber and Verdi who are not usually classed with the nationalists, but with the main stream of German or Italian music. Second, music by Fauré or Elgar which, for all its harmonic richness and subtlety, has a classical basis may be as national as music by Ravel or Vaughan Williams which reflects features either of folk music or of music of a previous period. Third, many 'nationalist' composers had no dominating political aspirations. Grieg loved Norway and Dvořak loved Bohemia but so did other Norwegians and Bohemians; all that 'nationalism' amounts to in these two composers is the aggregate of stylistic features which measure their originality. So far from feeling rebellion against foreign music Dvořak sent his scores to Brahms. Grieg was admired in Germany.

It should also be borne in mind that music which uses folk melodies and rhythms, modal and archaic turns of harmony, may not thereby reveal immediately *which* country it belongs to. Unwilling totally to jettison classical melodies and harmonies, composers fertilized their style by going beyond the major and minor scales used by Mendelssohn, Wagner or Verdi, which seemed to be 'played out'. Sometimes their nationalism is no more than a feature of technique, a small corner of the musical garden which was itself soon overworked. To sum up, 'nationalism' was a natural development both of the romantic movement and the growth of democracy, especially manifest through opera in the language of its country, since romanticism and democracy favoured regional stories, scenery and characters.

RUSSIA

The Russian composers of the nineteenth century formed the outstanding example of a school for which the designation 'nationalist' is a good one. It even reflected protest against foreign domination, not political – for Russia was the aggressor in that field – but social. French was the language of the court and upper classes and was spoken at social gatherings: Russian, the language of serfs, might be used informally by gentlemen but not in conversation with ladies. The musical language of Russia was also imported, and had been so since Cimarosa, Paisiello, Cavos and other Italians were employed at court and for the opera during the eighteenth century. The first Russian composers of importance – the nineteenth-century romantics – were privileged liberals whose native heroes were Pushkin, poet and dramatist, and Mikhail Glinka (1804–57), 'the father of Russian music'.

A charming hedonist and intelligent musician, Glinka enjoyed himself in various European countries and could command a cosmopolitan style. In *A Life for the Tsar* (1836), known in Russia by the name of its peasant-hero *Ivan Susanin*, Glinka intended to be nationalist. He used several recurrent motives, many of them contrasting Russian and Polish folk tunes, for the hero misleads the Polish army and so saves the Tsar's life by losing his own. The patriotic theme ensured a certain enthusiasm even from those who called the 5/4 bridal chorus and some of the soldiers' songs 'coachmen's music'. *Russlan and Ludmilla* (1842) is more original; adapted from a Pushkin fairy tale it gave scope for the fantastic, colourful and decorative in which the Russian genius has excelled in all arts. The sorcerer's music uses the whole-tone scale, beloved of Debussy, and an utterly racial and distinctive use of the orchestra can deceive the non-connoisseur into supposing that he is listening to work by Borodin, Rimsky-Korsakov or even Stravinsky.

Glinka's disciple Alexander Dargomizhsky (1813–60) made his first notable success with *Rusalka* (1856), also from Pushkin

and generally resembling Glinka's masterpiece. His setting of
Pushkin's version of the Don Juan story, *The Stone Guest*
(1872), is of greater importance both for its originality and for
its being almost totally in recitative-like declamation: it must be
admitted that whole tracts of this opera seem dull, yet from it
came inspiration for the most moving of all Russian operas,
Boris Godunov (original version 1869).

Modeste Mussorgsky (1839–81) has been called 'the patriarch
of impressionism' meaning the art of direct impact. The passing
harmony, turn of melody, or sound of certain instruments conveys a picture, a character, mood or purpose. It hits or misses;
and if it misses we shall not gain what we miss from the development or interplay of musical ideas. This does not mean that
Mussorgsky (or Debussy or Britten) lacks the ability to make
music expand, but that he presents the musical equivalent of
vivid photographs, as he does in his wonderful declamatory
songs, in the well-known *Pictures at an Exhibition* and *A Night
on the Bare Mountain* which evokes a witches' sabbath and is
used as the prelude to Act III of the comic opera *Sorochintsy
Fair*.

Pushkin's chronicle play of Boris begins in 1584, and con-
cerns a man who usurped the throne by a murder comparable
with that of the princes in the Tower by Richard III. It was a
fortunate choice for a composer whose outstanding abilities
were the realistic delineation of characters, emotions and scenic
background. In an outward arrangement of acts and scenes,
Mussorgsky set what he (and Pushkin) called ten 'pictures'. Not
more than seven can be presented in an evening performance,
and the big number of characters makes performance costly.
The Tsar appears in only five of the 'pictures', and the main
choice is between a version which will give us most of Boris and
one which uses all the choral sections and so presents a cross-
section of the Russian people from serfs and soldiers to boyars.

Mussorgsky said that he tried to avoid 'stylization'. The
revolutionary composer imagines that he has not arranged his
expression in deference to an inherited taste or style, yet he
defers to a modified style or to stylistic canons of his own.
Though it would take many pages to show some points of

Mussorgsky's style (e.g. intervals of fourth, fifth and second rather than the ubiquitous third and sixth of classical harmony) it is plain that he could not have integrated such magnificent sections as the coronation choruses or the famous 'I have attained' monologue without some recourse to traditional means of expansion. Marvellous is his power, in sparse chords or a few notes, to give full meaning to such ideas as 'Siberia', when Boris's little son is shown a map, 'a solemn tribute to the tombs of Russia's rulers' in the coronation, the ghastly hallucination of the murdered child in his coffin, the cruelty and scorn of the leading boyar and the peasants' helpless fatalism, or the fatuous luxury of the false Dmitri's court in Lithuania. Mussorgsky's influence has been enormous not because his life's work forged an esteemed style but because the series of impacts in one work add to an effect as impressive as that of a well-planned tragedy like *Macbeth*. Whatever the selection of 'pictures', whatever the version used, even Rimsky-Korsakov's,* we are moved by terror, humour, pity and intense pathos; we even accept the horror, shared by Tsar and serf, that a well-meaning man has arrogated an office invested by divine right in primogeniture. We respond to the guilty Boris as a noble creature in torture, and cannot find contempt even for the superstitious and bullied rabble. In all opera nothing is more harrowing than the last call of the Idiot to whom Boris, forbidding the boyars to drive him away, said 'Pray for me', and who answers 'No Boris: that I cannot do' – unless it be the Idiot's unaccompanied 'Weep ye, weep good Russian folk' on which the final curtain descends if the 'Revolution' picture is made the last.

Mussorgsky is one of 'The Five' or 'Mighty Handful', though the Russian group-name *Kuchka*, applied by the critic Stassov, is now internationally accepted. They were led and taught by Mily Balakirev (1837–1910), who must have had a strong personality to hold their allegiance until he gave up

---

* Rimsky-Korsakov has been castigated for bowdlerizing and smoothing *Boris*, of which there are three 'authentic' versions; yet Rimsky-Korsakov's services to Mussorgsky's masterpiece, like those of Mendelssohn to Bach's *St Matthew Passion*, made it acceptable not only in Russia but as far away as Italy.

music, for his arbitrary theories and judgements reached crankiness. He, more than any, believed in folk-song symphonies and symphonic poems, and it was he who set up the Free School of Music in opposition to the official Conservatory which was dominated by the German-trained Liszt pupil Anton Rubinstein and then by his brother Nicholas Rubinstein. Balakirev's career was cut short by nervous collapse and we know him chiefly by the brilliant piano piece *Islamey*, the symphonic poems *Russia* and *Tamara*, and a symphony. César Cui is inconsiderable as a composer. He was of French extraction and was valuable as propagandist and historian of the group. Like Mussorgsky, he was an army officer, but too much has been made of the fact that every member of the group was a musical amateur or dilettante: some of these Russian 'amateurs' were as knowledgeable about European developments in their art as was Glinka. Their reactions are another matter – Tchaikovsky first heard *Tristan* in the year of Wagner's death and was unmoved by it except to distaste!

The most naturally gifted of Russian composers, Alexander Borodin (1833–87), reflects in his lighter pieces what he had learnt as a cellist from classical chamber music and, by playing duet arrangements, of works by French composers, by Schumann, by Mendelssohn and by Liszt. He was the natural son of Prince Ghedeanov, feudal ruler of Georgia, and certainly owes to his native country east of the Caucasus the semi-Asiatic gorgeousness of his musical palette. His most characteristic melodies may be voluptuous or almost brutally energetic, expanded more by repetition-cum-variation and strong contrasts than by metabolic development; yet is it culpably romantic to suppose that the heroic grandeur of his *Prince Igor* and his great Second Symphony are a reflection of his own nobility? He would have been a great and good man even if he had been unknown as a musician. After a medical training he became fascinated by research into biochemistry and his work on the aldehydes contributed to modern developments in subjects as wide apart as benzine, fuels and plastics. He declined lucrative posts in Germany and France because Russia needed him more. He and his wife, whom he met when she was giving a piano recital for charity in Germany, did much to alleviate the lot of poor students, and he was the first professor to admit women to university courses. It must be admitted that (as is proved by the music of the exiled hero in *Prince Igor*) he could not convincingly express despair or high tragedy. Despite the overwork which prevented him from composing except during vacations and which hastened his sudden death from heart disease, Borodin's was a happy and triumphant life.

His friend Nicholas Rimsky-Korsakov (1844–1908) had not quite his genius, yet he was the most versatile and accomplished musician of the group, and his turning from a naval career to a musical one – indeed that of a conservatoire professor – enabled him to develop his rich invention and fantastic command of the orchestra. The popular *Sheherazade* suite represents his happiest vein – illustration of magical and fantastic stories from Russian legend. The best of his fifteen operas are not those in which he deals with history and human characters (*Ivan the Terrible* and *Mozart and Salieri*) but those of a highly-coloured dream-world in which clues to the symbolism hardly matter – *The Snow Maiden* (1881), an allegory of the seasons with gorgeous transformation scenes; *Sadko* (1896), set in an undersea kingdom with ballets of its creatures; *Tsar Saltan* (1900); the visionary and magical *Invisible City of Kitezh* (1904); and *The Golden Cockerel* (1907) in which the audience is informed by the Astrologer that the plot has no meaning and all characters except himself and the Queen imaginary; perhaps this very fact led the censors to suspect particular instead of general satire and to ban its performance. It has since become its composer's most popular opera. The others, alas, are infrequently staged, possibly because they are expensive, though probably because our century fondly supposes that serious entertainment is more 'real' than satirical fantasy.

Glazunov, though more cosmopolitan, is sometimes associated with 'The Five' centred upon St Petersburg, but it must not be supposed that Moscow composers such as Liadov and Tchaikovsky were antipathetic to the avowed nationalists. Tchaikovsky's wonderful 'Overture-fantasia' *Romeo and Juliet* (1869), the first of his orchestral works to be widely loved outside

Russia, was dedicated to Balakirev. The somewhat western-ized Glazunov finished and orchestrated some of Borodin's incomplete work, and Peter Ilyich Tchaikovsky (1840–93) would have impressed foreigners more as a Russian if he had not done so as a composer of symphonies and concertos. Their popularity adversely affected the dissemination of Russian music unlike his own or not composed for the concert room.

There is little point in cataloguing or describing Tchai-kovsky's concert music which is the most familiar in the repertoire. Yet one must defend it against disparagements which are motivated by hatred of its deserved popularity. To say on the evidence of his last and most wonderful symphony that Tchaikovsky's music is dominated by self-pity is in the first place untrue; and if it were true one might ask the objector how much of the greatest English poetry, from Shakespeare to Shelley and Keats and beyond them, expresses this emotion. Irrelevant to a great deal of his art is the fact that he was psy-chotic, for so probably were many of the great romantics.

As a man Tchaikovsky claims from any intelligent critic almost as much sympathy as does Beethoven. He lost his mother when still a boy and lived in near-poverty as a minor civil servant until given a teaching post at the Conservatoire. He promised marriage to an importunate pupil – a mode of life he was incap-able of fulfilling – went through the ceremony, fled, suffered a nervous collapse and recuperated in Switzerland. A 'pen admirer', Nadezhda von Meck, made him financially secure on condition that he never met her face to face; yet his extreme pessimism and the regularity of his nervous depressions made him little happier in his affluence and success than he had been formerly. He frequently imagined himself to be 'finished' and was exhausted by the ordeals of conducting his works in Germany, England and America; but as this was the composer of *The Nutcracker*, *The Sleeping Beauty* and *Swan Lake*, with their seductive rhythms and colours matched to Petipa's chore-ography, how foolish to draw a close parallel between his physical and mental weakness and his artistic achievement! We do him less than justice by recalling only such works as his superficially brilliant concertos. Why do we neglect his fine *Manfred* Symphony, which is not one of the numbered six? Why do we so rarely see any but one of his six operas? *Eugene Onegin* (1879) is certainly his finest work for the stage and the passionate character Tatiana is enough to prove how irrelevant his abnormality was to his artistic capabilities; but *The Queen of Spades* (1890), taken from a Pushkin novel, is fascinating and beautiful as well as sinister, and it is a pity we hear so little of his *Iolanta* (1893).

We can do little more than mention Anatol Liadov (1855– 1914) – known by his *Seasons*, *Enchanted Lake*, *Baba-Yaga* and *Music Box* – Taneyev (1856–1915), a brilliant pianist and erudite historical scholar of music – Grechaninov (1864–1956), composer of operas and symphonies but known chiefly for his fine songs and his attention to Russian church music; and Alexander Glazunov (1865–1936), hailed in his brilliant youth as 'the new Glinka' for a symphony played by Liszt at Weimar. Glazunov's musical nature may be judged from the fact that his nationality did not inspire operas, but only the local colour to classical structures which we meet in *Stenka Razin*, in his popular Violin Concerto and in some of his eight full-scale symphonies. He was, nevertheless, an excellent musician of second rank whose steady production of very good chamber music and of concert music gave us very few works which fail to reward occasional attention. His mastery of the orchestra also enabled him to score music by Borodin and others which was left in piano or piano-duet form. His appointment to directorship of the St Petersburg Conservatoire was a good one. He was Russia's Saint-Saëns. Our view of Russian music at the end of the century would be unbalanced unless we remembered the wealthy merchant Belaief who instituted concerts of orchestral and chamber music, founded a near-philanthropic music-publishing firm and further helped promising young musicians with his annual 'Glinka prizes'.

None of the composers mentioned in the last paragraph (except perhaps Glazunov) enjoyed the repute of those on whom, with varying degrees of justification, it was supposed that the mantle of Tchaikovsky had fallen. Anton Arensky

(1861–1906), known chiefly by his delightful Variations on a Theme of Tchaikovsky (the *Christ Child* carol) and his Trio in D minor, was simply a minor Tchaikovsky; but Sergei Rachmaninov (1873–1943), one of the greatest pianists since Liszt, combined Tchaikovskian lyricism and dark pathos with an original classic-romantic dignity and command of large-scale composition. This once-outmoded composer deserves his recent return to popularity, for though it is difficult to pin-point anything strikingly original in him, he has a recognizable personality not adequately measured by the 'distinguished' once applied to his work with damning frequency. One does not easily tire of his mannerisms and conductors are to be commended for recent revivals of his symphonies. His finest concert work is the splendid set of variations entitled Rhapsody on a Theme of Paganini and he also wrote one or two excellent songs. Had there been no more to discover in Rachmaninov than distinguished and careful workmanship he might have waited long for rediscovery, as has Nicholas Medtner (1880–1951), a romantic who reveals so little of his Russian birth that he has often been likened to Brahms, though his pianism is lighter and more ascetic than Brahms's. His piano concertos and sonatas are treasured by those who know them. Though they might be American or English as much as Russian, his sonatas and songs are splendidly fashioned and his piano 'Fairy Tales' are more considerable works than their titles suggest.

The 'problem' Russian composer of this period was Alexander Skriabin (1872–1915), also primarily a pianist. His early Chopinesque preludes are frequently met in recital programmes but we rarely hear his symphonies, *Satanic Poem*, *Poem of Ecstasy*, *Divine Poem*, *Prometheus* and other romantic orchestral essays which might be called post-*Tristan*esque but for their esoteric variants upon the chromatic discords. Like other unbalanced sensualists, Skriabin professed a pseudo-religion which did some disservice to Theosophy. He regarded the voluptuous and erotic as 'mystical', and called creative activity a 'religious observance'. His plan to compose a supreme work called *The Mystery* was foiled by his early death, but for his last twenty years he was preoccupied with the occult – 'deep in it' strikes one as meiosis. Skriabin's genuine *work* was the organization of rich harmony in response to a highly sensitive ear. It was often based upon his 'mystic chord' of superimposed fourths and their upper partials, as first fully advanced in *Prometheus – The Poem of Fire* of 1910, performance of which was to be accompanied by the projection of a synthesis of colours and shapes upon a cinema-like screen.

BOHEMIA

The country now called Czechoslovakia, embracing former Bohemia, Slovakia and Moravia, was the most deserving in Europe of a supreme musical genius. Burney in the 1770s marvelled at the teaching of music in all Bohemian village schools and at the making and playing of violins in poor homes. Gluck's ancestry was Czech but in him and other eighteenth-century composers it is difficult to recognize national characteristics. The music of Stamitz, Reicha, Wanhal, Dussek and others is as Europeanized as the spelling of their names. Distinctively Czech music came to general notice only during the nineteenth century when the Bohemians, like the Italians, were offended at Austrian rule, taxation to maintain foreign armies, Metternich's police and censorship, and the use of German as the official language. Yet since the Czech language did not match classical rhythms there was no considerable composer of Czech opera before Bedřich Smetana (1824–84), a young pianist and violinist who was befriended by Liszt, secured a conductorship in Sweden (Gothenburg) and returned to a politically stormy Prague in 1861, deliberately identifying his compositions with patriotic subjects.

His comic operas, *The Bartered Bride* (1866), *The Kiss* (1876) and *The Secret* (1878), were tumultuously received and are still popular in Prague although only the first has become an international favourite. Their original political excitement is unnecessary to commend colourful peasant costumes, spirited polkas and furiants, bright scoring and a rich fund of characteristic melody. The intensity of national feeling between 1848 and the end of the century may be judged, however, by the fanatical accusation that Smetana's serious operas *Dalibor* and *Libussa* were 'tainted with Wagnerism'.

Between 1874 and 1879 Smetana composed the six symphonic poems (or tone poems: printed scores use both names) called *Ma Vlast* ('My Country'). They are:

1. *Vyšehrad*. The name of the citadel at Prague.
2. *Vltava*. The name of the river Moldau.
3. *Šarka*. A heroine comparable with our Boadicea.
4. *From Bohemia's Fields and Forests*.
5. *Tabor*. A city associated with Huss.
6. *Blanik*. The place where the Hussite heroes lie buried.

It is a pity that only the second and fourth are widely known, and that deafness followed by nervous breakdown prevented Smetana from increasing his contribution to the concert repertory.

Seven operas and three symphonies by the patriotic Zdenek Fibich (1850–1900) are cultivated in Prague, but most Europeans seem to regard Antonin Dvořak (1841–1904) as Smetana's successor. Are they justified in doing so? It must be admitted that Dvořak was more of the folk than Smetana. Poverty almost drove him into taking up the family business of local innkeeping and butchery, but he persisted in making a meagre livelihood as a viola player. During his thirties both his heart and his purse rose, for his settings of folk verses and the first album of his Slavonic Dances were unexpectedly popular; then Brahms, who had a contempt for most young composers, admired what Dvořak sent and secured for him not only the patronage of his publisher, Simrock, but also a government grant. Brahms's friendship was lasting and enthusiastic, but the mutual admiration increases our reluctance to call Dvořak Smetana's successor. The best of Dvořak is not found in Czech operas, settings of Moravian poets, or works based upon Czech dances, but in symphonies and chamber works that were acceptably traditional yet sufficiently different from their German counterparts to be thought brilliantly original. Open-air freshness, trills and melismata evocative of bird song, unexpected harmony with modal flavours, melody with 'Bohemian' rhythms – these characteristics distinguish them from Leipzig and Paris products.

One should not minimize that difference, but Dvořak would have shown it whatever his nationality. In some twenty splendid movements (to make the most grudging estimate) the difference remains refreshing; in others it proclaims the authorship without greatly honouring it, for Dvořak's work is unequal. At best he displays an astounding command of structure as well as colour. He could advance a complex of ideas, as in the lusciously dark second movement of his great D minor Symphony, without seeming to imitate Beethovenian development – without doing what Beethoven did better; and in such pieces he seems even more profound than Brahms. Are his Symphonic Variations in G any less marvellous than Brahms's *St Anthony* Variations? What comparable work is so virtuosically improvisatory yet just as virtuosically integrated? Where is any obvious recourse to inherited means of integration? Again, a cello concerto with a large orchestra is notoriously difficult to compose, but how easily Dvořak seems to surmount the task, and with what eloquence! Yet Dvořak must have had more than a musical personality for he was brilliantly successful as Director of the New York Conservatoire from 1892 until in 1895 home-sickness hastened his resignation. His influence on American musicians was considerable. We shall not add to the pages which discuss the titles *New World* Symphony and *American* Quartet beyond observing that Dvořak denied using any New World folk music, and that there is much consanguinity between some types of folk expression. One has heard Krishna hymns in Bengal that could be passed off as English carols. Even when paying direct tribute to his own country's music, Dvořak invented afresh from what he had absorbed. A series of 'dumky' (plural of 'dumka') gave his Op. 97 the name *Dumky* Trio and Dvořak uses dumky in other works. (They consist of alternating sad-slow and angry-fast sections.) No collection has exposed his direct borrowing of a single dumka or furiant, yet his recourse to their shapes, especially in *scherzi*, can be mistaken for the requisitioning of authentic folk music.

He wrote nine symphonies, beginning with one called *The*

Bells of Zlonice in 1865, but only the last five are acknowledged as representing his mature personality. Remembering that Schubert died young, remembering also Schubert's songs and not pretending that Dvořak was his equal, we may cautiously regard Dvořak as a Czech Schubert. Dvořak's *Requiem* and *Te Deum*, like Schubert's last Masses, show grandeur as well as lyrical loveliness; in the works commissioned for Birmingham Festivals (*Stabat Mater* and *The Spectre's Bride*) the traditional and the characteristic are found side by side as in minor works by Schubert; and *Rusalka* outshines Schubert's *Rosamunde* as a romantic fairy opera.

Smetana's true successor was Leoš Janaček (1854–1928), a fiery soul within a home-loving and reclusive exterior. Consequently his genius was not recognized outside his native land until after his death. Despite performances of the Sinfonietta and the *Glagolithic* Mass we hardly knew Janaček until, during the 1950s, *Katya Kabanova*, *Jenufa* and the over-praised *The Cunning Little Vixen* began to enter the operatic repertoire. These masterpieces, like the works of two other Czech composers, Novak and Suk, belong to the twentieth century, but Janaček was greatly beloved at home long before 1900 because, like Kodaly and Bartok in Hungary, he was deeply interested not merely in native folk music but also in the music-making of humble folk. The wealth of fine music which he provided for the many male-voice choirs of Czechoslovakia makes most of our own part-songs and cantatas seem like tame academic exercises. Janaček thought incongruous the alliance of traditional harmony with the abrupt and energetic melody required to reflect the cadence of native speech. We should not judge Janaček's expression entirely from the jaggedly asymmetrical phrases and stark harmonies of operas which deal with savage jealousy and vengeance, for he is less violent in his instrumental works (such as the Sinfonietta and *Taras Bulba*) than in the *Glagolithic* Mass.

HUNGARY

The flamboyance of certain Hungarian tunes appealed to Brahms as much as to Liszt, and it might be argued that the first nationalist 'art' music was that of Hungary as presented in Brahms's Hungarian Dances and Liszt's Hungarian Rhapsodies. Alas for romantic deception! This urban and far from ancient music is a translation of gipsy expression by sophisticated purveyors of popular light music. The first collector of genuine Hungarian music was Bela Vikar, who began work as late as 1898, six years before Bela Bartok (1881–1945) and Zoltan Kodaly (1882–1967). These two collected folk music throughout Hungary and the adjoining Rumanian and Slovak rural areas. Their own music, however, belongs to this century and we must therefore leave Bartok as a brilliant nineteen-year-old pianist with radical political views. In 1900 the chief hope of Hungary was no artist of Bartok's intensity but the thirty-three-year-old Dohnanyi, whose musical allegiance is symbolized by the usual appearance of his name as 'Ernst von' rather than 'Ernö'. His musical language was Brahmsian, and he shone chiefly as a pianist and composer for the piano. Indeed the chief contribution of Hungary to music of the nineteenth century was not a nationalist school of composers but, as in the previous century, a number of wonderful performers – Liszt, Remenyi, Joachim, Auer, Hubay, Szigeti.

SCANDINAVIA

The Scandinavian countries had produced musicians of international repute before the nineteenth century but none was impelled towards distinctively national expression. Danish scenes and characters appeared in the ballets and operas of Johann Hartmann (1805–1900); the Swedes enjoyed similar music from Johan August Söderman (1832–76), whose *Missa Solemnis* and other choral works merit export, but they failed to see that in Franz Berwald (1796–1868) they had a better symphonist than Mendelssohn or Schumann.

Sweden's treatment of Berwald in his own day is more understandable than ours today, for as far as we can tell from plays and novels the supposedly educated classes of Sweden during the nineteenth century were almost as philistine as ours.

NATIONALISM

Berwald came from as long a musical ancestry as Bach, and most of his forebears had been musicians in the Swedish royal orchestra to which he himself belonged (violin and viola) until he undertook concert tours in Europe; yet neither his operas nor his concertos, performed in Berlin, Vienna and Paris, brought him an adequate livelihood. He thrived at one time as an inventor of orthopaedic appliances and later as manager of a glassworks where he was responsible for several enterprises and inventions. Only the second of his six symphonies, the G minor of 1841 called *Sérieuse*, received much attention. Although Berwald's genius is less dazzling than Dvořák's, his melodies and modulations, his unexpected turns of wit, provide a welcome contrast to the over-familiar procedures of Mendelssohn, Schumann and Brahms.

The music of the Danish composer Carl Nielsen (1859–1931) belongs chiefly to this century. It is carefully distinctive as if Nielsen were determined to be no facile imitator of Germans; yet he studied under a man whose considerable popularity was achieved for exactly the opposite reason, so great was the swing of taste between *c.* 1850 and *c.* 1900. No other Danish composer has enjoyed the international repute of Niels Gade (1817–90), who was not only sent to Leipzig with a government grant (his violin playing and orchestral composition having been admired by Mendelssohn) but also appointed Mendelssohn's deputy conductor at the Gewandhaus. Gade's facility and industry may be judged by reading the catalogue of his works in *Grove*, though it is hard to think of his music as Danish. It is scarcely national, and yet the titles of his overtures, cantatas, piano pieces, as well as his many works for Danish choirs, indicate love of his native land and language.

Because he did not become fully 'classical', and because he was indebted to Norwegians whose influence we have only recently recognized, Edvard Grieg (1843–1907) was the first distinctively Scandinavian composer. Berwald's distinction was personal; so also was Grieg's, but Grieg's modal and chromatic progressions, which fascinated artists as different as Liszt and Delius, were derived from folk music and Norwegian musicians who did not travel abroad. From the moment in Rome during

1869 when Liszt rose delightedly from playing the 'mixolydian' final cadence of the A minor Piano Concerto, Grieg gradually became an international favourite.

There is good reason why a Norwegian, even the shy, small-built and delicate Grieg, should be the first distinctly 'nationalist' composer of Scandinavia, for Norway alone among Scandinavian countries witnessed a general nationalist movement, securing her full independence from Swedish rule only in 1905. She took pride in the purification of her literary language and among her nationalist heroes were Ibsen the dramatist and Björnson the poet. Grieg's association with them is enshrined in the incidental music to *Peer Gynt* and in several fine songs to Björnson's verses, comparable with but unmistakable for Schumann's Heine songs.

Though Grieg's mind was formed within this strong but not violent movement, Scandinavian musical talent sought education in Germany. Grieg's life in Leipzig and elsewhere seems to have been happy, yet it provoked in his homely nature just sufficient sense of romantic exile to justify indulgence in that nostalgia which characterizes his longer works like the Piano Sonata and Cello Sonata or his charming pieces for the drawing room. To despise the charmers in his albums of *Lyric Pieces* is insensitive as well as snobbish. As Rachmaninov said after playing the very popular *Papillons* as an encore: 'He may have been a *petit-maître* but let there be no doubt of the *maître*'. His evocations of rustic Norwegian drone-and-drum music; his piano pieces that rivalled copies of genre paintings in bringing idealized village, mountain or coastal scenes into the home along with the rhythms of the *springer*, *halling* and *slatter*; his 'parallelisms' which anticipate Debussy's technique; his fondness for ninths and thirteenths – all these mark an original artist whose unpretentious pieces can never be mistaken for Chopin's mazurkas, Mendelssohn's *Songs Without Words* or Schumann's genre pieces.

Grieg owed much to Ludwig Lindemann (1812–87), the first serious collector of Norwegian folk dances, and to Rikard Nordraak (1842–66), one of those fascinating links which are perforce missing in short histories. As Paer to Beethoven or

Hoffmann to Weber, so was Nordraak to Grieg, and if he had not died at the age of twenty-four he might have robbed Grieg of his uniqueness. Composer of the Norwegian national anthem, Nordraak was an anti-Swedish patriot with the fervent idealism of a consumptive. He caught Grieg returning from Leipzig, persuaded him that his artistic duty was to express himself as a Norwegian, accompanied him on a projected tour to Italy but died in Berlin before completing it. We possess little music by him except settings of poems by Björnson which are indistinguishable from Grieg's own early pieces.

Norway's Paganini, the violinist Ole Bull (1810–80), performed caprices and fantasias upon Norwegian tunes but his music is insubstantial. He encouraged Grieg, persuading him to go to Leipzig. Christian Sinding (1856–1941), remembered chiefly by a fine Piano Quintet and *Rustle of Spring*, seems to have been only a Norwegian counterpart of Gade, cosmopolitan not national. Johan Svendsen (1840–1911), son of a military bandmaster and an adept performer on both wind and string instruments, was admired by Grieg for his ability to achieve classical structures of some length and to command the orchestra as conductor, arranger and composer.

FINLAND

National feeling against Russia, from whom Finland did not wrest independence until 1917, resembled Norway's against Sweden, for its first artistic manifestation was literary. In 1835 Elias Lönnrot published *Kalevala* in fifty cantos of Nordic alliterative unrhymed verse; it is a compilation from all known folk legends of Finland, nature and magic being more prominent than in the mythology of other nations. The pioneers of Finnish music – Genetz, Hannikainen and Kajanus the conductor – composed only patriotic choruses, songs, choral works and theatre music that did not travel beyond Finland. Not until the last years of the century did music pay its magnificent tribute to three inextricable subjects – Finnish national feeling, the *Kalevala*, and the vast forests and lakes of Finland – in the first major works of Jean Sibelius (1865–1957).

He studied in Vienna as well as in Berlin yet was so unequivocally national that in 1897 the Finnish government settled upon him a sufficient annuity to free him for composition. Like Borodin, Dvořak, Grieg and Vaughan Williams he is not known ever to have used his native folk song or dance except by direct acknowledgement, and western researchers have still to demonstrate how his own musical ideas are indebted to his native legacy. Not everyone shares the present writer's opinion that Sibelius is the greatest symphonist since Beethoven, but it is undeniable that his is the most impressive fertilization of original genius by national idiosyncrasy apart from Bartok's. Only the first of his symphonies (1899) was written before the end of the century – a classical structure which, whatever influence it shows, cannot be mistaken for work by a previous symphonist. His stature was first established by the vivid *En Saga* of 1892 and the bright suite of pieces honouring the south-east province, *Karelia* of 1893. There followed in 1895 the first overt evocations of the *Kalevala* in *Four Legends*, the last two being *The Swan of Tuonela* and *The Return of Lemminkäinen*. The popular *Finlandia* was an item composed for a patriotic pageant in 1899 and it roused such political excitement that performances were prohibited.

Sibelius draws no firm line of method and style between a work with a specified subject and one without; *Tapiola* or *Pohjola's Daughter*, or even a shorter piece from incidental music (e.g. to *The Tempest*), could have been included in a symphony. These works are no less impressive than Sibelius's symphonic movements with their constant suggestions of vast landscapes and powerful natural forces. No feature of today's concert programmes more pathetically reveals the inability of this age to let intelligence overcome ephemeral fashions than its temporary distaste for Sibelius.

SPAIN

Rhythms marked by the feet and elaborated by guitar and castanets have sufficiently distinguished Spanish music to make it a perennial export and object of fake, since only its devotees recognize its particular forms, places of origin and purposes. Until the late nineteenth century 'Spanish music' was merely the name of one form of local colour, akin to the 'Turkish music' supplied by bass drum and triangle in such works as Mozart's *Die Entführung aus dem Serail*. Even a brilliantly served *Capriccio espagnol* or *Symphonie espagnole* did not raise it from association with entertainment, and probably Domenico Scarlatti's harpsichord sonatas were the sole alloy of great musical invention with the guitar idioms.

The revival of old Spanish music and a movement to raise the status of Spanish theatre, church and concert music owe much to Felipe Pedrell (1841–1922), doyen of European musicologists and a magnificent teacher. Unfortunately his picturesque national operas did not prove him a vital composer, and we revere him chiefly as the editor of the collected works of Victoria and of Cabezón. The fruit of his ideals in composition came through his devoted pupils Enrique Granados (1867–1916) and Manuel de Falla (1876–1946), but the honour of being the first Spanish nationalist of distinction goes to a slightly older man, Isaac Albeniz (1860–1909), a child pianist duly admired by Liszt. He was educated chiefly in Paris and became a member both of the d'Indy and of the Debussy circles. The slight but vivid pieces which make him popular with young pianists are no more to be despised than, say, Chopin's waltzes, but the twelve pieces called *Iberia* are his best. Some of them are known in their orchestral version by Enrique Arbos. Granados made his reputation through the two sets of *Goyescas*, each piece illustrating one of Goya's pictures and therefore incurring some reflection of humanity beyond the picturesque. The attempt to make *Goyescas* into an opera (staged in New York) was not successful, and it is worth noting here that the *zarzuela* (or popular 'musical' which flourished in Spain during the nineteenth century) has not been successfully exported.

Falla was undeniably an artist of wider and greater gifts than Albeniz or Granados. His *La Vida breve* (1904) was the first really fine Spanish opera and the music for the ballets called in English (the first not accurately) *Love the Magician* and *The Three-cornered Hat* indicate his technical brilliance and dramatic power. Falla's maturity, however, came within the twentieth century.

ITALY

Unfortunately Italy's resolve not to live in her operatic past was also deferred until the twentieth century. Before 1900 (Malipiero was not born until 1882) she had not even recognized that her great past was more than operatic, and that one of her greatest services to music would be the editing of her instrumental and vocal music of the renaissance and baroque eras. Consequently all we need record concerning Italy up to 1900 (having dealt with Verdi) is the staging of some of the most popular operas of Giacomo Puccini (1858–1924) – *Manon Lescaut* (1893), *La Bohème* (1896), and *La Tosca* (1900). About these more will be said later.

FRANCE

The most civilized of European nations needed no political chauvinism to integrate the ideals and advances of her writers, musicians and painters. At the close of the nineteenth century her wonderful crop of impressionist painters, like her symbolist poets, had much recourse to the technical vocabulary of music – 'volume', 'harmony', 'rhythm' – because their quest was suggestion rather than representation, evocation of mood rather than delineation of character. They envied the emotional and symbolic power of music. At the same time many of France's leading musicians were adept writers and painters. Debussy could write well and had considerable skill as a painter.

An interesting treatise could be written upon the love-hate for Wagner experienced by French artists, especially musicians. They could not ignore his sheer technical advances, and they helped themselves to *Tristan* harmonies; after all, how very impressionist were such pieces as the *Forest Murmurs* and the wood-bird music in *Siegfried*, and how fascinating the light construction of the *Siegfried Idyll*! How could they ignore a musician who had conceived a unification of the arts! Though composed after Debussy had turned against the Wagner who had once been his idol, *Pelléas et Mélisande* is more a *Gestamtkunstwerk* than any constituent of *Der Ring*. We have already noticed the Franck–d'Indy school with its open allegiance to Wagnerian methods; it remains to trace the beneficiaries-by-reaction of the Conservatoire rather than the Schola Cantorum, and our key-figure is the patriarchal Gabriel Fauré (1845–1924), the quintessence of Gallic refinement, of conservatism fertilized by marvellous imagination and feline subtlety. If wit, unlike humour, is drawn not from outside an art but from past mastery of the artistic medium, then Fauré in some of his most sensuously lovely passages is supremely witty. One such passage must suffice to illustrate the point. These modulations which take us far far away from key and back to it within four bars symbolize '*chemins perfides*':

The classical in Fauré's nature and his excellence as a pianist are largely attributable to his friendship with his master at the Conservatoire, Camille Saint-Saëns (1833–1921), whom he followed as organist at the Madeleine. Saint-Saëns has received considerable castigation because so little of his enormous output of composition has survived – *Samson et Dalila*, *Le Rouet d'Omphale* (the first French tone poem), the delightful A minor Cello Concerto, the somewhat amusing Third Symphony which includes organ and piano parts, and those of his piano concertos in which vivacious movements compensate for *longueurs*. Saint-Saëns shone most brilliantly where his intent was humorous. His *Le Carnaval des Animaux* is superb, not merely in its subtle references to Berlioz, Offenbach and Rossini, but in such an item as *The cuckoo in the lonely wood*, the harmonies of which Fauré or Debussy might have been proud to have written. Almost a parody of its composer's brittle, classical clarity is Saint-Saëns's Trumpet Septet, composed for a Mardi-gras meeting. Curmudgeonly though some of his serious compositions must have seemed to the *avant-garde*, his influence was wholly beneficial. What other pianist could claim that, in his twenties, he publicly performed all of Mozart's piano concertos? What should we know of Lully, Rameau and other French worthies but for Saint-Saëns's vocal scores?

Fauré and Saint-Saëns made their trips to Bayreuth, and, of all artists the least like Wagner, Fauré composed extremely Wagnerian passages in his lyrical drama *Pénélope*. Despite his noble *Requiem* (1887) and his dramatic incidental music, Fauré was of a sensibility most happily engaged in chamber music and songs, and in these he exerted an influence over other French composers, particularly Debussy and Ravel. His piano music may have been even more influential than the orchestral work of Franck and the Franckists. His String Quartet of 1924 affords remarkable proof that his style advanced with his keen interest in new developments, yet as surely as any work by Fauré's English counterpart, Elgar, it can be recognized as coming from a musician of the nineteenth century. It is one of many many pieces (among which one may mention the last of Sibelius's or of Mahler's symphonies and the last of Puccini's or of Strauss's operas), which dissuade one from halting at the year 1900 this account of music in 'the romantic century'. Wherever one cuts a slice in history there must be, so to speak, a raw end to cauterize and hide under the bandage of valedictory sentences; but if we can draw out and avoid cutting in their middles those channels of expression which do not extend far beyond the point of separation, the effect of the operation is less crude.

The French national or impressionist movement is one of those channels, for despite the dates attached to works in the last paragraph Debussy did not secure a considerable national or international audience until the Paris Exhibition of 1900. By that year no major work by Ravel had been composed although some of his permanent mannerisms can be savoured in the popular *Pavane pour une Infante défunte* of 1899. Fastidiousness and a distaste for Teutonic rhetoric were not entirely a bequest from Fauré to his most gifted pupil, Maurice Ravel (1875–1937); Fauré's influence seems merely to have confirmed natural taste which is manifest in Ravel's wilful restriction of emotion to sentiment. Ravel's restriction makes for piquancy; mannerisms which from other composers seem but the affectations of a period still fascinate us from him. Similarities between his Quartet of 1902 and Debussy's of 1893 show that not every point of his style is uniquely personal. He was indebted to Debussy as well as to Fauré and former French musicians, but he did not display the chauvinism which led Debussy to write '*Compositeur français*' after his name on pre-war scores.

Ravel and Debussy were interested in all the arts; both were highly intelligent and made sensuality attractive by delicacy. Yet they differed considerably. The less pleasant, because the more obviously hedonistic and wilful, is regarded as the more original artist because he made more stylistic advances. Claude Debussy (1862–1918) was a natural revolutionary. Asked what he was studying at the Conservatoire he retorted '*Mon plaisir*', and he studied other composers less to proceed from them than to react against them ... a point already noted regarding *Pelléas et Mélisande* (begun 1892 and produced 1902). Like the cantatas *L'Enfant prodigue* and *La Demoiselle élue* this unique opera owes much to Wagner's '*Tristan*' harmony, yet members of the cast were instructed to 'forget that they were singers'; parallel with this is Debussy's request that the pianist engaged on his *Préludes* should make the instrument sound as if it had no hammers! The opera is so original a masterpiece that one tires of hearing what it owes to *Parsifal* according to Strauss or what it owes to *Boris Godunov* according to Stravinsky. One can conceive no imitation that would not become continuous and tedious recitative, yet Debussy's magical undeclamatory parts do not flag, his delicate orchestra does not lose intensity by avoiding rhetorical developments, and we do not tire of diaphanous half-lights and subdued elaborations. At the height of emotional tension there is no *fortissimo*, no Straussian or Puccinian outcry; the orchestra merely stops, and the most tense words in the work ('*Je t'aime . . . je t'aime aussi*') are treated in a way that would today be called 'dead-pan'.

For most listeners Debussy is the composer of *Prélude à l'après-midi d'un faune* (1892), the triptych called *Nocturnes* (1898) consisting of *Nuages*, *Sirènes* and *Fêtes*, the three vivid symphonic sketches forming *La Mer* and the almost equally dazzling set called *Ibéria*. He would have been a major artist if he had left only these pieces which make him the counter-part of France's impressionist painters. A few piano pieces in his two books of *Préludes* enable the home player to savour points of musical character – occasional wit and parody, recourse to the whole-tone scale and to augmented fifth chords as vehicles of the mysterious, and fondness for *scrappets* and arabesques of melody; yet he was very much a professional musician demanding professional performers. So was Ravel, who uses some of his colours, but not all. Ravel was not fond of the whole-tone scale nor, despite his brilliant command of the orchestra, did he normally conceive pictures as large and full-blooded as those in *La Mer*. He is often said to have revived classical forms and formulas. He was not a neo-classicist but his short, clear-cut sections of melody and crisp textures recall the genre pieces of eighteenth-century *clavecinistes*. Most of his admired scores (e.g. *La Valse*, and the suites *Ma Mère l'oye* and *Le Tombeau de Couperin*) were originally piano works, and he is widely thought to be most himself in piano music. This includes *Jeux d'eau*

(1901, dedicated to Fauré), the Sonatina and *Miroirs* of 1905 and another suite, *Gaspard de la nuit*, of the following year. Indeed apart from the suites from *Daphnis et Chloë* he seems to have written little originally for orchestra except *Rapsodie espagnole* and the two Piano Concertos of 1931, the second of which was for Paul Wittgenstein who lost his right arm in battle. Nobody excels Ravel as a demonstrator of the art of translating piano music into orchestral terms. He called the notorious *Bolero* 'orchestral effects without music' and produced his exquisite score of *Alborada del gracioso* from *Miroirs* because challenged to translate a piece so idiomatic; this aptitude is perhaps best known through Ravel's orchestral version of Mussorgsky's *Pictures from an Exhibition*. Similar sensitivity to texture characterizes his chamber music, the best examples of which, apart from the Quartet, are the *Introduction and Allegro* for harp, flute, clarinet and string quartet, and the Sonata for violin and cello without piano which he dedicated to the memory of Debussy. His two operas, *L'Heure espagnole* (1907) and *L'Enfant et les sortilèges* (1925), show consummate mastery of the medium. Though humorous and whimsical respectively, they include enough mordancy and mock pathos to make us wish that Ravel had finished the other operas he contemplated, notably that on his own libretto for Don Quixote. Opera elicited from him a richer spate of melody than did other music, and he was as sensitive to voices as to instruments.

Before leaving the French renascence we should mention Paul Dukas (1865–1935), if only because of his symphonic poem *L'Apprenti sorcier* and his opera *Ariane et Barbe-bleu*. Like Franck's pupil Florent Schmitt (1870–1958), Dukas should be classed with the d'Indy school rather than the impressionists. Not so the eccentric Erik Satie (1866–1925), who claimed to be a major influence upon Debussy. He is known chiefly by short piano pieces with silly titles (e.g. *Trois Morceaux en forme de poire*) and directions (e.g. *léger comme un œuf* or *ralentir avec politesse*); yet it is undeniable that in the *Gymnopédies* of 1888 he used the parallel fourths, modal and unresolved chords and barless arabesques of the impressionists, and that in *Socrate* (1918), consisting of songs with small orchestra to translations from

Plato, as well as in the Cocteau ballet *Parade* (1919), Satie revealed veins anticipating some of Stravinsky's. His astringence and anti-sentimentality take him from the impressionist to the neo-classical movement, which we shall discuss when dealing with Roussel, a greater musician than any mentioned in this paragraph.

BRITAIN

If Burney had written *The Present State of Music* fifty years after the 1770s he would have reported that Britain approached her musical Dark Ages while Vienna reached the zenith of her glory. The dearth of great composers was no shame. Why should even one be granted every century to a small country when not a dozen are allocated to the whole of Europe in two centuries or three? The shame lay in general Philistinism as reflected in education. Having lost eighteenth-century classical values, our literary and architectural taste was as uncertain as our musical taste during the Napoleonic era. What evidence of serious interest in the arts is shown by Austen's or Scott's wealthy characters? Ambitious music is scarcely mentioned by English men of letters of the early nineteenth century.

> I would not give a fig to visit
> Sebastian Bach, or Batch, which is it?

Lamb's verses to his friend Novello might well be truth in the mouths of most of his contemporaries among the British aristocracy and intelligentsia. No feudal rulers in these islands had left theatres and orchestras supported by public subsidies, enforcing a modicum of musical culture and providing professional employment as in German states. The provincial meetings of professional with amateur orchestral players (over a hundred were flourishing while Burney was alive) became moribund as communications improved, and most people enriched by the industrial revolution merely increased audiences for 'show' performers in the new big cities. Girls learned the piano for the marriage market, but a musical schoolboy might be despised as effeminate, or as preparing for a servile profession.

London, Edinburgh, Dublin, Manchester, Birmingham and the cities of the Three Choirs Festival invited distinguished foreign musicians. Beethoven's Ninth Symphony fulfilled a commission from the Philharmonic Society; Weber's *Oberon* was first directed by the composer at Covent Garden; Spohr made six visits as the new kind of conductor and Mendelssohn was *persona grata* with the Prince Consort and Victoria; before Bayreuth days Wagner conducted festivals of his work in the Albert Hall; Rossini, Berlioz, Chopin, Liszt, Joachim, Verdi – we heard them all; but the only names of our own to put well after theirs were those of Irishmen – Field (who became an exile), Balfe and Wallace whose *The Bohemian Girl* and *Maritana* are the sole survivors of their dramatic essays, and Thomas Moore who published *Irish Melodies with Symphonies and Accompaniments* in 1808. Next we mention Sterndale Bennett, a Leipzig product like Gade, whose piano concertos were so admired in Germany that Schumann dedicated to him his *Études symphoniques*. They are now less familiar than a few of his songs and piano pieces and the accomplished overture *The Naiads* which was influenced by Mendelssohn's *Melusine*.

The Philharmonic Society and London's two most prominent music critics, Chorley and Davison, were hostile to new ideas. Britain was a conservative German colony in the concert room and an Italian one in the theatre. The most prominent musical activities of the industrial towns were the choral societies, some formed mainly for an annual *Messiah*, others for works by Haydn, Mendelssohn, Spohr, Gounod and a host of minor purveyors of cantatas and choral ballads. 'The English Choral Tradition' sometimes indicates an inferiority complex, for there was no less choral activity among artisans of Germany, especially the Lower Rhine cities. Even today, if we made a list of the best fifty choral works, British composers would not appear to have contributed a majority.

Queen Victoria, herself not as musical as her husband, felt it her duty to bestow honours upon conductors, cathedral and university musicians, and the directors of the Royal Academy of Music and the Royal College of Music when those schools had been instituted. New concerts began in the Crystal Palace and

Albert Hall, those of the Reid foundation in Edinburgh, and those run by Hallé in Manchester. Although 'festivals' increased, the social status of any but highly successful musicians showed that for most English people music was no more than an innocent pastime, an adornment of living rather than an expression of life.

Even our cathedrals, ancient colleges and royal chapels were musically in a squalid state until well past the middle of the century, and improvement was to stem from religious and educational reforms rather than a musical renaissance. One detail will testify to our infertile insularity; by 1850 most English organs still lacked pedals. Yet many a talent with little outlet but church music can be misjudged in general disparagements. It is sometimes forgotten that Sir John Stainer (1840–1901) was a notable Bach player at Magdalen College and St Paul's, and that when he returned to Oxford as professor he was among the first Englishmen to engage in musicological research and the publication of old music. Much in his popular *The Crucifixion* serves to show how his facility was wasted because England had no permanent *opéra comique*. Sir Frederick Gore Ouseley (1825–89), his predecessor as Heather Professor, was a dignified composer himself and founded St Michael's College, Tenbury, as a school maintaining a choral establishment for the best Anglican music. He himself edited much by Gibbons.

Some writers regard what were miscalled the Savoy Operas as the first fruits of the 'English Renascence' – a phrase that has been questioned for various reasons, the strongest being that improvement owed more to Nature's bounty than man's effort, depending upon the flourishing of musical talent in British soil. The crop was overdue and, though considerable, not of the very first quality until what was sown after the first harvest came to a second one just before 1900 to be enjoyed in the new century. Naturally the talents of the first harvest, Arthur Sullivan (1842–1900), Hubert Parry (1848–1918), Frederick Cowen (1852–1935) and Charles Villiers Stanford (1852–1924), sought expression in oratorio and church music, though only one of them can be said to have shone as a church musician and all of them achieved better secular music than did their predecessors. That comment applies notably to Sullivan, the son of an Irish bandmaster and one of the brightest students at the newly founded R.A.M. His teachers did not overestimate his command of the processes of composition. His musical wit is international, indebted to other musicians from Mozart to Offenbach, whereas Gilbert's verbal wit is insular and often dated. True, Sullivan's invention is patchy, but study in Leipzig did not stifle its originality except when he tried to be solemn in cantatas and church pieces which exhibit not only the sentimentality of their time but also a disconcerting pseudo-piety to which the theatrical secularity of Stainer is preferable.

Sullivan's operettas have been undervalued and overvalued by generalization. His early overtures like *The Tempest* and *Di Ballo* reveal a love of orchestral colours which many of our British composers still lack. It is shameful that patrons so rarely hear Sullivan's operettas without alterations, cueings or depletions. The overture to *The Yeomen of the Guard* is, for instance, a better concert piece than several that are regularly played. Sullivan's command of structure is seen when he works up ensemble or chorus finales in *opera buffa* style. From *Cox and Box* (1867), throughout the series of successes that extended to *The Gondoliers* (1889), he constantly drew upon the resources of an unusually well-stocked memory – not always in such direct parody as the waltz-song in *The Pirates of Penzance*, the Rossinian ensembles and choruses of *The Gondoliers*, the glee called a madrigal in *The Mikado*, the music for Mad Meg in *Ruddigore* or the Beethovenian 'orchestral recitatives' for Lady Jane in *Patience*. Sullivan's resources were needed most where Gilbert was least helpful, for though Gilbert's wide range of verse forms stimulated rhythmic invention, the composer alone sometimes saved the situation when the metre was humdrum. To observe this one must secure a copy of Gilbert and read, say, 'In a contemplative fashion' (*Gondoliers*), 'Oh the doing and undoing' (*Yeomen*) or 'How beautifully blue the sky' (*Pirates*), afterwards turning to the Sullivan settings. They testify to the composer's devotion to Schubert. (Sullivan accompanied Grove to Vienna in quest of Schubertian treasure.) His apostleship equipped him with striking modulations, varied accompaniments, enchanting orchestral introductions and connective passages, and the ability to break the repetitive chain of a strophic song.

> When Britain really ruled the waves –
> (In good Queen Bess's time)
> The House of Peers made no pretence
> To intellectual eminence,
> Or scholarship sublime.

How easily this could have been set one-syllable-one-crotchet in a 4/4 jogtrot, or to the alternating crotchet-and-minim of a facile 3/4! How easily Sullivan might have cocked a snook at *Rule, Britannia*! Instead he recalls, probably unconsciously, Schubert's *Fischerweise* and produces just the music for a satire on arrogance. Sullivan should not be judged by vocal scores simplified to suit the home pianist, who is unaware of such a detail as the quotation from Bach at 'Masses and fugues and ops' (*Mikado*).

Sullivan's nimble facility passed to another Irishman, Stanford, but the Savoy operettas were produced during the 1870s and 80s, and during the next decade it was not Stanford but Parry who disturbed British audiences with several choral-orchestral works, most of which are shelved precisely because they disturb today's audiences too infrequently and too mildly. Items from *Job* and *Judith* have survived as hymns or songs but only *Blest Pair of Sirens* (1887), Parry's magnificent setting for eight-part chorus and orchestra of Milton's ode *At a Solemn Musick*, is still treasured as a whole. *Prometheus Unbound* (1880) has not returned to repertory, yet in that work Parry's original vein of dignified lyricism made notable impact. In it one rarely recognizes the direct influence of his musical heroes, Bach and Brahms; nor are there echoes of Schubert or anyone else in his English Lyrics or his part-songs, of which the best known are in the set called *Songs of Farewell*. It is easy to gibe at the 'English gentleman' qualities – cleanliness (more often elicited by philosophic reflection than by the countryside), staid dignity that can be ponderous – but they were striking when taste favoured sentimentality and jejune elaboration. The contrast between his music and Stanford's shows his originality. The Irishman's is generally more inventive, yet when inspired Parry had unique command of the slow-moving, spacious rapture enjoyed in *Blest Pair* and the anthem *I was glad* associated with coronations and other ceremonial occasions.

Parry's influence at the R.C.M. and Oxford was enormous – not merely because of his compositions and scholarly books (his *Bach* is still valuable) – but as a new kind of musician. Philistine society could not disregard a landed squire, a popular, games-playing Etonian and keen yachtsman who chose daily hard work as a musician, writer and teacher, and it has been pointed out that many of the British composers who achieved distinction between the advent of Parry and Stanford and that of the Welfare State were able to maintain themselves during student years and to avoid uncongenial occupation later.

Yet a greater technical mentor than the R.C.M. director and Oxford professor was his R.C.M. subordinate, the Cambridge professor. Tributes to Stanford from Ireland, Holst, Vaughan Williams, Howells and other distinguished pupils make him legendary but have not directly assisted an overdue reappraisal of his secular compositions. (His church music will be considered later.) Like Brahms whom he admired and Franck whom he did not, Stanford composed as a daily discipline; most of the result had distinction when new, but does not remain distinguished when flanked by the work of his pupils. Posterity has largely rejected his many chamber and orchestral works, but cherished his settings of words. His instrumental work was not wasted, since he acquired the ability to set poems expressively yet to thematically organized music, as he shows in many a fine song, part-song and suite-like work with orchestra which he called 'choral ballad', e.g. *Songs of the Fleet* and *Phaudrig Crohoore*. This ability belongs to an opera composer, and eleven operas (though not in any styles of the Wagner he admired) show that Stanford knew what German composers gained from a vital tradition of dramatic music. An Irish cast is essential for his *Shamus O'Brien* (1896), an opera of such verve that the rarity of its production reproaches us. Beecham gave *Much Ado About Nothing* (1901) and *The Critic* (1916) to enthusiastic audiences.

The Critic transforms Sheridan's burlesque into 'The Opera Rehears'd' and contains aptly comic quotations such as the first phrase of *Blest Pair of Sirens* after Whiskerandos's 'O cursèd *parry!*'. It has the disadvantage of works which do not occupy a whole evening but, along with *The Travelling Companion*, which has twice pleased Sadler's Wells patrons in revivals, it should be in the repertory.

CHURCH MUSIC

British Church Music

Stanford needs no advocacy as almost the only Anglican church composer since Boyce or Greene who could command lengthy and thematically integrated structure. At the opening of the nineteenth century the national church was at a nadir of moribundity; its music remained squalid until after the middle of the century when improvement came in the wake of religious revivals and educational reforms. Yet Samuel Wesley (1766–1837), who became a Roman Catholic in 1784, was one of the first English champions of Bach. He edited Bach's trio sonatas and *Well-tempered Clavier* and published an English edition of Forkel's book. Because he composed dramatic and orchestral music, including symphonies and piano concertos, his magnificent motets are some of the only church pieces of the whole century which enable us to apply to another English composer the comments just made upon Stanford.

Unfortunately they cannot be applied to his son, Samuel Sebastian Wesley (1810–76), who wrote *only* church music and depended upon words to suggest ideas and structure. Even his organ music consists chiefly of trifles, and the ambitious exceptions make one regret (as does *Choral Song and Fugue*) that he lacked the German training enjoyed by his juniors; with that he could have excelled his father, for if the sum were as fine as the parts many of his church works would rival the best of any period. His strength incurs his weakness, for the great paragraphs of *Thou wilt keep him*, *Cast me not away*, *Ascribe unto the Lord* and *Wash me thoroughly* would have been impossible from one of the older composers who, inheriting baroque ideals, subjected the words to an integrated preconceived structure. S. S. Wesley's exquisite textures, dignified dramatic effects, expressive vocal lines, sensitive accompaniments and feeling for the Anglican resources give him pre-eminence among Victorian church composers, though the best single Anglican work of the reign is probably the Evening Service in D minor by Thomas Attwood Walmisley (1814–56), the professor of music at Cambridge.

Reform in the education and treatment of boy choristers was begun at St Paul's through the remonstrances of Maria Hackett ('the Chorister's Friend') who regularly visited other cathedrals between 1810 and 1835. S. S. Wesley himself was influential as a fine organist and teacher, and also through his crusty writings and verbal complaints against conditions worse than those reflected in Trollope's novels. For all their worldliness, Barchester clergy and lay clerks were not absentees lacking regard for beautiful buildings and traditions. Before the Barchester period Wesley held appointments at Hereford, Exeter, Leeds, Winchester and Gloucester. The mention of Leeds, where there is no Anglican cathedral, is important; Hook, vicar of Leeds, sought new standards of worship and evangelism in great industrial populations, and Leeds played a leading part in the formation of robed chancel-choirs, cathedral-like treatment of the liturgy, and the abolition of a service read from a 'three-decker' and interspersed by metrical psalms 'lined out' by the parish clerk on the bottom deck and performed by 'charity children' in the west gallery to the accompaniment of a double-bass, bassoon, trombone or barrel organ, if not by a heterogeneous collection of instruments. In Hardy's *Under the Greenwood Tree* there is an amusing account of objection to the change in a country church. True, the movement was to bring hundreds of ugly-looking and -sounding organs into parish churches as well as facile and jejune imitations of cathedral settings and anthems; yet its social and musical value remains unspent. It gave experience of sight-reading and concerted music to thousands of boys from parish schools whose teachers became organists and directors of local choral and operatic (i.e. operetta) societies. After the 1870 Education Act, singing and sight-reading music were introduced into the syllabuses of the new elementary schools.

Utility Music

We should be cautious in our condemnation of much Victorian and later music for churches, schools, brass bands, choral societies, etc., that is not of a quality to earn specific mention in histories of music. Little of it equals Mendelssohn's *Songs Without Words* or the genre pieces by Schumann and Grieg which appealed to home pianists, but not all of it is by composers who 'wrote down'. Monk and Dykes (to name the two most popular composers of hymn tunes), Ouseley or, in secular music of a later period, Edward German are examples of composers who exercised to the full their limited invention to supply what was needed but not forthcoming from first-rankers. *Gebrauchsmusik* was needed at several levels before Hindemith invented the word in our own century, and it is still needed. The publication of *Hymns Ancient and Modern* in 1861 provided the most widely disseminated manual of harmony, and its enormous popularity was as much a triumph for Dissenters as for the High-churchmen it was said to favour. Only a few decades earlier the only Anglican churches to use other hymns than metrical psalms were those influenced (as the Wesleys had originally intended) by Methodism. Objection to hymns and organs persisted in Scotland until the end of the century.

European Church Music

When romantic aspirations find expression in religious words and symbols, as in Beethoven's *Missa solemnis* or the *Veni Creator Spiritus* of Mahler's Eighth Symphony, unorthodox listeners may be more pleased than churchfolk. Some writers on church music praise no nineteenth-century music except that by minor composers, for they reflect the age of the papal *motu proprio* of 1903 which is widely approved by Protestant musicians. Yet, disregarding such works as Berlioz's *Messe des morts* and *Te Deum* which were not intended for church, we are still reviving a quantity of splendid religious music from Schubert to Bruckner which was once thought too personal, theatrical, passionate or colourful for the sanctuary; indeed, in direct contradiction to writings on the subject by Liszt – once the most disparaged of church composers – it has been asserted that the romantic values, being 'humanistic', are antipathetic to church music, which should be 'mystical'. (People differ in their applications of those epithets.)

Detraction of Schubert and Liszt does not come only from naive people who have no ear for music unlike that of their native church tradition, but from intelligent and culture-conscious men who set up plain-chant of the late Middle Ages, treated by themselves to accompaniments derived from six-teenth-century harmony, as 'the music of the early church', and who regard 'the spirit of the sixteenth century' as ideal for composers living three or four centuries later. They might find the crude vigour of the early church or of Palestrina's singers 'unspiritual', and there is no single 'spirit' of one century. Palestrina is as often sumptuous as austere, and composers are most sincere when they offer the church the best of themselves instead of trying to do what Palestrina or Byrd did better. Official conservatism too often makes the musical equivalent of a church shop, and the anti-romantics could not see that they were themselves children of the romantic movement, along with such medievalists as Scott, William Morris and the Pre-Raphaelites.

Comprising so many nations and traditions, the Roman church during the nineteenth century was artistically tolerant. The movements leading to the *motu proprio* were admirable and timely, reform being notably overdue in the country which con-tained the seat of authority and so loved opera and the theatre band that the sacred text was broken up to make noisy choruses and solo cavatinas of inordinate length, the organ supplying Rossinian, Bellinian or Donizettian accompaniments and connective passages. In 1869 a *Requiem* at St Peter's in honour of Rossini was patched by the music director there (Melchorre Balbi) from portions of that composer's operas, the officiating cardinal leading the applause that produced a repeat perform-ance! Moreover the reforming clerics who prepared the *motu proprio* were influenced, if not directly inspired, by a branch of musical activity for which the nineteenth century deserves special credit, though in a survey of this size it can have only passing mention – the discovery and republication of old music.

The original impetus to historical revival came from the Protestant north of Germany, the centres of performance being the Prussian court chapel, St Hedwig's cathedral in Berlin and Bach's church at Leipzig. The mystically inclined Friedrich Wilhelm IV was aware that Lutheranism had steadily declined in vitality since Bach's day but he was ill-advised to try to impose uniform worship and historical music – a mistake not made by Luther. Against this must be set editions of Praetorius, Schütz, Buxtehude, Bach and others undertaken by such scholars as Spitta and Liliencron, Mendelssohn's cantata-like psalms, Brahms's motets and other new contributions to Protestant church music. There followed the undertaking of the *Denkmäler* collections of music by composers from various German-speaking states and, since the King's religion had a Catholic tinge, the editing of music by Palestrina. The Catholics of south Germany, however, had two advantages over the Prussians; they could put to immediate liturgical use whatever they published by Palestrina, Victoria, Lassus and other polyphonists, and they had in their ranks several excellent priest-scholars such as Haberl and Proske. Consequently Regensburg (or Ratisbon as it was called on title pages) became the chief European centre for editions of church music from the Golden Age and, since a school was attached to its cathedral, its performances rivalled those of the famous Munich churches. In Bavaria was formed the first 'Society of St Cecilia' pledged to the improvement of church music. Cecilian societies sprang up in other countries during the last years of the century, and composers like Gounod and Saint-Saëns, though offering church music with orchestra or full organ parts, would claim to have composed a 'Cecilian Mass' if it was reasonably brief and did not chop up or unduly repeat words. Latin composers, however, rarely emulated the Bavarian, Franconian and Rhenish Cecilians in producing unaccompanied or very simply accompanied music in neo-Palestrinian style.

Of far greater importance than the Cecilian movement was

one which, by coming into conflict with the Ratisbon school, incurred delay of Vatican approval. In 1833 Prosper Guéranger, abbot of the Benedictine community at Solesmes, a village near Le Mans, challenged what he called the 'hammered', mensural singing of plain-chant which could hardly be avoided by those who used the official seventeenth-century or Medicean edition or, like Ratisbon, accompanied it by too many chords. Why sap its fluid vitality by clogging accompaniment? Guéranger and his successors – Pothier, Mocquereau and Gajard – were at least able to prove false the underlay of syllables in the Vatican edition by publishing photographs of codices belonging to the Gregorian period. Without presuming to weigh differing opinions about performance of the chant, we may safely say that the Solesmes scholars should take the greatest credit for restoring a text and style that commends this wonderful music to non-churchmen whereas formerly it was by no means generally enjoyed by Catholics.

The papal advisers had the sense to commend the use of plain-song and polyphony without issuing peremptory orders which would have been widely disregarded, not in defiance but because they could not have been carried out. In Italy and France, church music like Mercadante's, which recalled the operatic styles of Donizetti and Verdi, gave place to 'Cecilian' utility music by purely church composers such as Perosi, Ravanello and Refice; but in the larger churches of Austria, Bavaria, Franconia, and parts of Rhineland the orchestral or fully accompanied tradition from Haydn's time was allowed to continue, and visitors may still hear Masses composed for Salzburg by Mozart, for the Liechtenthal parish church by Schubert, or the more difficult and lengthy settings by Bruckner. Even the shortest and most 'Cecilian' of Bruckner's Masses, that in E minor of 1866, needs eight-part chorus and fifteen wind instruments, and his *Grosse Messe* in F minor of 1876, as well as his later *Te Deum* and Psalm CL, is more likely to be heard in a concert hall than a church.

The one composer rarely heard during a church service is Liszt, most ardent churchman among composers of our period before Bruckner, destined to be ordained and to end his life in cloistered meditation. Though he was an enthusiast for the romantic evocations of plain-chant (in the corrupt form known to him) and used its phrases as themes (notably in his mass for men's voices of 1848 and his *Missa choralis* of 1865), though he also liked the flavour of the ancient modes, he wrote in 1834: 'It is necessary to invoke a new church music which we may call humanitarian. ... It should combine the theatre with the church and be at the same time holy and dramatic, restful and stormy. ...' In the *Graner Festmesse* (1855), for the dedication of the basilica at Gran, seat of the Hungarian cardinal, we meet an extreme contrast of ideal from that of the Cecilians, and in the Hungarian Coronation Mass of 1867 we even find Magyar gipsy rhythms; moreover Liszt applied to many of his church works the motivic principles of his symphonic music. Here one cannot discuss at further length their fitness for liturgical use, but any reader who has relished the extraordinary modern-sounding organ and choral effects of Liszt's treatment of *Via crucis* (the devotional service of the Stations of the Cross) will agree that not to know some of Liszt's church music is to miss acquaintance with some of the most remarkable testimonies to his genius. It is not enough just to hear occasional broadcasts of excerpts from *Christus*, *The Legend of St Elizabeth* or his solo pieces for organ: the catalogue entitled 'Sacred Choral Works' occupies nine pages of the article on Liszt in *Grove*. Some of it has been explored recently but the mine is a very rich one.

4. The Indian Summer

GERMAN ROMANTICISM

OUR survey has already passed beyond 1900 because of the persistence of a stylistic time-lag in British music dating from the seventeenth century; but in the twentieth century the phenomenon was not only insular. We are often reminded that Schoenberg composed music that was radically new in the 1920s, that most British composers and teachers, to say nothing of ordinary music-lovers, have not given that music or Webern's their careful attention, and that Vienna is to be envied by *avant-garde* musicians; in fact fewer Viennese citizens heard Schoenberg's and Webern's new music while the composers were living than heard Beethoven's third-period quartets while their composer was living. Viennese concert audiences, like Roman opera-goers, hear chiefly the classics of their own people, and they have less opportunity than radio listeners in London to know a wide or modern international repertory. The time-lag is no longer national but cultural. When the classics of all ages are available in recordings it is possible to cultivate historical connoisseurship rather than insight, and to thwart interest in urgent expression; and the man who lives only in the past can claim interest in *some* music of this century. Several great composers still living after the two great wars continued not only the romantic expression of the past century but also its unadulterated technical resources.

It is impossible to separate them clearly by technical criteria. Bartok and Britten, to name two utterly different composers, are thorough romantics unless the designation is meaningless, yet despite the young Bartok's worship of Strauss and despite reminders of Verdi and Mahler in Britten's lyricism, we do not feel the warmest sentiments of these two to be a 'hang-over'. On the other hand *Elektra*, as disturbing as any subsequent opera worth hearing, projects in more brilliant technique both the kind of violence and the kind of rapture expressed by Strauss before 1900. The main romantic stream is characterized by two dominating features, observed in the contrasting 'groups' of Beethoven's first movements. The first is evocative of adventure, heroism, assertion (tragic or genial) or struggle, and in Beethoven, Wagner or the Strauss of *Heldenleben* it normally incurs rhetoric; the second *may* incur rhetoric or it may attain its varying levels of climax by less articulated rhapsody; it is evocative of yearning – for permanence of beauty, love, peace or spiritual vision that is transient in the human condition. When the yearning strikes us as morbid we speak of 'the romantic malaise'. Morbid or not, if the yearning, pain, poignancy or nostalgia seems unaffected and predominant in the composer's artistic personality, he belongs to the nineteenth century even if he were born in the next, whose true composers use it either satirically or to relieve stark expression by a concession to the sensuous.

Strauss and Mahler are therefore the two pre-eminent 'hangover' figures. The best of Strauss's symphonic poems were heard before 1900; his operas came after that year – *Salome* (1905), *Elektra* (1909), *Der Rosenkavalier* (1910), *Ariadne auf Naxos* (begun 1911), *Die Frau ohne Schatten* (1919), *Arabella* (1933) and *Capriccio* (1942). The list omits a few, for it is generally thought that Strauss's genius in opera declined after his collaboration with Hofmannsthal, his magnificent technique showing best after 1914 in smaller works such as the *Metamorphosen* for twenty-three solo strings. Mahler lived for only eleven years of the new century, but after 1907 he was not committed to regular conducting. In his last five symphonies, *Das Lied von der Erde*, the *Kindertotenlieder* and other songs he showed that his greatness measured his limitations. The verses he chose for his exquisitely orchestrated songs show that he was obsessed by suffering and death, and he is admired chiefly as the musical poet of the second vein of romantic expression described above; in the first vein he was sometimes merely grandiose and, because of his Lisztian bedevilment with banal themes, occasionally garish. His command of the orchestra usually prevents his being dull, yet to play the piano scores of his symphonies after playing those of *Elektra* and *Rosenkavalier* is to recognize, even in such a detail as modulation, that in all professional skills except instrumentation Strauss was the more brilliant technician. The young Strauss was wise to be so fervent an admirer of Mahler; and Mahler was wise, though he *knew* more about opera 'from the inside' than do most musicians, not to emulate the younger master but to put his best into the beautiful song cycles.

Mahler's tenth and last symphony, recently revealed through Deryck Cooke's realization of its composer's indications as to scoring, has been called the threnody of German romanticism. Carl Orff (b. 1895) and Werner Egk (b. 1901) continued much of the Straussian technique but, though both were Munichers, declared themselves to be in reaction to the nineteenth century and especially to Straussian expression. The most sincere continuation of the main German romantic vein is found in the very composers associated with revolution – Schoenberg of *Verklärte Nacht* (1899), *Pelleas und Melisande* (1905), passing moments in Five Orchestral Pieces (1908), *Gurrelieder* (begun 1904, first performed 1912) and even works after the technical change, and Berg (1885–1935) in almost every work, especially the operas *Wozzeck* (1917–21) and *Lulu* (begun 1928) and the valedictory violin concerto (1935). This is not because phrases and figurations, sometimes movements, by Schoenberg and his famous disciple derive from the nineteenth century when their melody harmony has turned to the twelve-note basis, but because the effect upon us of their most moving passages is similar to the effect of parts of *Tristan*, except that the yearning is more akin to that described in Freud's case books of dreams and nightmares; it is paralleled in Schoenberg's own expressionist paintings.

EARLY TWENTIETH-CENTURY –ISMS

There is not room here to define 'expressionism', which serves as a label for the graphic arts rather than music. During the early twentieth century several such labels appeared in articles and manifestoes – barbarism, neo-classicism, naturalism, even brutism. One or two have remained because they are still useful (not for explanation but for classification) and are attached to artists who drew inspiration from romantic emotions but who, unwilling to be stagnant, sought odd corners of the technical garden, so to speak. One of the earliest to do so was Alexander Skriabin (see above p. 189). He may be under-valued. At present it is widely thought that he invented little which Stravinsky and others have not used to better purpose.

The metaphor of the garden may help us to explain the period of –isms, beginning with Debussyan impressionism itself. The gardener may find a corner that has not been fully tilled and fertilized, and there he may make a rockery, a water-garden, or a place in which to grow exotic plants under glass; but space and fertility is likely to be exhausted by the first culti-vator or the first two. Others can produce nothing valuable, and the dreaded day when familiar ground must be left is merely postponed for a few years. A postponement of radical change was made by cultivating neo-classicism or 'Back to Bach'. It seemed a thorough reaction against both romanticism and impressionism, and where it proved so we are not concerned with it in this book. Yet Paul Hindemith (1895–1964), regarded between wars as an *enfant terrible*, reached romantic expression in what (probably for that very reason) are considered his finest works – the opera *Mathis der Maler* (performed 1938) and the ballet about the conversion of St Francis, *Nobilissima visione*. He does not belong to the romantic twilight and therefore not strictly to this study, yet he shows how unsafe it is to declare that the romantic sun finally set at any specific date. His revolt proves to have been, at heart, less against romantic expression than against traditional technique, against the chords of thirds built on the dominant–tonic hierarchy of the major scale and against the shapes of phrases and rhythms from 1800 to 1900.

Albert Roussel (1869–1937), non-sentimental and classically clear-cut in manner, allied himself with no school and did not apply to himself the label neo-classic. He first followed a career at sea and turned to music via the Schola Cantorum, maturing as a composer when in his thirties and at first reflecting in a somewhat pedestrian manner the style and discipline of his master, d'Indy, and to some extent his admiration of Debussy.

By 1914 a distinct personality emerged in some orchestral pieces recalling his travels in India and Indochina, but more notably in *Padmâvatî*, really an *opéra-ballet* (to use a French eighteenth-century title) with a Hindu setting, the best scenes being those of a temple with its dancers. Roussel uses genuine Hindu scales and raga variations yet the music is not sham-oriental in its total effect. The most prophetic part of the work, however, comprises the dances, for in these as in Roussel's symphonies and string Sinfonietta we seem to meet another Stravinsky – paradoxically both sterner and more full-blooded than the neo-classical Stravinsky – and yet we know that, for all the composer's determination not to be lured by romantic yearning or by the languorous and sensuous veins in Debussy, this is music of the romantic Indian summer. Through d'Indy it has an *ampleur* not found in most French music, and we can specially relish a musical wine that is dry and not cheap-sour when Roussel relaxes harmonic astringence and rhythmic tautness to make the beautiful lyric climaxes of his slow movements.

Another thorough and German-trained romantic who was determined not to be a mere imitator was the Swiss-born Ernest Bloch (1880–1959), who became a greatly respected professor at Berkeley. It did not occur to Schoenberg or Mahler to be dedicated to Jewish music, but many of Bloch's works, such as the noble *Schelomo* ('Solomon') for cello and orchestra, the '*Israel* Symphony', which is in fact a cantata, or the almost traditional (at times Brahms-like) *Sacred Service*, a series of psalms with responsories set to an English text, have led people to call Bloch a 'Jewish nationalist'. The label is questionable, for is there an '–ism' where there is no 'school'? It is obvious that Bloch found his escape from traditional and early Debussyish technique in the exotic evocations, the augmented seconds, melismatic decorations of melody, even the quarter-tones, that were part of his racial inheritance. Moreover his finest works, despite the excellence of *Schelomo* and the *Sacred Service*, are supremely the Piano Quintet of 1923 and then the last two of his four string quartets, and none of these is overtly Jewish. The finale of the Quintet is one of the most wonderful movements composed since 1900, opening with a Bartokian ferocity and finishing in an after-storm-light, beautiful and uncanny, which few men have captured since Beethoven. The professional may admire the composition technique (including microtones in the lyrical themes) and the expert knowledge of the medium; the naive listener is exhilarated by the sheer physical impact and fervour, and spellbound by the heavenly closing section.

After Strauss and Mahler, the most obviously traditional romantics outside Britain were the German-influenced Russians, already discussed above (p. 186), followers of Tchaikovsky rather than Borodin and Mussorgsky. But towering above most of the late romantics is the figure of Sibelius, still not properly known where he is labelled (as earlier in this study) 'nationalist' and regarded, with Carl Nielsen or Vaughan Williams, as standing out of the main stream of music – outside an apostolic succession in which Richard Strauss was pontiff just after 1900. To recognize Sibelius's occasional closeness of expression to Wagner's one has only to play a minute or so of the beginning of Sibelius's Fourth Symphony and then a similar length of the prelude to *Siegfried* – an experiment which temporarily baffled the present writer when asked to identify the excerpts. Sibelius's last thirty years (he died aged ninety-two) saw no publication of his music, the last orchestral work being *Tapiola* in 1925. His symphonies from No. 2 to No. 7 therefore span the period 1901–24. The Second and Fifth, with the lighter Third, strike the general public as the most romantic, though younger listeners favour the grimly impressionist Fourth; the Seventh secures regular performance in admiration of its one-movement structure. Outside opera no other non-stop complex of this length has been so perfectly integrated since Beethoven's *Leonora* No. 3 Overture. It moves too easily and expansively to be no more than a compression of thematically linked movements; it is a total unified conception. Perhaps the most intimate and charming of all Sibelius's symphonies, No. 6, is unjustly neglected still.

ITALY

The Latin temperament, quick to anger or laughter, overtly

passionate and unashamed of sensuousness, is less prone than
the German to the sublimation of morbid emotions in artistic
expression. Because the romantic assertion and romantic yearning are more directly expressed than they are among Nordic
races we find that the radical difference between Verdi and
Wagner has persisted even in serial music. Unfortunately
Verdi's followers did not approach him as nearly as Strauss and
Mahler approached Wagner. Pietro Mascagni (1863–1945),
composer of *Cavalleria Rusticana* (1890), Ruggiero Leoncavallo
(1858–1919), composer of *I Pagliacci* (1892), and Giacomo
Puccini (1858–1924) all succeeded in moving audiences to pity
and terror, so that there is still debate as to whether their music
rises to tragedy or only to the melodrama of the stories they
chose. Since the first two men maintain popularity only in the
two short pieces which normally share an evening's entertainment, we must examine their limitations and abilities as they
are observed in the more gifted and versatile Puccini.

Let it be noted that because the style of a novel or novelette is
vulgar, jejune, sentimental and melodramatic, its story is not
necessarily productive of a play or opera to be similarly described; on the other hand the source of an opera may be Sopho-
cles, Shakespeare, Goethe or Sheridan and the musical result
be the equivalent of the feeblest novel. To make an *effective*
opera the story must be 'good stage' or rather 'good music-
stage', for not all 'good stage' allows time for music to extract
lyricism from the action, provides the particular emotions and
situations that music enhances instead of encumbering, or
enables music to grow by its own processes without being at
variance with the drama. First-rate musicians have failed to
produce a successful opera where the story would not make
'good music-stage', whereas the musically third-rate *Andrea
Chénier* (1896) by Umberto Giordano continues in the continental repertory because the action moves swiftly – the story is
about the Robespierre 'Terror' period – and the composer is
content just to heighten its effect for naive listeners. '*Cav*' and
'*Pag*' and at least five of Puccini's popular favourites are
effective operas because they are based on stories capable of
'good music-stage', and they are by musicians with the dram-

atic sense and grasp of technical means to use their opportunities. To make a *great* opera, however, there must be a composer with the versatility of expression commanded by the great dramatist or poet – in short a great composer. Puccini was not that, and if he had dared, like Verdi, to deal with Othello or Falstaff his music could not have covered what previous artists had already revealed to us of those characters. But Puccini shines brilliantly because he was no such fool; he knew his own capabilities and limits, and we do him far less than justice if we think him merely an Italian Massenet whose operas hang upon a thread of facile sentimental melody, supremely appealing when it comes from a young and ailing heroine more sinned against than sinning.

The word 'realism' or *verismo* or the phrase 'a slice of real life' are foolish except to denote imitation that is no longer art, such as the importing of the nightingale's song via gramophone recording in one of the items of *The Pines of Rome* by Ottorino Respighi (1879–1936), a brilliant orchestrator grossly flattered by those who called him 'the Italian Debussy'. We need spend little time examining the aptitude of applying 'verist' to composers who avoided exalted personalities and heroic settings, just as recent dramatists have abandoned 'drawing-room' in favour of 'kitchen-sink' plays, drawing just as much romanticism and just as much sentimentality from the 'low' as from the 'high' social ambience. No post-Verdi Italian has equalled the musician and music-dramatist of *Carmen* but Verdi's followers made no mistake in pursuing ideas that fascinated them after enjoying the 'low-life' scenes in Bizet's masterpiece.

Puccini did well to proceed from his first notable success, a *Manon Lescaut* which eclipsed Massenet's, to modern-dress slices of the seamier side of life, which he romanticized as Mussorgsky would not have done. He had powers of musical characterization to match the protagonists of *La Bohème* (1896), *Madama Butterfly* (1904) and *La Fanciulla del West* (1910), which are not revealed as many-sided personalities like Mozart's or Verdi's heroes yet are not merely simple personifications of jealousy, constancy, disdain or pity. Showing just two facets of personality, e.g. cruelty and tenderness, Puccini can bring a character to life, and in *Tosca* (1900) he nearly achieved tragedy as distinct from melodrama by disregarding the political element in Sardou's novel and concentrating upon the drama of persons. From this work and *Turandot*, not quite finished before Puccini died, we could draw convincing evidence of Puccini's ability to suggest greater violence and more complex emotions than are actually witnessed, yet of producing no hotch-potch of contrasts. To a musician inclined to underrate Puccini one commends two works which for obvious reasons are not among the popular melodramas – the two 'outside' one-act operas of *Il Trittico* (1918), an admirably contrasted sequence, a genuine triptych. *Il Tabarro* ('The Cloak') is set in Grand-Guignol fashion among Seine barge people, and *Gianni Schicchi* is a deliciously fast-moving comedy about the Floren-tine rascal who outwitted other 'vultures' at a death-bed, the comic fantasy banishing gruesomeness. The middle piece of the triptych, *Suor Angelica*, is a tragedy set in a convent, and one would suppose it too sentimental for sophisticated audiences, yet in it Puccini's melody achieves unusual breadth and distinction.

Ermanno Wolf-Ferrari (1876–1948) was German-trained, like Busoni, and reflects this in his orchestral scoring and use of traditional counterpoint. There is little popular naïvety even in his only sentimental opera, *I Gioielli della Madonna* (1911) of which we rarely hear more than the Intermezzi. His cultured personality is more evident in comedy. Without writing neo-classical pastiche he recaptures features of Mozartian and Rossinian *opera buffa* in *I quattro Rusteghi* (1906) on a libretto from Goldoni, known at Sadler's Wells as *The School for Fathers* to a nimble translation by Edward Dent. Better known is the one-act *Il Segreto di Susanna* (1909) – Susanna's secret being cigarette smoking. It is to be regretted that *Sly* (1928), since it is based on the opening of *The Taming of the Shrew*, did not also reach England through Dent's services.

Ferruccio Busoni (1866–1924), a wonderful pianist, was even more of an intellectual than Wolf-Ferrari. His *Fantasia contrap-puntistica* includes a Bachian fantasia on the chorale *Allein Gott in der Höh' sei Ehr*, the transcription and elaboration of two pieces from *The Art of Fugue*, a treatment of its unfinished

Contrapunctus XIV, an intermezzo on B–A–C–H with variations, a cadenza and a huge finale. Busoni went to E. T. A. Hoffmann for *Die Brautwahl* (1912),* to the renaissance Comedy of Masks for the one-act *Arlecchino* (1918), and to Gozzi for *Turandot* (1913) which connects incidental music with spoken dialogue. Busoni's last and greatest work, *Doktor Faust*, finished by his pupil Jarnach, was performed at Dresden in 1925, and we lose little by knowing its intensely imaginative but non-sensuous music only through concert performance and not stage presentation. It is not an opera based on Goethe – for one thing there is no Gretchen – but an orchestral, vocal and choral essay which treats the Faust legend as received by Marlowe in a way which may be compared with Berlioz's treatment of Goethe in *La Damnation de Faust* though Busoni transcends Berlioz in depth of thought. *Doktor Faust* is a great and unique work.

AMERICA

If we set aside Stephen Foster (1826–64), composer of songs about Negro life, J. P. Sousa (1854–1932), the Washington bandmaster and 'march king', together with the suppliers of tunes to various touring hot-gospellers and the purveyors of popular songs, dances and 'musicals', we shall find difficulty in mentioning a native American composer, except the German-trained Edward MacDowell (1861–1908), who secured any considerable international reputation before 1900. MacDowell's picturesque pieces are not likely to disappear from albums but his piano sonatas are rarely heard and of his orchestral works only his two piano concertos receive occasional performances. He has been not unfairly called the American counterpart of Grieg, with this difference, that Grieg is recognizably Scandinavian. Even now it is hard to identify any distinctively American music (a nationalist American music is ethnologically impossible) except where there is deliberate evocation of scenes, or of races (Red Indian or Negro) or of an American-born class of music such as jazz.

* Dates are those of first performance.

Recently much interest has been focused upon Charles Ives (1874–1954), and his junior by two years, Carl Ruggles. Little was discoverable about these two until after the last war when Ives was still regarded as cranky and Ruggles as intellectual and remote. Ruggles still lacks an entry in *Grove*. Those who think that Ives now receives more than compensatory adulation do not question his sincerity or the novelty of his experiments but his significance as an artist – a matter depending upon communication, which depends upon apprehensible form and style, which in turn depends upon wilful self-limitation. There can be no distinctive trumpet style if the trumpet may have any notes given to the violin; Fauré would not be valued as one of music's aristocrats if his expression had been as unbridled as Strauss's. A distinct style, be it no more arresting and personal than MacDowell's, has so far been necessary to the survival of a man's music. It does not affect Ives's standing *as an artist* that he anticipated isolable procedures used by later composers – the permuting of notes of a theme (without conditions demanded for a serial *style*), the abandonment of tonality (impressionistically not functionally) or any systematic rhythm, superimposing strands of polyphony each in a different key. A child may find an effect which the 1990s will include in a style, and the trouble with Ives is that many of us find childish both his effects and his intentions. The attempt to regard him as an amateur or as a naive, musical backwoodsman who became a Robert Frost of music (though incomprehensible) is nonsensical; he was the son of a musician and a student of music at Yale; he was also a good pianist, violinist and organist. As director of an insurance company he could afford the rural retreat of a commuter, but after his university and organist days he had no public. From about 1920 he ceased to compose, and when the third of his four symphonies was accorded a prize in 1947 the performance that secured it was a première given thirty-six years after the work was composed.

Ives also wrote several choral works, five violin sonatas, a string quartet and two piano sonatas. From the little of his music that has been heard in this country we can acknowledge him to have had a vigorous imagination and to have been a

thorough romantic even in his most inchoate and original procedures. His most accessible work is the second piano sonata,
Concord, finished in 1915, its four movements named respectively after literary heroes of Concord – Emerson, Hawthorne,
The Alcotts, Thoreau. Unlike integral stylists, e.g. Schubert,
who did not risk incoherence by deferring to a passing word or
image if it were recalcitrant to the general expression of a passage, Ives attempts to express many ideas either simultaneously
or in close proximity, and we depend upon his verbal declara-
tions for the clue. Thus he wishes to convey Hawthorne's
'Puritan sense of guilt' along with evocations of sights and
sounds in Hawthorne's memory and in his writings (e.g. a
dance, a circus band); to produce the phantasmal effect the
pianist must use a strip of cardboard for the veiled, *pianissimo
glissandi*. Because Beethoven's Fifth Symphony is said to have
been played on the Alcott piano the next movement gives us its
first theme, but why rhythmically transformed and with added
hymn-tune chords that falsify the key? We are baffled because
we know the purpose is not satirical like Debussy's quotation of
our national anthem in *Hommage à S. Pickwick, Esq*. So far
posterity has been harsh with merely interesting music and
indulgent to bad music in a clearly personal or period style. It
will watch the game when it knows the rules – which means the
limits. Ives seems to have recognized no limits.

A reference to America would be utterly misleading if it left
the assessment of her music after mentioning only composers
with a considerable international repute. Time may reveal a
distinctive American style if not a number of highly personal
styles and then up-grade several composers not mentioned in
this short account. It has been observed already that favourable
conditions do not guarantee the emergence of supreme genius.
(Unless we lack standards no supreme genius has come from
Russia since Mussorgsky.) A vast tract of high mountains may
contain no Everest. The size and wealth of the U.S.A. normally
enables musical and artistic talent to secure public or private
patronage, if only in excellent university faculties, most of which
modify the German pattern of a link between university and
conservatoire training. Yet these conditions alone do not explain

the very great number of symphonists and writers of operas, choral and chamber works whose names swell the pages of larger histories than this both before 1918 (the year at which it was intended to close this survey) and since. Many of them hold university chairs.

ENGLAND

Almost self-taught, owing something to Parry, Schumann, Franck, Wagner, Tchaikovsky and others, Edward Elgar (1857–1934) leapt to international fame not by his cantatas but the Variations on an Original Theme (*Enigma*) of 1899 and *The Dream of Gerontius* of 1900. After hearing the latter at Düsseldorf, Strauss proposed a toast to 'Meister Elgar'; if he had heard the former he surely recognized his own equal in mastery of the orchestra. Elgar's music as a whole is entering a period of new popularity after the inevitable reaction against its opulence and the identification of its magnificent panache with political imperialism. Even if we were small enough to prefer marches of psychotic problematology to marches of pomp and circumstance we could not fail to see in Elgar a sensitivity that occasionally reminds us of his contemporary Fauré, dissimilar though their styles in general. Without prejudice we need no more apologize for the pageantry and gusto in Elgar than for his haunting melancholy and religious mysticism. Should there be less of trombones and big drum because a civil servant instead of the Emperor of India cuts a tape?

Thematic organization does not secure for *The Apostles* (1903) and *The Kingdom* (1906) the dramatic integrity and appeal of *Gerontius*. Its 'Everyman' story is admirably suited for an oratorio with a central hero who expresses the fears, aspirations, pain and glory of the human condition, and makes us receive them unimpeded by a material stage setting. In the first decade of the new century Elgar also produced a uniquely brilliant application of the *concerto grosso* principle in his Introduction and Allegro for string quartet and *ripieno*, and also his romantically impressive First Symphony, its outer movements sharing a motto theme, its inner ones linked by theme transformation. The Violin Concerto of 1910 is also haunted by forms of its opening theme. The work was dedicated to Kreisler by a composer who was himself no mean violinist; at first it caused surprise by two original features – the fact that the soloist replied to the opening theme instead of repeating it, and that in the magnificent cadenza the orchestral strings were directed to accompany the soloist holding their instruments like lutes, and thrumming the harmonies. In the following year the Second Symphony – headed by the quotation from Shelley, 'Rarely, rarely comest thou, Spirit of Delight' – was heard by audiences which knew neither the symphonies of Mahler nor those of Sibelius. Many members were unaware that the twentieth century had brought forth any other essay in the genre to match it in quality or competence. Despite faults not associated with Sibelius,* this is still recognized as one of the last really great romantic symphonies. Elgar's last two major works are among the finest proofs of his calibre. They are the symphonic study *Falstaff* of 1913 and the Cello Concerto of 1919. Elgar's shyness changed to taciturnity at Lady Elgar's sudden death in 1920, after which he composed little. Theirs had been a union as enviable as the Schumanns'. His supposition that his music was no longer wanted was manifestly mistaken, for at the peak of natural reaction, which was strong after the war when the rising generation discovered British ignorance of continental music, his *Enigma* Variations, *Gerontius*, the concertos, the Introduction and Allegro and the ever-popular Serenade for Strings were not only frequently performed but also recorded, some of them under the composer's direction.

Lacking Edwardian rodomontade, the elegiac Cello Concerto was and is a favourite, partly because it has been honoured by a series of internationally famous soloists; yet Elgar's supreme orchestral achievement is probably *Falstaff*. It is not inferior to

---

* If not faults then what yet seem like evidences of the price a symphonist must pay if he gives us the pleasure of a continuously lyrical texture to which rhetoric sometimes seems applied to secure a preconceived design. Thus the *reprise* section in the first movement sounds inflated and the approach to it contrived, and the sequences in the splendid finale sometimes make for sectional rhythm.

any of Strauss's symphonic poems though more complex in imagination and technique. Shakespeare's Falstaff cannot be presented in music that suggests only the scenes and events of two plays, and Elgar uncannily translates what the dramatist revealed of the fat knight's longings and dreams as well as his escapades and jests – his humours as well as his humour. Elgar, like Shakespeare, portrays with sympathy.

Among Elgar's contemporaries, Granville Bantock and Henry Walford Davies are remembered by a few compositions, but both were very influential teachers, Davies being the first to draw a vast number of old and young pupils to classes he could not see, for he taught them by radio. Rutland Boughton should not go without mention though his work is widely regarded as an unrealized ideal. An ardent socialist, he saw in the Arthurian legends material for a Celtic parallel to Wagner's *Ring*, and he chose Glastonbury, richly associated with Celtic legend, for summer festivals between 1914 and 1925. The envisaged Arthurian cycle reached only choral scenes, more Gluckian than Wagnerian, but the Celtic Twilight of *The Immortal Hour*, from Fiona Macleod's novel, appealed enough at the time to secure a long London run. Legends and static dramaturgy failed to draw crowds, and the turn of politics in the 1920s was not in Boughton's favour. He inspired the shrewder and better trained Alan Bush (b. 1900) whose *Wat Tyler* and *Men of Blackmoor*, to our discredit, are better known here by broadcasts than stage performances; in them proletarian heroes and subjects find expression in declamation and chorus work which contribute vitally to the drama, and successful productions in Germany confirm this impression.

Frederick Delius (1862–1934), born in Bradford of German ancestry, did not leap to fame. Before 1900 he had already composed his best opera, several of those orchestral pieces which identify him with Wordsworthian nature mysticism and are characterized by voluptuous 'blues' chords, though they never seem to suggest any indoor or sophisticated locale. The full richness of Delius's harmony is unique, so much so that one is not reminded of him by, say, Gershwin or other composers who enjoy the pleasure of hearing themselves sag. Rhythmic invention is inconsistent with Delian harmony and Delius is usually content to keep the music going without boiling; yet there are places in his huge choral symphony *A Mass of Life* (1907; to texts from Nietzsche) and other works in which he temporarily abandons dream-like reflection, even the suggestion of a horizon (of nature or of thought) to which one yearns, and with it there also disappears the harmonic luxury and easy-going rhythm. He *can* express harshness though not rhetorical energy. It would be ridiculous for anyone who has conducted one of his master-pieces, long or short, to say that it lacked form and coherence. Though so much more full-bodied and, indeed, limited than a French impressionist, Delius had a sense of form and integrity.* He did not think recognition of design to be a valuable con-comitant of listening.

Learning kills instinct. Never believe that one must hear music many times to understand it. That is the last refuge of the incompetent. Music is simply the expression of a poetical and emotional nature.

In this tirade Delius makes the generalizer's and the egotist's mistake. 'Instinct' did not bring his spontaneous-seeming 'expression'. Its overflow as well as much of its coherence came from a mind stocked by previous romantics – Chopin, Wagner, Debussy and Grieg (Delius's favourite). We do not deny him his unique artistry by saying that he could have been articulate only in the autumn of romanticism. 'To secure form all you need is a sense of flow.' Delius did secure it, with or without a text to suggest the 'flow'.

That is why his most satisfying big work is *Sea Drift* (1903). Whitman's verses about the bereaved seagull and the musings of a boy observer are admirably suited to the Delian palette and emotional range, as also the medium of baritone solo with chorus; yet if this piece were wordless, the orchestra and voices

* He sometimes passed makeshift – the transition, join or variation that he himself could have improved; but in this he differs only in degree from the most formal artists. Even Bach's works (though not the few he published) contain botching which their composer would certainly have revised before putting before a pupil.

evoking the seascape and the boy's reactions, it would still be moving. 'O past, O happy days!' – unlike Debussy in *La Mer*, Delius is less concerned with a brilliant picture than with emotions. The Frenchman leaves the moralizing to be done by us; the Teuton must preach even when antipathetic to religion and the preaching of others. Delius wisely omitted Whitman's philosophic reflections on death (which Mahler would not have resisted), and it is a pity that he did not use the pruning knife more heavily on Nietzsche. The quintessence of Delius is yearning for the transience of natural beauty and vigour, so that even in *A Mass of Life* the most memorable passages are those of Zarathustra's contemplation of 'Midnight' (Nietzschean meiosis for Death) while still 'glowing noonday sleeps on the meadows'.

Delius's life was itself romantic. Music was cultivated at his home, despite opposition to his wish to make it his career, and he became a good violinist. After employment as a rather un-commercial foreign traveller for his father's wool business, he managed an orange grove in Florida and sought the company of a Jacksonville organist and Bach-lover, though the 'blues' harmony of the Negro singing on the plantations fascinated him. Grieg's advocacy secured him training in Leipzig and his first works, including *Paris* (1900), *Appalachia* (1905), and the operas *Koanga* and *A Village Romeo and Juliet* (1901), had a vogue in Germany, though not in France, where he lived in a village some seventy miles south of Paris. His music made no headway in England until Beecham became its stalwart champion from about 1910, a climax being the Delius Festival of 1929 to which the composer, though paralysed and going blind, was brought in a wheel-chair. There are signs, after the usual reaction of taste, that Delius's 'nature' works are attracting revived interest, especially *Appalachia* and *Brigg Fair* (1907), which are in the form of joined variations with 'atmospheric' episodes. Perhaps the most appealing of all to English nature-lovers are two of free rhapsodic structure (whatever variation element they contain) – *In a Summer Garden* and the exquisite piece for small orchestra, *On hearing the first cuckoo in Spring*. What most calls for regular hearing, however, is *A Village*

Romeo and Juliet, a dramatically competent and musically most beautiful *Tristan*esque opera dealing with the love and death of two lovers who, to escape the long feud between their families who hold adjoining farms, seek 'The Paradise Garden', a lonely riverside inn. One of the scenes is their dream of a village wedding, and though the whole work is dream-like we are still aware of the natural beauty of country and river.

Some of the seven symphonies of Arnold Bax (1883–1953) are also likely to be revived. Bax called himself 'a brazen romantic'. More elaborate in texture and astringent in harmony than Delius or Elgar, Bax showed that *Tristan* did *not* push chromaticism to its limits. Many parts of his works sound like incredibly fervid and rich improvisations with a large and powerful orchestra, but they usually lead to huge paragraphs of lyricism (likely to be interrupted by more angry 'boiling over') which seems to have a legendary import. In fact Bax was fond of Celtic literature and though his symphonies are not programmatic he had, between wars, international success with his symphonic poems *The Garden of Fand* and *Tintagel*.

Frank Bridge (1879–1941), the teacher to whom Britten has often acknowledged his gratitude, a fine string player and pianist, should be honoured for chamber works, the merits of which are most appreciated by their performers, and for his determined attempt to combat natural facility and to advance his style. The piano music and songs of John Ireland (1879–1962) as well as his *A London Overture* and Piano Concerto have advantage over most of Bridge's work in their wider appeal, for they are more conservative, though finely wrought. Apart from some of his songs from *A Shropshire Lad* his best pieces are probably for piano, e.g. *Amberley Wild Brooks* and the much later impressions called *Sarnia* (Guernsey).

No English songs since the seventeenth century equal those of Philip Heseltine (1894–1930), who issued music under the name Peter Warlock, reserving his proper name for scholarly researches into early seventeenth-century music (especially Dowland's) and trenchant articles and reviews. As a man he presented two personalities – one of a debonair and gentle scholar, the other of a bibulous roisterer – and the fact led to a rather too summary classification of his music into Heseltine's and Warlock's. He commanded a diversity of veins of which we have space to mention only a few. First the hauntingly romantic one, owing something to the harmony of Delius (who befriended him) and seen at its most exquisite in 'Take, O take those lips away'; secondly a tragic but uncannily unsentimental one, found in *The Fox*, *My gostly Fader* and his finest work, *The Curlew*, a setting of Yeats's poem requiring string quartet and cor anglais accompaniment; thirdly works in which skilful archaism is mingled with humour, as in the *Capriol Suite* using Arbeau's dances from *Orchésographie* (1588); fourthly quasi-medieval or quasi-Elizabethan songs which, coming from a mind so steeped in the genuine article, would pass for originals but for the deliberate avoidance of 'fake' implied in the fully professional accompaniments; finally the roistering tavern-like 'Warlock' songs.

Conclusion

THE year 1918 was originally mooted as a closing date for this survey. Its line has often been crossed, perhaps inconsistently. Why speak of Sibelius's symphonies and not Vaughan Williams's? The answer is not simply that Sibelius was a national hero many years before works by Holst and Vaughan Williams could be heard at Wood's Promenade Concerts, but that (*a*) one cannot securely include Holst and Vaughan Williams in an Indian summer of romanticism; and (*b*) others must agree, since these composers are included in the Pelican book *European Music in the Twentieth Century*. (Composers examined in that book have received only passing mention here.) A skilful pen may close the account of a period neatly, yet if the writer's historical sense is vivid so, in his eyes, is the bleeding tissue he has bandaged after cutting history.

It remains to indulge in one reflection after a determination to stop this short account of music in the great Romantic period. Will European music cease to reflect that period during the next century or even longer? Read a notice of some contemporary work by a young critic, wholly sympathetic with *avant-garde* music, and deeply moved by it. His words, although one may not know the music to which they pay tribute, seem those which one would use if one's romantic emotions had been aroused. He writes about something by Stravinsky, Henze or Gerhard exactly as an older man would write about something by Wagner, Mahler or Fauré! Is music essentially a romantic art? Can no musician claim greatness until he shares the appeal to our common humanity notably achieved by the great romantics?

Books for Further Reading

I. THE ENLIGHTENMENT AND THE REVOLUTION

Barea, Ilsa, *Vienna, Legend and Reality*. Secker & Warburg, 1966.

Barford, Philip, *The Keyboard Music of C. P. E. Bach*. Barrie & Rockliff, 1965.

Blom, Eric, *Mozart*. Dent, 1935.

Blom, Eric (ed.), *Mozart's Letters*. Penguin Books, 1956.

Burney, Charles (ed. Percy Scholes), *Musical Tours in Europe*. O.U.P., 1959.

Carse, Adam, *The Orchestra in the Eighteenth Century*. Heffer, 1940.

Deane, Basil, *Cherubini*. O.U.P., 1965.

Dent, Edward J., *Mozart's Operas*. 2nd edn, O.U.P., 1947 (Oxford Paperbacks, 1960).

Einstein, Alfred, *Gluck*. Dent, 1936.

Einstein, Alfred, *Mozart, His Character, His Work*. 2nd edn, Cassell, 1956.

Geiringer, Karl, *Haydn, A Creative Life in Music*. Allen & Unwin, 1947.

Geiringer, Karl, *The Bach Family*. Allen & Unwin, 1954.

Graf, Max, *Composer and Critic*. Chapman & Hall, 1947.

Grout, D. J., *A Short History of Opera*. Columbia University Press, 1947 (O.U.P., 1967).

Hauser, Arnold, *The Social History of Art*, Vol. 3. Routledge Paperbacks, 1962.

Hutchings, Arthur, *A Companion to Mozart's Piano Concertos*. O.U.P., 1949.

Jacobs, Robert L., *Harmony for the Listener*. O.U.P., 1958.

Kerman, Joseph, *The Beethoven Quartets*. O.U.P., 1967.

Kirkpatrick, Ralph, *Domenico Scarlatti*. Princeton University Press, 1953.

Landon, H. C. Robbins, *The Symphonies of Joseph Haydn*. Rockliff, 1955.

Lang, Paul Henry, *Music in Western Civilization*. Dent, 1942.

Mellers, Wilfrid, *The Sonata Principle* (*Man and His Music*, Vol. 3). Rockliff, 1957.

Simpson, Robert (ed.), *The Symphony*, Vol. 1 (Chapters 1–3). Penguin Books, 1967.

Sullivan, J. W. N., *Beethoven*. Cape, 1927 (Penguin Books, 1949).

Tovey, Donald Francis, *Beethoven*. O.U.P., 1944.

Yorke-Long, Alan, *Music at Court*. Weidenfeld & Nicolson, 1954.

Handbooks from *The History of Music in Sound* (O.U.P.):
Abraham, Gerald, *The Age of Beethoven*. 1958.
Wellesz, Egon, *The Symphonic Outlook*. 1957.

II. THE NINETEENTH CENTURY

Abraham, Gerald, *A Hundred Years of Music*. Duckworth, 1949.

Calvocoressi and Abraham, *Masters of Russian Music*. Duckworth, 1936.

Cooper, Martin, *French Music* (c. 1850–1924). O.U.P., 1951.

Einstein, Alfred, *Music in the Romantic Era*. Dent, 1947.

Harman and Mellers, *Man and His Music*, Vol. 4. Barrie & Rockliff, 1962.

Hartog, Howard (ed.), *European Music in the Twentieth Century*. Kegan Paul, 1957 (Penguin Books, 1961).

Hindemith, Paul, *A Composer's World*. O.U.P., 1952.

Lang, Paul Henry, *Music in Western Civilization* (Chapter 15 to end). Dent, 1942.

Lambert, Constant, *Music Ho! A Study of Music in Decline*. New edn, Faber & Faber, 1966.

Schoenberg, Arnold, *Style and Idea*. Williams & Norgate, 1950.

Tovey, Donald Francis, *Essays in Musical Analysis*, Vol. IV (Illustrative Music). O.U.P., 1948.

The following volumes in Dent's *Master Musicians* series:
Beckett, Walter, *Liszt*.
Calvocoressi (ed. G. Abraham), *Mussorgsky*.
Dean, Winton, *Bizet*.
Elliot, J. H., *Berlioz*.
Hedley, Arthur, *Chopin*.
Hussey, Dyneley, *Verdi*.
Jacobs, Robert, *Wagner*.
Latham, Peter, *Brahms*.
Lockspeiser, Edward, *Debussy*.
Suckling, Norman, *Fauré*.

Index

The numbers in heavy type are the more important references

THE PELICAN HISTORY OF MUSIC 1

ANCIENT FORMS TO POLYPHONY

Edited by Alec Robertson and Denis Stevens

The '1066' of our music lies somewhere in the Middle Ages, when the Western tradition seemed to spring, fully armed with tonality, harmony, and rhythm, from the head of medieval man. It is easy to forget that musical languages had been evolving, both in the East and the West, for at least five thousand years before music in Europe began to assume the laws we are tempted to regard as perfect and unalterable. This first volume in the Pelican History of Music traces the story of music from the earliest known forms as far as the beginnings of the polyphonic period in the first half of the fifteenth century. A full section on non-Western music indicates how our tradition is linked with or has evolved from the forms of music prevailing in other parts of the world.

THE PELICAN HISTORY OF MUSIC 2

RENAISSANCE AND BAROQUE

Edited by Alec Robertson and Denis Stevers

This second volume of the Pelican History of Music is particularly concerned with the social and artistic environment during the two centuries associated with Renaissance and Baroque music. By the mid fifteenth century the Church's monopoly of influence was gone; alongside its rites a wealth of courtly and civil occasions demanded music and opened the way to every kind of experiment.

Europe knew no musical frontiers and it is possible to trace a whole pattern of influence and counter-influence: the motet, the chanson, and early opera are much alike in their regional forms and adaptations.

Towards the end of the period the musician, like the artist, has become emancipated. Composers such as Monteverdi, Vivaldi, Purcell, and the Bachs are as individually distinct as the works that make them famous.